PRAISE FOR

HER FINAL GAMBLE

"A lawyer with nothing left to lose uncovers a nest of family secrets in this layered murder mystery that keeps the twists and turns coming right to the very end."

—**KELLY SIMMONS**, author of *Not My Boy*

"I was so excited to dive into *Her Final Gamble* and was thoroughly impressed by both the story and the characters. Each was well-developed and very interesting. I found myself on the edge of my seat the entire time, constantly second-guessing myself about 'whodunit.' The multiple storylines were seamlessly woven together, making me feel like I was living the story rather than just reading it. It's exceptionally well-written, with characters so relatable you feel as though you know them personally. I can't wait to see what she writes next!"

—**LUISA LIVORNO RAMONDO**, Author of *Beyond the Cobblestones*

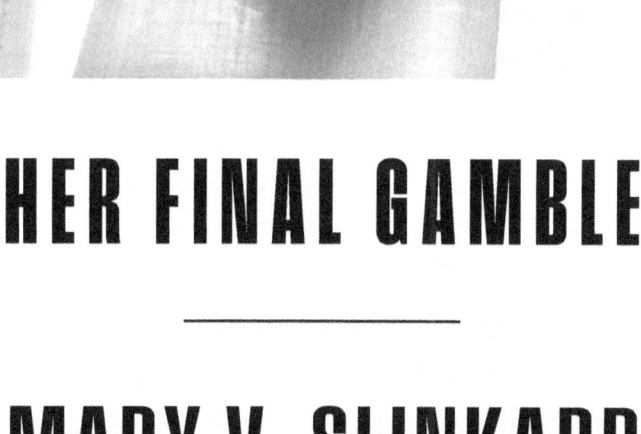

HER FINAL GAMBLE

MARY V. SLINKARD

KEYLIGHT
BOOKS
AN IMPRINT
OF TURNER
PUBLISHING

KEYLIGHT BOOKS
AN IMPRINT OF TURNER PUBLISHING COMPANY
Nashville, Tennessee
www.turnerpublishing.com

Her Final Gamble
Copyright © 2025 by Mary V. Slinkard. All rights reserved.

Cover design by Emily Mahon

Book design by William Ruoto

Library of Congress Cataloging-in-Publication Data
Names: Slinkard, Mary V., author.
Title: Her final gamble / by Mary V. Slinkard.
Description: Nashville, Tennessee: Turner Publishing Company, 2025.
Identifiers: LCCN 2024026127 (print) | LCCN 2024026128 (ebook) | ISBN
    9781684428472 (paperback) | ISBN 9781684428663 (hardcover) | ISBN
    9781684428670 (epub)
Subjects: LCSH: Stone, Jacqueline. | Criminal defense lawyers—United
    States--Biography. | Defense (Criminal procedure)—United States.
Classification: LCC KF373.S749 S55 2025 (print) | LCC KF373.S749 (ebook)
    | DDC 340.092 [B]—dc23/eng/20240614
LC record available at https://lccn.loc.gov/2024026127
LC ebook record available at https://lccn.loc.gov/2024026128

Printed in the United States of America

To the Loves of My Life—Rob, Kaitlyn,
Jacqueline, Robbie, and Michael

Thank you for all your support and encouragement.
You are my purpose in life, my big why, the reason I
do everything. I love you more than life itself.

He would build empires
And he would have sons
Others would fall
Where the current runs
He would find love
He would never find peace
For he must go seeking
The Golden Fleece.
All of the things he was going to be
All of the things in the wind and the sea.
—Jacqueline Bouvier Kennedy

Four Years Earlier

IT WAS OVER. AND AT THE SAME TIME, IT WAS JUST beginning.

The day began like any other. The sun rose. The waves crashed. The light pierced through the windows of Jacqueline Stone's beach-front dream home in Stone Harbor. And although most of the rest of the world woke to the sound of an alarm clock or a baby crying, like any other normal day, for her nothing would ever seem normal again.

Instead, she woke to a throbbing headache and an aching body. The empty cabernet bottle and restless night on the couch their origin. Legal papers spread all over the coffee table. She actually welcomed the pain though. At least she felt something. She searched the embers of the fire for any evidence of the black dress. None. Gone. A sad smile crossed her face. She did it. The funeral was finally over.

Yet she dreaded this new beginning. She forced herself to get up. Still wearing John's faded gray Boston College hoodie, she debated about going outside. She opened the sliding doors, sucking in the cool salt air. The smell of ocean and sand swelling in her body. If she could only stand like this forever.

Move, she thought she heard someone whisper. *Go*. She opened her eyes. Of course, no one was there. It was a beach town in early April. Deserted. Only the seagulls greeted her. She noticed something out by the water. She shook her head. *Look*, the wind whispered to her. Her eyes followed the breeze. And there, by the water, a vision of a little boy playing with his toy boat. With blond curls. Wearing a red Phillies cap.

She shut her eyes, trying to block out this madness. She wanted to cry, but she had nothing left. Her doctor had warned her. She just didn't listen. Instead, she stood there. Too paralyzed to move. Would this be her new normal?

A strong gust of wind snapped at her. Her eyes became wide with surprise. Her insanity immediately replaced with shock. Reality gripped her spine. It wasn't a ghost. A living, breathing child stood on the water's edge. She scanned the beach. No one else around. Except the crashing waves, remnants of last night's angry storm. The ocean waited, luring the child with its churning power. He didn't stand a chance. And like all good taunts, it worked. The little boy put down his tiny boat and the current grabbed it, encouraging the innocent captain to follow into the rushing white water.

Jacqueline watched in horror as the little boy heroically raced after it.

"Stop!" she screamed. But the crashing of the waves muffled her voice. She sprinted toward the ocean. He continued bravely after the boat, tiptoeing to keep his head above the waves. Jacqueline spotted his red cap. But just as quickly, a wave engulfed him, his head disappearing under the water. The hat resurfaced. The boy did not.

Jacqueline dove in, ignoring the sting of the freezing temperature. She had to find him. A wave crashed on her, pulling her down. Her body slammed against the hard sand floor. She gasped for breath. His red hat caught in a rip current and floated out to even deeper water. "Where are you?" she screamed. She didn't see him anywhere. She swam out farther, diving under to feel for the boy, rising only to catch her breath. The churning water made it impossible to see the ocean floor. Long seconds passed. Then she saw his blond head bob to the surface.

"Help!" he cried, stretching his tiny hand above the water as another wave crashed over him, dragging him back under the murky water.

She swam out in his direction, as the water level rose well above both of their heads and the waves made it impossible to stay afloat.

Jacqueline couldn't stand. And that meant the little boy...she refused to entertain the thought. She sensed the large wave forming behind them, threatening to crush them with its might. She had to get to him. And fast. She dove again. The salt water stung her eyes as she searched. She flung her arms around, hoping to connect with him. Something grazed her arm. His body. But the undertow pulled even harder, warning of the looming wave building just feet away. Her panic rose. Her fingers finally brushed his arm. She grabbed his tiny hand. Pulling his little body to her, she pushed toward the light shining above. *Hold on, little guy. We're almost there.* As she hit the surface, she saw it. *He can't die* was her last thought as the wave engulfed them.

Chapter 1

TERROR RAGED THROUGH RYAN MITCHELL'S BODY. Somewhere deep in his soul he remembered this uncontrollable fear. It had happened once before. Seeing something but understanding nothing.

"Stay with me, Patrick," Mitchell ordered as he slammed his black Range Rover to a stop in front of the emergency entrance of Penn Central Hospital, the front tire jumping the curb. Angry bystanders rushed to move out of its way. A woman screamed as the SUV missed her by inches. She turned to face her almost assailant, but no words emerged from her mouth. Her eyes froze. Mitchell bolted from the car, grabbing his son, Patrick. Both were covered in blood.

The medical staff had already moved into action, bringing the gurney with them. "Mr. Mitchell, lay him down here."

Fearing Patrick would try to escape again, Mitchell refused. "No. I'll carry him inside."

Mitchell followed the array of medical personnel to a private room through the hallway, bypassing the registration desk while wrestling to hold on to Patrick's flailing body. His son's tiny arms pounded against Mitchell's massive chest, his legs thrashed wildly. Three orderlies used their collective strength to transfer him to the hospital bed.

A young nurse tried to calm Patrick down. "Sweetie, it's okay. You're safe."

Exhausted, Mitchell fell back against the wall. He stared at the creature that had replaced his beloved son. Patrick wrapped his arms tightly around his knees and rocked back and forth.

Mitchell's reputation had its benefits at the hospital. But unlike in their interactions at various fundraisers and gala events, Dr. Patricia Vassallo was all business here. "Mr. Mitchell, can you tell me where Patrick is hurt?"

Mitchell shook his head. "I couldn't find any injuries. But he wouldn't talk. I tried to examine him, but he wouldn't let me. So I just grabbed him, jumped in the car, and called you. Thank you for having your team meet us on the drive."

Mitchell ran his hand through his hair. *This can't be happening. Not to Patrick. Not to us.* "Doc, what's wrong with him? He just sits there, rocking back and forth. I can't get through to him, he just starts screaming."

Mitchell locked eyes with the doctor, the gravity of the situation crashing down on him like a tidal wave. His legs buckled under the immense weight of his fear.

"Catch him," he heard someone shout, and an orderly swiftly materialized at his side. The full force of Mitchell's huge, muscular frame almost knocked the man to the ground. A nurse slid a chair under Mitchell.

Mitchell pushed the chair away, balancing against the wall. "I'm fine. Help my son."

Mitchell watched helplessly as the doctor examined Patrick. It had been years since he'd set foot into a church, and he couldn't recite or even remember any prayer. But he begged whatever god there was that Patrick didn't see what happened to Tiffany. Mitchell squeezed his own eyes shut, trying to block out the image seared into his mind. Finding Tiffany's lifeless body in his arms. Blood everywhere. Then, seeing Patrick. That feeling of complete horror. Despite spending a lifetime learning to control his every emotion, Mitchell wanted to collapse. His training refused to let him. He needed to focus. "Doctor, what's wrong with him?" he repeated.

But before the doctor could respond, a familiar voice outside the room demanded that security move. Mitchell looked over to see Tyler Hines, his mentor, face to face with security. For not the first time in his life, Mitchell welcomed Tyler's fatherlike protection. "He's with me. Let him through."

"Mitchell, I got here as soon as I could..." Tyler gasped at the sight of Mitchell's crisp white oxford covered with blood. "Oh my God, Mitchell! What happened to you?"

Anger surged through Mitchell as he saw the medical staff momentarily divert their attention from his precious son. "Don't you dare take your eyes off him!" he roared. "I'm fine. Okay, for the last time, I'm fine." He ignored Tyler's attempt to console him.

"Mitch, they are only doing their job."

"Well, then do it," Mitchell ordered the young nurse who stood paralyzed nearby. "What didn't you understand?"

Without waiting for direction from the doctor, the nurse returned to Patrick. Tyler and Mitchell waited. And watched.

"Tyler, Patrick wasn't supposed to be home. He's never home on Fridays. I don't understand."

Dr. Vassallo interjected. "Mr. Mitchell, I need your attention, please. Are you able to help me?"

Mitchell moved toward her. "What do you need?"

"I cannot find any physical trauma, cuts, bruises, or wounds on Patrick's body. So physically, your son appears to have no injuries. But he is clearly in shock from whatever he saw or experienced, and that shock is causing his mind and body to react. I can only surmise that he has experienced some very serious mental trauma."

"Can you tell me if he saw what happened?"

She shook her head. "I am not a psychiatrist. So I can't tell you what he did or didn't witness. But we need to give him immediate medical treatment. Starting with something to calm him down so he can rest."

Mitchell nodded. "Do it."

She turned to the nurse. "Give him one milligram of Ativan IM now." Turning back to Mitchell, she explained, "This will sedate him. Then we'll run a battery of tests to determine our next steps."

Remembering Patrick's fear, Mitchell demanded, "I have to hold him. He hates needles."

"Are you okay to stand?"

Mitchell ignored the doctor, moving to Patrick's side. "Please just help him." He grabbed his son's hand. "Patrick, listen to me. It's Daddy."

At the sound of Mitchell's voice, Patrick's pale blue eyes opened, and he seemed to be trying to register the voice. But a split second later, his body erupted, and he started wailing again. The medical staff instinctively held Patrick down.

Mitchell turned to the nurse. "Please, help him." Patrick pulled Mitchell's hand to his face and sank his teeth into Mitchell's finger. Mitchell ignored the pain. "Patrick, listen to me. You are safe. No one is ever going to hurt you. I promise you."

Mitchell hoped Patrick would look at him. Instead, Patrick focused on the ceiling, his eyes void of any recognition.

As the needle pierced his tiny arm, Patrick cried out in pain. "Noooo…"

Mitchell watched as the sedative flowed through his son. He could almost see the monsters leaving Patrick's personal hell as he collapsed into the hospital bed. Mitchell shut his eyes in relief. At the last moment, Patrick turned to his dad and whispered, "Daddy… No, don't hurt my mommy!"

Chapter 2

"LET MOMMY DECIDE. SHE FIGHTS THE REAL BAD guys," Jack yelled as he raced into his mom's study, his Batman cape flying in the air. Just as Jacqueline Stone looked up from her legal briefs, Superman barged in, grabbed Batman, and started flying him around. The giggles broke the silence of the once-quiet study.

"Okay, put me down," Jack commanded. "Let Mommy see." Having played this game a million times, her husband, John, did as instructed. Batman stood in front of the make-believe Judge of Superheroes, his blond ringlets hanging out from under his black mask. Superman stood next to him, a much taller version of Batman, looking ridiculous in his blue tights, his muscles not nearly as defined as actor Christopher Reeve's. John didn't care that his buddies laughed at the suit. He strutted like a proud peacock in costume through the neighborhood that Halloween with his family of superheroes. She stared at their beautiful faces as they stood erect, each trying to outdo the other in bravado.

"Mommy, decide! Who's the best superhero in all the world?" Jack asked, gazing up at her with his crystal eyes. "Mommy, do you hear me? Mommy, are you okay? Jacqueline?"

Jacqueline's eyes flew open at the sound of her name. She blinked, trying to focus. She watched in horror as her beautiful antique desk morphed into the modern, sleek one of her new law offices. Her beloved home study in calming hues of federal blue and Shaker beige transformed into her sterile, sophisticated office space, purposefully devoid of all family memories. And worst of all, reality came slamming back. Jack's sweet voice was replaced by her worried associate's. Her beautiful boys were gone. Their funny faces vanished into thin air, replaced by that of a concerned colleague. Lisa hovered over her, her face filled with a combination of fear and anxiety. "Jacqueline, are you okay?"

Jacqueline stood up. She never fell asleep at work. Or at least she never let her associates see her asleep. Or at least she hadn't ever before. "Lisa, please forgive me." She needed to come up with an excuse and fast. "You know these insurance cases. A little boring. I've been researching case law for that Anderson brief. We can't lose at trial." Jacqueline mindlessly shuffled papers on her desk, hoping to change the subject. "What's up?"

Lisa leaned against the desk, forcing Jacqueline to face her. "You know you were calling his name again, right?"

"Excuse me?" Jacqueline's heart skipped a beat.

"You kept calling out for Jack." Lisa turned around to shut Jacqueline's office door. "Jacqueline, I think you need help. I can't even imagine what it is like to lose them, but they've been gone for over four years now. I think..."

Jacqueline held up her hand. "Lisa, stop. I appreciate your concern, but I'm fine." Jacqueline pretended to review the papers in front of her. She knew if she looked at Lisa, she'd lose it. "Please don't worry. We need to focus on the Anderson case. Do you have the research I requested?"

Before Lisa could respond, Jacqueline was saved by the receptionist's call. A surprise visit from a client. A paying client. "Send him in," Jacqueline answered. "Lisa, I'm sorry, but David is here," Jacqueline smoothed down her hair, trying to erase all the evidence of her unexpected nap.

Lisa inspected Jacqueline. "Don't worry. Somehow you do an amazing job of masking your pain to everyone else but me. You look beautiful as ever. But this discussion isn't over. I know you're my boss, but I don't care. I worry too much about you."

As Lisa left, she nearly collided with David Lawson, one of their most important clients. Jacqueline silently prayed for good news. As the in-house counsel for GEICO Insurance, David was the one who decided which law firm handled its litigation claims. In other words, he was the one who essentially paid her firm's fees. And judging by his expression, he didn't look happy. Jacqueline put on her brightest face. "David, what a nice surprise."

David sat down. "Unfortunately, I don't think you will think so after our meeting."

Jacqueline waited. She wasn't going to make it easy on her friend of over fifteen years.

"Jacqueline, I'm sorry, but the company is not going to send you any more cases. I felt like I owed it to you to tell you personally."

"David, you know how important your cases are to this firm. Please don't do this to us." Jacqueline shut the door.

David put her firm's bill on her desk. "I got your bill. What are you thinking? This is a car accident case, for Christ's sake."

Although Mr. Anderson was technically the client, the insurance company paid her fees. Jacqueline couldn't look at David. Right now, he was the sole reason her law firm was still alive. "David, please don't do this. I think there is still a chance to settle, and I won't charge you. The plaintiff is a lazy thirty-year-old who can't keep a job. He's just looking for a quick buck. He doesn't deserve those damages. And the doctor. Wait 'til you hear what I found out..."

David threw up his hand. "Stop. Just stop. This isn't one of your criminal cases. There isn't a life on the line."

Ouch.

David saw the pain in her face. "I'm sorry. But you can't research these cases to death. Jax, you've done some good work, but GEICO won't pay for all this. The plaintiff's last demand was four thousand dollars. Just pay it."

Jacqueline couldn't look at him. Her bill for this case alone was almost that amount.

David lowered his voice. "I'm sorry, Jax. But this is coming from above." He looked at her. "I do have to admit, the arguments in your briefs are amazing. And for the record, if this was *Brown v. Board of Education*, you'd have changed the world too."

Jacqueline laughed. "So you read them?"

David smiled. "Of course. There's some good stuff there. You're an incredible lawyer. Always have been. How in the world did you figure all that out?"

Jacqueline shrugged. "You know me. I don't really know why. That's what I've always done. Gather all the information possible, then dig and dig. The answer lies somewhere in it. My gut told me there was more to the story. I've always prided myself on being able to read people. I never believed the plaintiff. And Mr. Anderson is a good guy. Cautious. Careful. He wouldn't have just run the red light. So I gathered everything I could get my hands on to find the truth."

"I guess that's why they called you the Quiet Queen," David said, referring to the nickname the media gave her when she won a case that everyone thought was a dead loser.

"Called is right. Now they don't even call. I'm nobody."

David smiled. "Where's that bulldog I remember? The teacher's pet? Come on. No pity party for you. You still have that killer instinct. You'll bounce back. I know it."

Jacqueline hated pity. "Please, David, forget it. You're right. I'll be fine."

"I'm really sorry. It's just that insurance law isn't right for you. We make money by settling the cases quickly and cheaply. You never know how a jury will rule. It's all about the mighty dollar. And Jax, you have that poor Mr. Anderson so confused. He doesn't understand any of this and calls my office night and day, scared shitless that they are going to take his house if they get a settlement over his policy limits."

Jacqueline collapsed into the chair. David was right. She'd spent way too many billable hours on a case she could have easily settled. No one cared about justice. Yet she had nothing better to do than this case. Her law firm was it.

David moved next to her. "I did try to fight for you, but now it's my job on the line. I'm sorry, but after this one I can't send you any more cases."

Jacqueline thought of her boys and put on her Supergirl face. "David, I totally understand. Thank you for going to bat for me."

David sighed. "Jax, you know you always have me as a friend. I can't imagine what you are going through. Losing John and Jack like that...but Jax, someone has to say it. It's been four years." David turned to face her. "I'm saying this because I care about you. You need to move on. What happened wasn't your fault. When are you going to forgive yourself?"

That answer she knew.

Never.

Chapter 3

RYAN MITCHELL PACED THE PRIVATE HOSPITAL SUITE like a caged animal. Its size, four times that of any normal hospital room, still wasn't enough to contain his raging mind. He couldn't escape. Not without Patrick. And with all the tubes and medical gear attached to the boy's tiny frame, running wasn't an option. *Think*, Mitchell demanded himself. Usually, he had an uncanny ability to devise a plan under even the most challenging circumstances, circumstances where most men would collapse. But instead, Mitchell only saw red.

The murder scene replayed in his mind. *What did I do?* He stared at his hands, still smeared with Tiffany's blood. He couldn't bring himself to wipe it away, driven by a relentless need to understand what had happened. He was always meticulous, planning everything down to the smallest detail, no matter how unlikely. Ever since his days alone in foster care, he had vowed to maintain control over his life. And now this. He had called in valuable favors with some powerful people to receive certain courtesies, but once Patrick was sedated, the police needed to perform basic forensic testing on him. The hourglass of his influence to manipulate events was running out of sand, and he knew it. But he didn't think forensics would reveal anything he hadn't already admitted to. Tiffany's mother had seen him holding Tiffany's dead body.

"What happened?" Tyler asked, his voice barely a whisper as he returned from the nurses' station with some water. "Here."

Mitchell accepted the glass, not to quench his thirst but to avoid Tyler's interrogation. "Are you asking if I did this?" Mitchell couldn't look at Tyler's face. As his father figure for the last thirty years, Tyler had witnessed Mitchell's unexplainable rage. Mitchell knew both men feared it had resurfaced, despite Mitchell's years of training and commitment to control his emotions.

"Look at me," Tyler pleaded. "We'll get through this. I promise. Mitch, talk to me."

"Please leave."

"Are you kidding? I can't leave you alone. Let me help you."

Mitchell turned to look at the distinguished man sitting next to him. Tyler's eyes pleading to let him help, just like he had decades ago. His mind flashed to a memory of Tyler in a dark suit, looming over him, saying he was there to help. Marie explaining, "He's the hospital lawyer who is here to help us." Mitchell refused to believe anyone would actually help, especially a stranger. In his tumultuous eight years of life, no one had ever helped Mitchell or his family. Instead, he did what he'd learned to do. Shoved Tyler away with all his might. Waiting to be slapped back, Mitchell raised his arm to protect himself. But despite his fight, he was no match for Tyler. Tyler grabbed him and wrapped him in a bear hug, his strong arms engulfing Mitchell's scrawny body. The stress of those weeks of hell in a dilapidated foster home came crashing out in tears. Mitchell was all alone, both his parents gone. And there was Tyler, comforting him in his unimaginable depth of grief. Ultimately helping Marie gain custody. Restoring a small amount of hope that there were good people left in this world.

Since Tyler had no children of his own, he checked in on Mitchell and Marie from time to time. And although he never admitted it, Mitchell craved Tyler's approval. He was determined to someday pay Tyler back for all he had done to help him. And Mitchell did. He made Tyler more money than either of them had ever imagined.

For the first time since that day in foster care, Mitchell again felt like that small boy, desperately longing to confide in Tyler. To seek his counsel like he'd done for years. But Mitchell dismissed the idea as quickly as it came. He had moved into warfare mode the moment he heard Victoria scream. The brutal years of intense training kicked in. His movements became robotic. He'd spent years training for this exact type of moment. Learning to master his emotions, to assess the situation, read the room, and control his facial expressions and eye movements before he uttered a word. Become the Iceman.

He refused to fall prey to the loving eyes looking back at him, the eyes of the man who had saved him. Over the last few hours, he forced himself to be objective. Analyze the situation, pros and cons. Victoria Harrison Westerfer believed he murdered her daughter. She had transformed into the enemy. Mitchell knew that despite Tyler's care for him, his love for Victoria would always win out. Growing up, Mitchell quickly learned the importance of relationships and loyalty. Tyler had been the Harrison Westerfer family lawyer after his own father retired from the position. Way before Mitchell came into the picture. And Tyler's original relationship with the hospital was because of the Harrison family. After Victoria's husband died, Mitchell wasn't surprised when she and Tyler started dating. He knew Tyler had carried a flame for Victoria for years. And with Tyler's marriage to Victoria now weeks away, the battle lines were drawn. Despite their history and Tyler's true love for him, there was no need to ask where he stood. Tyler's allegiance would always be with Victoria.

"Go home to Victoria. See how she is." There would be no arguments. No pleas. No tears. Theatrics never worked on Mitchell.

As Tyler turned to leave, he bumped into Eric Conceillo, Mitchell's college roommate, business partner, and brother-in-law. "Take care of him."

Eric nodded. Mitchell watched as the two men exchanged knowing glances. Except for his adoptive mom, Marie, and his wife and son, Eric and Tyler were the only sort of family Mitchell had.

As Eric laid bags of food down, Mitchell assessed him. People always misjudged him. Eric's slim, small build screamed nerd, making him likable and nonthreatening. A major advantage they had both learned to use masterfully. The giant and the nerd, as the kids from Penn called them. They meant it as an insult, but like everything else Mitchell touched, he turned it into a badge of honor.

"You know Marie would have a fit if she saw us eating like this," Eric joked.

Mitchell debated internally. He trusted Eric. Their longtime friendship had weathered many battles. So many that they never agreed who had befriended whom first. Mitchell never argued with Eric when he claimed he started the friendship. But Mitchell knew the truth.

He remembered it vividly. After enduring a grueling season as the star football player at Penn, he finally allowed himself a rare moment of respite at the campus hangout bar. He deserved it. As usual, the entitled fraternity brothers were present, drowning themselves in alcohol. Mitchell had previously tolerated their behavior, considering them potential allies in the future. But on that night, he'd reached his breaking point.

The obnoxious frat boys targeted the nerdy kid. They were relentless in their torment. Mitchell felt a surge of memories from his own past as an outcast. The scholarship kid. The poor guy was just sitting there, fidgeting with his glasses, attempting to make conversation with a girl well out of his league. Drunk beyond reason, the bros decided to have a little fun, cornering the kid against the wall, explaining how he was infringing on their territory. In a last-ditch effort to reason with them, the nerd presented what Mitchell thought was a sound argument, but they were either too stupid or drunk to comprehend it.

Unable to witness the injustice any longer, Mitchell intervened, grasping a frat boy's arm before he could strike Eric and delivering a powerful blow, sending the guy sprawling to the ground. Naturally, as the scholarship student without influential parents, Mitchell paid for it. The football coach sidelined him for a week. But his friendship with Eric was much more valuable. He'd do it again in a heartbeat.

Through their Penn years, Mitchell and Eric used their differences to make them an unbeatable pair. Two loners, willing to bet the odds, perfectly different, yet complementing each other in unique ways that worked. And had always worked. First on campus and then in the boardroom. Together they accomplished their dreams and more. But not this time.

Mitchell didn't need to be a mastermind to assess the danger of this situation. His life and freedom, not to mention Patrick's, were being threatened. He wouldn't confide in Eric or seek his counsel. He needed to act alone and protect himself. He glanced at Patrick, his stuffed animal Bear secure under his arm. Unbeknownst to all of them, that picture was safe. Hidden. In Bear's secret compartment. Mitchell was grateful once again that Victoria hadn't seen the picture fall from Patrick's bear.

Mitchell remained guarded as Eric put out the food, his answer to everything. But Mitchell refused the distraction. He forced his brain to replay the events. Shutting his eyes, he tried to return to that afternoon at his house. Despite his normally uncanny sense of recall, there was nothing new. Blank. That next awful moment he'd never forget. Waking to Victoria's screams. Tiffany's beautiful head in his hand. What the hell happened between opening the door and Victoria coming in? Mitchell felt that old sense of being trapped. He wiped sweat from his face.

Attempting to control his panic, Mitchell felt Patrick's arm, lying on Bear's chest. The picture was secure. He didn't need to look at it. The image was cemented in his memory. When no one was looking, he would remove it to a safer place. But, more importantly, what was Patrick doing with a picture of her? And where did he get it?

Eric broke the silence. "Mitchell, you look like shit. You need to rest." Still in a sort of trance, Mitchell felt Eric move in front of him. "I'm serious. There are all kinds of things in that bathroom you could use, including a razor, shaving cream, and mouthwash. God knows you paid for that fancy shower."

Mitchell felt his mind stirring. The memories overwhelming. The picture, the murder scene, red, Victoria's distraught face. It all agitated a rage he'd thought was buried inside him. Mitchell moved into protective mode. He shot off the chair, attacking Eric from behind and slamming him against the wall. Mitchell lifted Eric off the ground and choked him.

He stared at Eric gasping for breath, but didn't release his choke hold. Anger, loss, and confusion took over his body, and he felt paralyzed. He no longer saw his business partner. His lifelong friend.

"Mr. Mitchell, what are you doing? Let go of him." Dr. Vassallo was in the room now. As small as she was physically, she managed to pull Mitchell off Eric. "What the hell is going on in here?"

As Eric hunched over and caught his breath, Mitchell came to his senses. *What has taken over me?* He put his hand on the wall as the doctor checked on Eric.

Satisfied that Eric was okay, Dr. Vassallo lashed out at Mitchell. "Mr. Mitchell, I have no idea what you think you are doing or who you think you are, but there will not be any fighting in this hospital. Do you understand me?"

Mitchell refused to turn around. "Yes. I'm sorry."

She checked Patrick's monitors. "Mr. Mitchell, I know you have been through a lot, so I will let that go. This time only. I don't think you understand what a fragile state your son is in."

Eric regained his breath. "Doctor, please forgive us. It's been a horrible few days."

Dr. Vassallo appeared to accept Eric's apology and continued her task of checking on Patrick. "As I said last night, your son is suffering from a form of post-traumatic stress disorder, commonly referred to as PTSD. While this is not my specialty, it appears that he is traumatized. That is why he must be monitored and sedated."

Still confused, Mitchell muttered, "Doctor, do you have any idea what happened?"

"We don't. Sometimes events happen that are so traumatic, the brain blocks them out because it can't deal with it. Sometimes people don't remember for years. They block it out completely."

"Could something have happened to Patrick physically?"

Dr. Vassallo hesitated. "Unfortunately, we can't say for certain. I don't want to alarm you because it's very rare, but people can become so scared and panicky that their minds create physical trauma to their bodies. Plus, there is the mental stress that he is experiencing. That's why it is very important we limit conversations and keep visitors to a minimum. And trust me, Mr. Mitchell, I will have no problem kicking you out if I believe it's medically necessary for your son's well-being."

Mitchell looked at Patrick, his secret safely hidden.

Chapter 4

JACQUELINE STEPPED OFF THE ELEVATOR TO HER Rittenhouse Square apartment, waved to Mrs. Feeney, her nosy neighbor, unlocked both the lock and dead bolt, and opened her front door. It had been a long day. As she took off her winter coat, she collapsed to the floor. And silently wailed. *Don't let Mrs. Feeney hear you*, she commanded herself. So she bent her head into her lap and just rocked herself. Rocked for all the loss she knew. For Jack. For John. For herself. No one greeted her. She had no one to confide in. No one here to hand her a glass of wine after her trying day. No amazing trial wins to celebrate. Just all alone.

She wasn't sure how long she'd been rocking when her phone rang. She wiped her face and forced herself to sit up against the door. She had no intent of answering the call, but she recognized the number. And not answering would be worse. Thank God he doesn't want to FaceTime. "Hi, Dad."

"How's my killer attorney? Did you win those motions today?"

Jacqueline shut her eyes, willing herself to sound normal. "He took them under advisement. We're trying to settle the case." It was okay to lie because her father worried enough about her. No reason to tell him even the clients knew she was finished.

Jacqueline glanced at her watch. Four p.m. California time. "Dad, do you mind? Can I call you later?"

"Jax, what's wrong? You weren't crying, were you?" She could hear his concern from thousands of miles away. "I shouldn't have come out here."

Jacqueline made her way to the kitchen. "Dad, stop it. What are you going to do here? Let's change the subject. How are Caroline and my newest niece doing? I loved the pictures you sent."

Jacqueline opened a bottle of La Crema chardonnay as her father relayed the stories of the birth of his newest granddaughter. Selfishly, Jacqueline was glad when she heard her sister had another girl. In her fragile state, a baby boy would have put her over the edge.

"Dad, Caroline knows I would have been there if I hadn't had the Anderson case, right?" Again, Jacqueline thanked the stars and wondered if John was looking out for her from above. While no one said it out loud, they all knew Jacqueline couldn't handle being at the birth. The trial worked as a great excuse. Even if it was nonexistent. They would never know since her cases were no longer headline news.

"Yes, of course she does, and she's overwhelmed with all the presents. And Emily loves her rocking chair."

Jacqueline choked back tears, recalling the pictures of her older niece rocking in the personalized chair with her Big Sister T-shirt on, her long dark hair in pigtails with matching bows. "I'm glad."

"Did you talk to your doctor?"

"Dad, seriously though. Can we talk about this later? I just got home. I'm exhausted." Jacqueline knew that would work. No one wanted Jacqueline exhausted. They all knew what happened then.

Her father gave in. "Okay. But this isn't over. Jacqueline, we need to discuss this. You work too hard. No one sees you. Please make sure you take your medicine."

"Goodbye, Dad."

Jacqueline hung up the phone and gulped her wine. She decided to change, taking her wine glass with her. Her therapist would suggest she go for a run, but she was too drained to fight with running leggings. She had just enough energy to change into her pajamas.

She walked down the freshly painted hallway, which was now devoid of any mementos of her former life. Gone was the small hole in the wall where Jack had smashed his tricycle into the door, failing to maneuver the turn into his bedroom. Instead, modern art gave off an air of sophistication and adultness. Why everyone—her therapist, Caroline, and her father—believed changing the interior of her home would help her only proved that no one understood her pain. Her beautiful memories were her pain, and no amount of paint could erase them from her mind. The detail and the fine accents made it more welcoming, less obvious, but the pain remained. It still lived. Because it never existed on the walls or in the furniture. Jack and John were her. Her very being.

She walked past Jack's room and gave a long, sad smile. She'd stuck to her guns on that one. She refused any changes. No lecture, no screaming match, no medical data would change her mind. She didn't care how absurd or irrational she was acting. Jack's room stayed as Jack had it. His small trophies stood on the shelf next to his superheroes; his comic books rested in his bookcase, still waiting to be read. His last obsession, *The Flash: Green Arrow's Perfect Shot*, still rested on his nightstand, the bookmark saving his place. She couldn't part with his things. She wondered if she ever would.

The one thing she knew for sure was it wasn't happening today. She smiled and moved on to her bedroom. As she opened her closet door, another reminder of her new life hit her. Just like the bland new decor of the rest of her apartment, she had transformed her closet. She no longer wanted to see any cute little black dresses or sexy silk blouses. They weren't necessary. She didn't go out anymore. Instead, she gave them to Lisa to enjoy. Her professional clothes invaded the entire closet, erasing any trace of a social or maternal life. Her suits were hanging there, like boring friends, in stuffy beige, brown, gray, navy, black. Everything was so orderly now. In its proper place. No one played in her closet or ran sticky fingers all over, causing her to send clothing back to the dry cleaners. She felt sick. She grabbed her nightgown and matching robe, defiantly leaving the cushioned hanger in the middle of the floor. At least the silk fabric would pamper her.

She grabbed her novel and fell into bed. John and Jack stared back at her from the frames on her nightstand. There was Jack, as a toddler, dressed as Batman. Her favorite wedding picture of her and John. How did things change so quickly? She grabbed her prescription bottle and took out her medicine, adding an extra pill to help her sleep. She picked up the picture frames to kiss them goodnight. *Help me, boys. I need my superheroes,* Jacqueline begged as she popped the pills in her mouth.

Chapter 5

ERIC CONCEILLO RUBBED HIS NECK, THE RED SPOTS A reminder of Mitchell's rage yesterday. He wanted to go home and get a shower and comfort his wife, Katherine, to process everything. She must be a wreck. Although Katherine and Tiffany were not close, Eric knew his wife loved her sister very much. They were so different in so many ways, but the sisterly protection was always there. Eric smiled to himself as he remembered Tiffany grilling him about his intentions when he and Katherine first started dating. He looked at his phone. Eight missed calls. Eric was torn. He wanted to be there for Katherine, but he couldn't leave his friend of twenty years. Mitchell had always protected him, and he wasn't about to abandon him now, even with his doubts. As he watched Mitchell check the hospital monitors for the third time in thirty minutes, Eric shook his head, desperately trying to remove the dangerous thoughts from his mind. Tiffany had been so upset about something. But she refused to tell him what she discovered.

Eric knew only too well that Mitchell had a volatile rage. Eric flashed back to college when he was covering the football team's practice before the big homecoming game for the school newspaper. Mitchell on the football field. The final practice before the big game. And then that idiot Tommy, kicking him after Mitchell got sacked, talking shit as he lay there on the ground. Mitchell exploded. The linebacker's physical advantage didn't stand a chance. It took five guys to pull Mitchell off him. Tommy spent three days in the hospital. If it wasn't for Coach Fay, Mitchell would have faced jail time. All those hours Coach spent teaching Mitchell to channel that rage. That rage disappearing. But did it disappear? Did Mitchell feel attacked by Tiffany?

Eric knew about Mitchell's past, but they never talked about it. And now he didn't know where to begin. He decided to be the straight shooter he always was. "I think we need to be prepared. I've made a few calls. I still have some lawyer friends who work in the district attorney's office."

Eric realized they'd switched roles. Normally Mitchell had his own reliable sources among the city's players. But Eric watched as Mitchell declined all their calls.

"Spill it," Mitchell said.

"Word around town is that Victoria is using her connections to get Frank Cunningham to charge you with murder."

Mitchell sighed. "Classic. Guess you do learn who your true friends are. When he needed money for his campaign, he acted like we were college roommates."

Eric didn't answer. They both knew lots of people were cheering for Mitchell's demise. He'd made too many enemies over the years, and they were coming out of the woodwork, now that Tiffany was no longer here to keep them at bay.

Eric pulled one out of Mitchell's playbook. Studying him over the years, he'd learned a few tricks. "Mitchell, you need to listen. For Patrick's sake."

"I am. I'm just surprised it's so soon. I thought our friend Cunningham wouldn't have acted so fast. Guess I should've known where his true allegiance lies. Gotta hand it to him, though. He did warn me that money only buys you so much status."

Here we go again. The "wrong side of the tracks" reason why everyone hates Mitchell. Eric turned away so Mitchell couldn't see his face. That excuse was getting old. Eric had always feared that Mitchell's obsession with becoming blue-blooded would be their downfall. He handed Mitchell some papers. "I've compiled a list of the best criminal attorneys in town. Just say the word, and someone will be here immediately."

Mitchell didn't respond.

Eric walked over and put the papers in front of Mitchell. He had been up all night creating a dossier on every criminal attorney he thought worthy, listing their credentials and schooling as well as their number of losses and wins. Eric didn't know what else to do, so he did what he always did. He prepared the stats. "We need to get you an attorney."

"You might want to listen to your friend." They both turned to see the intruder.

Mitchell stood up immediately, blocking the man from coming further into the room. Despite the man's impressive build, Mitchell still towered over him. "How the hell did you get in here?"

Eric moved back as the man flashed his detective badge. "I'm Detective O'Neill. Normally I don't go barging into hospital rooms, but since you failed to answer my calls, you left me no choice."

Mitchell didn't move. "This is not a good time."

The detective didn't budge. "I'm sorry about that, but I need to ask you some questions. We normally talk to the spouse within hours, if not minutes of the murder. To go without questioning you for over"—the detective glanced at his watch—"twenty-four hours is very rare. Now, please, don't make me do this the hard way."

Fearing a confrontation, Eric extended his hand. "Detective, I'm Eric Conceillo, Mr. Mitchell's brother-in-law and business partner. Please forgive us, it's been a difficult time."

As Eric shook hands, he maneuvered the detective into the room while warning Mitchell with his eyes against picking a fight.

O'Neill searched his notebook. "First, Mr. Mitchell, I'm truly sorry for your loss. I was at your home after the murder. I promise you I'm going to catch your wife's killer."

Eric witnessed the exchange between the two alpha males. Blank stares. The underlying disdain in the detective's voice indicated he hadn't ruled Mitchell out as a suspect. O'Neill turned to Patrick.

"How's your son doing, Mr. Mitchell?" Wrong move.

"What do you think? We are still here, aren't we?"

The detective refused to take the bait. "Again, I'm sorry. But I'm not the enemy here, Mr. Mitchell. I want to find the person who did this to your family."

Eric watched as hints of the calm, calculating real estate tycoon returned.

"Yes, I know," Mitchell said. "Please forgive me. As you can imagine, this has been an extremely difficult time. I'd rather focus on my son's health, so if we could please get this over with quickly."

"Could you please take me back to when you found your wife?"

"Where do you want me to begin? I found her dead."

The detective looked at his notes. "Thank you for that. According to a neighbor's lawn crew, you flew into your driveway at 5:45 p.m. But your mother-in-law, Mrs. Victoria Westerfer, didn't call 911 until 6:05 p.m. What was the delay? Why didn't you call 911?"

Mitchell didn't skip a beat. "What gardener? How the hell does he know it was 5:45? And, I'm sorry, Officer, but I didn't time myself. This is all new to me. First time I ever found my wife murdered."

Eric decided to end it. "Detective, do you think we can do this at another time? Mr. Mitchell is rightfully still upset about the entire situation."

"Mr. Conceillo, I'm afraid I need to ask Mr. Mitchell a few more questions."

Mitchell put his arm on Eric. "It's okay. Let's get this over with."

The detective looked at his notes again. "Just so we are clear, you have no explanation for the delay?"

"No." Anticipating his next question, Mitchell added, "And no. I don't remember what time I got home."

"Did you see a gun?'

"No, I didn't see a gun. Would have mentioned it, don't you think? Did your idiots not find one? Why don't you ask them?"

This time Eric got in between the two men. "Maybe we should wait for appropriate counsel. I don't like the tone of this."

Detective O'Neill closed his book. "I just have one last question regarding the night when you brought Patrick in. According to hospital staff, you were covered in blood and Patrick said, 'Daddy, don't hurt my mommy.' Do you know what he was talking about?"

Eric jumped up, physically leading the detective out of the room. "If you have any more questions, you can talk to Mr. Mitchell's counsel. We are done here."

With the detective gone, Eric faced Mitchell. "You need to look at that list. This is not good."

Mitchell put up his hand. "Not another lecture. I've already decided. She should hopefully be here soon."

"She?"

Mitchell refused to look at Eric. "Yes, Jacqueline Stone."

Eric didn't say a word. He knew the name. He just wondered if it could get any worse.

Chapter 6

FOR ONCE, JACQUELINE FELT GOOD. SHE WOKE UP with the sun, something she hadn't done in a long time. Her father answered on the first ring. "Jacqueline, what's wrong?"

Jacqueline forgot the time difference. "Oh, Dad. I'm sorry. I didn't mean to wake you. Go back to bed."

She heard him shuffle to sit up. "No, wait. Do I actually detect some excitement in that voice?"

She took a deep breath. "I'm closing the firm and coming out to see you and Caroline."

"What?"

Jacqueline recoiled. "Well, I have to admit that wasn't the reaction I was expecting. You keep saying I need to get my life in order."

"Yes. I did. But not by quitting. Jax, you are a brilliant attorney. You were meant to do that. I've seen you in action."

She sat back down. "Dad, please. I need your support right now. I need time. I just know I can't do this without John."

"Then take a vacation. But don't close. I'll give you the money to stay afloat." Her father paused. "Listen to me. John would never want you to do this. You know he was your second greatest supporter."

Jacqueline smiled, thinking back to all the times her dad and John had joked about which of them believed in her more. Only out of respect did John ever concede. "But Dad, John isn't here."

"Jacqueline, trust me, I know what it's like losing your soulmate." Her dad still got choked up talking about losing her mother to cancer. "But it gets easier. And the beauty is your mother is now with me every day, every moment. And she is with you. And so is John. And Jack. Think about it. Please."

Jacqueline hung up the phone and headed to the shower. She still thought she'd made the right decision. Everything reminded her of them and it paralyzed her. She just couldn't do it anymore. She looked around her home. She hated all the expensive vases and tchotchkes. She wanted to worry whether Jack would throw a football and knock them over. To hear the crash of things breaking. Or the rip of drapes when he dragged his tricycle over them. None of those precautions were necessary anymore.

She knew she didn't need the physical things. Those memories were a part of her. They lived in her heart. But the car accident haunted her. What happened that fateful day? Why couldn't she remember? She needed to leave. Take a trip. Stop thinking about the past. Maybe being with Caroline and around family was exactly what she needed. Find something that would bring a little joy back into her life. If that something even existed.

She splashed water from the shower on her face, hoping to find comfort. But it was useless. Death still haunted every aspect of her miserable existence. He seemed to be lurking around every corner. No matter what she tried to do, she couldn't escape his unimaginable power.

Last night, she'd reviewed her firm's financial status, and it was worse than she thought. The most recent text alert from TD Bank seemed like another nail in the coffin. The operating account for her law firm was negative and her line of credit was depleted. She'd maxed out her credit cards long ago. Yesterday, she'd met with a nerdy bank consultant for another small business loan but she hadn't heard back yet. The bank consultant politely but firmly told her he wasn't optimistic.

But at least she had her savings. She'd use that to pay her people. They didn't deserve to suffer. Her heart broke for Lisa. Lisa never should have followed Jacqueline when she left her family firm. It was such a bold, adventurous move, believing in Jacqueline, believing they could start their own firm. And now Lisa was pregnant. *How the hell am I ever going to tell her?* Since there were only four employees, she had enough to give them a few months' severance. Plus, she'd make sure they all got unemployment and health care benefits. Jacqueline forced herself out of the shower and got dressed. The least she could do was tell them all in person.

As she put on her favorite suit, Jacqueline slipped her pendant around her neck and stared at herself in the mirror. God, she looked like a ghost. Pale, bony, fragile. No wonder no one hired her. Nervous about her meeting, she tugged at her pendant, a slender gold tube that hung from a delicate chain. She lightly shook it to make sure her safety net—her pills—were still there, knowing full well they were. She laughed as she remembered the horror on the sales clerk's face when she had thrown out the tiny piece of paper that came with the necklace. Jacqueline had no intention of writing a goal or prayer on it and carrying it around her neck. It had no calming or soothing effect for Jacqueline. Instead, it felt like a noose.

As she packed her bag to go to the office for the last time, Jacqueline picked up her cell phone. The screen indicated a new message. O'Neill. Would he ever stop checking in on her? She could see his handsome grin as if he were standing there. In another time, another place, things could have been different. He was completely different from John, but a good man. Lisa had begged her to accept his invitation for coffee. But Jacqueline couldn't. Not yet. Maybe not ever.

Her cell phone rang. Lisa. Dread filled Jacqueline's heart. Lisa had been with Jacqueline from the start. Always positive and motivating, telling Jacqueline that their next big client was around the corner. Lisa was always trying to appear sophisticated, with her dark-rimmed glasses, long auburn hair in a fancy updo, and a crisp pin-striped pantsuit. But the lack of lines on her beautiful face gave her away. Lisa was young, innocent of the tragedies of life. Two things Jacqueline was not. Jacqueline hit accept right before it went to voicemail. "Hi, Lisa. I'm sorry I'm running late. I'm on my way in."

Jacqueline heard the excitement in her voice. "Uh, Jacqueline, we need to gather our team right away." Despite her misery, Jacqueline smiled. When they first started out, Lisa announced that "team" sounded much more impressive in the courtroom and in front of clients, even though most clients were too poor or worried to care. "Team" was code for her and Lisa since there were no other lawyers in the firm. But according to the world of positive Lisa, if they talked like they were a big firm, someday they would be. Jacqueline couldn't break her spirit.

"Lisa, I think you misunderstood my message. There is no good news, but I do need to speak to everyone." *To tell them I have to let them go.* Jacqueline felt vomit rising in her throat.

"No, boss. You don't understand. I need you to come in now. We have a new client."

Chapter 7

TO AN OUTSIDER, THE WESTERFER MANSION STOOD elegant and regal, its façade a testament to timeless beauty. While the cold air added a crisp serenity to its appearance, inside, Victoria Harrison Westerfer sat devastated in her beloved library at her Chippendale desk, where her mother and her grandmother had sat years before. She looked up at the priceless books, the artwork that lined the shelves, and her meticulous photo books. She had taken years to design everything in this house, including the people, so her life was perfect. Just perfect. She looked up at the portrait of her father, Bryon Charles Harrison III. Her parents had passed the responsibility of the family name, their reputation, the Harrison image and its allure to her. And she had not only protected it, but made it into something much grander, much more coveted. Unparalleled class, the society pages called it, and Victoria made sure the term followed the Harrisons, and then the Westerfers, from then on. And it wasn't an easy feat. Her mind wandered to her husband, Preston Westerfer. She'd thought *he* was a challenge. But that monster Mitchell. Ugh. She shuddered at the thought of his name. Damn Tiffany for letting that monster enter their lives. *Damn him, and damn you, Father*, she silently cursed, throwing her Baccarat tumbler into the marble fireplace. If her father had been able to control himself and his gambling, their family fortune would have lasted for generations to come. But no...

"Mrs. Westerfer, please allow me to clean that up."

Victoria gave her assistant a small nod as the girl quickly cleaned up the mess and retreated. *A Harrison never loses her composure, especially in front of others*, Victoria could hear her mother demanding. And Victoria never did. Until. *Well, Mother, you never lost a child. Or had a monster destroy your life's legacy.*

Victoria laughed to herself as she remembered her mother's reaction to Victoria's late husband, Preston. *We will have to help him. Educate him on how we do things.* Victoria's mother always placed an emphasis on *we* because Harrisons were different, better than others. Preston's blood wasn't blue, but together Victoria and her mother made him as blue as they could. God, was it painful to teach him. But he had the one thing the Harrisons needed. Money. When her father's favorite pastime finally caught up with him, Victoria paid the price.

But Preston's money wasn't evil. No, not like the monster's. Ryan Mitchell tried to ruin her family. But Victoria refused to give up. She willed herself to stay strong. For her grandson, Patrick.

Her assistant returned. "Excuse me, Mrs. Westerfer, there's a Detective Daniel O'Neill to see you."

Her plan for revenge began. "Please send him in." Victoria's anger rose as the detective walked in.

He extended his hand, which Victoria took solely out of protocol. "Mrs. Westerfer. Once again, I'm so sorry for your loss."

"Thank you for coming, Detective. But I must say, I'm not pleased that that monster hasn't been arrested yet."

Victoria stood perfectly still as she observed the detective taking in her and the room. She knew her resemblance to Tiffany was uncanny, and he probably expected her to be the mess he met the night of the murder, a very rare sighting of Victoria Westerfer. That would never happen again. Her skilled ability to apply makeup concealed most of her pain. She knew there were no signs of her tears and nights of hell. Instead, she gave him a moment to appreciate her beauty. Like her daughter, Victoria could captivate any man with a pulse, even at her age, and she intended on using every weapon in her arsenal. A fire blazed in the marble fireplace of the dark, impressive library.

Her son, Harrison, entered. She nodded to him. *You're up.* With golden hair just like hers and tan skin, he could be the poster child for the country club. He was dressed in a wool tweed sports coat with patches on the elbows, and Victoria stood proud next to him. He was finally acting like a Harrison.

He extended a well-manicured hand to greet the detective. "Thank you for coming. I'm Harrison Westerfer, Tiffany's brother. As you can imagine, my family is devastated."

The detective glanced at the shotgun resting against the fireplace. "I assume that isn't loaded?"

Harrison followed Detective O'Neill's gaze. "Oh, that. I just came back from trapshooting. I needed a diversion from this tragedy. Don't worry. Unlike him, I don't shoot humans."

O'Neill shook his head. "Let's back up. I promise you that we will do everything we can to find the person who did this to your sister, but I need names here. Are you referring to her husband, Ryan Mitchell?"

Despite her attempts to hide her pain, Victoria shivered. She appreciated that Harrison put his arm protectively around her.

Harrison continued, "We asked you to come here today to give us an update on my sister's murder. What are you doing about it?"

"The investigation is going full speed. As you are aware, we questioned Mr. Mitchell at the scene but found no concrete evidence linking him to the murder. He claims he discovered his wife dead upon arrival. Due to the urgent medical attention needed for his son, we conducted a search of Mr. Mitchell for possible weapons and evidence. But, we did make a rare exception and allowed him a police escort to the hospital to ensure his son's well-being. We have confiscated his passport but permitted him to remain free, considering his strong ties to the community. The district attorney is currently reviewing the case to determine if there is sufficient probable cause to bring charges against Mr. Mitchell."

Utter disgust raged through Victoria. She wanted to throw another glass. She spoke through her teeth, trying to control herself. "The last few days have been the worst of my life. Every day that he isn't behind bars is its own death sentence to me."

"Yes, Mrs. Westerfer. I read your statement."

"Well, what part of it did you not understand? My daughter called me that day hysterical. She feared for her life. So I rushed—"

Detective O'Neill interrupted. "Mrs. Westerfer, you didn't actually speak with your daughter then, correct?"

She waved her hand. "Must we do this again? Technically, you're correct. We never spoke. But did you not listen to the voicemail?"

"Yes, I did. And I agree with you that your daughter was upset." He referred to his notes. "But she said she needed you to come to the house immediately. That message was left much earlier, but you didn't call 911 until 6:05 p.m. Why the delay?"

Turning her head in disgust, she held up her hand. "Please, stop. Are you really going to make me relive that day? I will never forgive myself." Genuine tears flowed from her eyes.

O'Neill searched for a tissue box, but Harrison beat him to it. He handed her a monogrammed handkerchief. "I don't think this is necessary. As my mother told the other detective, she had a standing appointment at Spalon. She explained that the other night."

"Understood. But, as I am sure you agree, we have a duty to ensure we find the person responsible for your sister's murder."

Mrs. Westerfer stood. The years of being complicit with Tiffany's plan to help that monster control his violent tendencies overcame her. "I went to the house as quickly as I could. I knew all along that man was evil. He has always had a rage in him, and to think we helped him hide it. Do you understand the guilt I feel?

"When I walked in, he was holding my daughter. Her blood was all over him. He had shot her to death. In their family room. With my grandson seeing God knows what. Traumatized. Now that evil man has the only thing I have left of my daughter. My grandson. And you stand there and say you need more evidence? He didn't even pretend by calling 911. I had to."

"Mother, please sit down. Remember what the doctor said. You must take care of yourself."

"Harrison, stop."

Victoria regained her composure and moved to face the detective. Her height and heels put her eye to eye with him. "I may look like a lady to you, but, mark my words, I will not rest until Ryan Mitchell is behind bars. I should have never let him in this family. That was my mistake. But no more. Do you understand me? There is no question that animal killed her. And now he has forbidden me to see my grandson. Your captain, with whom I am very good friends, I might add, assured me that you are the best. Now prove it. What are you doing to ensure my grandson's safety?"

"Mother, I need you to sit down. Please forgive my mother. She is just very upset. No one will tell us how Patrick is doing."

Detective O'Neill nodded. "I'm sorry, but Mr. Mitchell is his legal guardian and only he can give us permission to speak to anyone about Patrick's health. Unfortunately, that's the law."

Victoria did not need a reminder. "Please. Don't. I couldn't care less about your apologies. I will get custody of my grandson by myself. Because clearly, Mr. uh, uh—"

"It's O'Neill," Harrison cut in.

"Detective O'Neill," the officer added.

"Yes, whatever." Victoria waved her hand dismissively. "Mr. O'Neill, if you do your job properly and arrest him, I can get custody. I don't think you fully appreciate the situation. My grandson is in grave danger and you people refuse to do anything about it."

The detective ran his hand through his hair, his gaze fixed on his notepad.

Victoria Westerfer was used to getting answers. "Well?"

"Mrs. Westerfer, it's not that easy. Mr. Mitchell is a well-respected businessperson in the community. He claims he just found your daughter murdered. Also, the preliminary results show no gunshot residue on his hands."

Her crystal eyes bore into Detective O'Neill. Clearly, his captain did not send the best, and he would be her next call. "Listen to me, O'Neill. That animal is well respected because of his ties to my family. There is nothing else to respect about him. He should be caged, and the key thrown away. And, I said he was evil, not stupid. He's smart enough to manipulate the evidence and you."

Victoria pushed her son's hand off her shoulder. "And if you ask me, this isn't the first time he's killed. Look into his background. He almost beat a fellow teammate to death. And if I was a betting person"—the pain of all her losses momentarily made her pause—"I'd say that bastard killed my sweet Preston."

"Mrs. Westerfer, those are some strong accusations. Do you have evidence to support those claims? When did your husband die? Was his death investigated?"

Victoria moved in front of Detective O'Neill, her face inches from his. "I don't think you understand how our world works. What has happened to my family since that man has come through our doors is unspeakable." Victoria lowered her voice to a whisper, as if exposing a world secret. Pointing to the portrait, she explained, "My family, the Harrisons, are a direct line from English royalty. And in our world, people don't *murder* people. The idea of opening up this family to scandal is unthinkable. My father would turn over in his grave."

She physically shuddered at the thought. "But now that we are in this place, I may consider exhuming my husband's body." Victoria pointed to a smaller portrait. "That's Preston. When he died, it was a shock to all of us. A man of good physical health suddenly dies of a heart attack right in the middle of the election of our family business.

He'd felt it was time for him to retire and turn the reins over to Harrison here. Everyone convinced me, including our stupid family doctor, that it was stress-related. But now I'm not so sure. Preston died, and suddenly that animal was CEO."

"Mrs. Westerfer, I understand that you have suffered some great losses. I'm sorry for that. But I assure you that we are working quickly and diligently to bring your daughter's murderer to justice."

While Victoria faced the fire, Harrison spoke up. "Detective, that is why we called you here. We have prepared a package for you which contains all the documents you need. First, as you will see, he—"

"I assume you are referring to Mr. Mitchell."

"Yes."

"I need you to use his name."

"Fine. But please understand our pain. Mr. Mitchell is a ruthless monster. I knew he was trouble the minute he entered our lives, but obviously we did not appreciate the depths of his destruction. I watched him connive his way into this family, first by befriending my older sister Katherine, then he deceived my father with all his manipulation, and finally he abused my sister Tiffany. We don't understand what you are waiting for. For God's sake, he killed Tiffany while their son watched."

"I'm not sure what you're asking. Do you want us to investigate your father's death too? No disrespect, but didn't your mother just say your father died of a heart attack?"

Victoria shook her head, realizing Harrison was getting nowhere with the detective. Once again, she needed to do everything. The information she put together for the detective explained everything and put the nails in Ryan Mitchell's coffin. Victoria handed Detective O'Neill the package. "Here is everything you need. Tiffany and that animal owned fifty-one percent of our family company, while my other daughter and Harrison had the other forty-nine percent.

For the record, we have no idea how that happened. It wasn't my husband's wishes."

"So if Ryan Mitchell and your late daughter, Tiffany, were to divorce, Mr. Mitchell would lose the company?"

Victoria nodded her head. "Yes. And Tiffany just received this."

She handed him the printout of a text chain. Watching the detective examine the paper gave her the first small glimpse of satisfaction. "My daughter received that text three days before she was murdered. She was filing for divorce with our lawyers."

Chapter 8

JACQUELINE ENTERED HER LAW FIRM THROUGH THE back door and told Lisa to meet her in her office.

"What is Tyler Hines doing here?" Jacqueline whispered. Like every other respectable attorney in the Philadelphia area, Jacqueline knew Tyler. Or at least knew him by reputation. Always behind the scenes and never getting his own hands dirty, he was the mastermind behind every successful business matchmaking deal in the tristate area. The gossip in the legal circles was that if Tyler Hines put his seal of approval on a deal, money poured out. His touch was green. But it wasn't his business acumen that originally drew Jacqueline's attention to this legal legend. After her brief but profound encounter with Ryan Mitchell, she felt compelled to follow his career. Once Mitchell entered the real estate world, Tyler dropped many of his A-list clients, focusing solely on the Mitchells and the Westerfers. With Tyler's years of legal expertise and connections, no one was surprised when he and Mitchell were dubbed the *Dream Team of Real Estate*, a nickname both had outright disclaimed. And given the latest news about the death of Mitchell's wife, it could only mean one thing. But that was impossible.

Lisa looked as confused as Jacqueline felt. "Boss, how would I know? But isn't this exciting? You know who he is, right?"

Although it was well deserved given her behavior over the last few months, Jacqueline ignored the question. "Of course I know who he is. But what is he doing here?"

Lisa shrugged. Jacqueline slumped in her chair, exhausted before the roller coaster began. An hour ago, she'd decided to close shop. Now the biggest case in Philadelphia in decades, or potentially ever, sat in her conference room. Lisa stared at Jacqueline, waiting. Jacqueline wanted to find within herself the lawyer Lisa followed to this hellhole.

Lisa broke into her thoughts. "Boss, what do I tell him?" Jacqueline sat in silence. "Come on. It can't hurt to just hear him out. We don't even know what he wants. Just talk to him."

Jacqueline stared at her associate, her eyes full of hope and excitement. Lisa had taken a chance on Jacqueline. When Jacqueline's father-in-law fired her, Lisa didn't hesitate, marching right out of the offices alongside her. And she continued to stay by Jacqueline's side, believing in her abilities. Lisa bet her own career and her young family's financial future on Jacqueline. And up until today, everything Jacqueline had done had let her down. Now she had a chance to prove herself.

"Okay, I'll talk to him," Jacqueline said. As soon as the words left her mouth, Lisa's face lit up like fireworks. Jacqueline grabbed Lisa's hand. "Please. One step at a time. Let's not get our hopes up. Give me five minutes and then send him in."

Despite Jacqueline's warning, Lisa beamed. "Okay, boss. Got it."

Jacqueline collapsed against her office door. *Breathe*, she instructed herself. It was one client meeting. Robotically, she switched out her walking shoes for the Christian Louboutin pumps John bought her at Neiman Marcus. She loved wearing them. *Remember, the red sole means we love you.* Then she decided the red soles were too flashy, so she went with a pair of plain black Manolo Blahnik pumps. She needed the height boost. This case could change everything. She retreated to her desk and opened her top drawer with shaking hands.

Her superheroes stared back at her. God, how she missed them. In this picture, taken just after she won her first criminal trial, Jack was dressed as Green Arrow, holding a pink card that said *My mommy is the best layer.* Later, they laughed at his attempt to spell *lawyer* at The Cheesecake Factory. When she started that trial, John created her collage of encouragement: pictures of the three of them, at the beach, at home, Jack in his various superhero costumes. And during every trial after that, the collage became her superpower. Right next to her real medicine bottle. She thought about taking one and then decided against it. She needed a clear head.

Jacqueline shut the drawer and checked her reflection in the mirror. Tyler Hines. In her office. Unbelievable. She ran her hand through her hair, smoothing down the imaginary flyaways. Checked her clothing. Although it was a little loose from the lack of eating, she wore her St. John suit with an air of confidence. She at least gave the outward appearance of an expert counsel.

She hit the intercom button. "Please send Mr. Hines in."

When Tyler Hines entered Jacqueline's office, his imposing frame towered over her. Her high heels were like a Band-Aid for a gunshot wound. Jacqueline felt like she was shrinking with every step he took forward. No surprise that he and Mitchell crushed their opponents. *Breathe*, she reminded herself. "Mr. Hines, I presume. I'm Jacqueline Stone."

"Ms. Stone, thank you for seeing me on such short notice." Jacqueline accepted his outstretched arm. His handshake was firm as his eyes met hers, a welcome sign of a man who regularly dealt with professional women. Skillfully, he examined her private office without being overly obvious. Jacqueline noticed that he glanced at her diplomas, most likely confirming his research: Boston College undergraduate, BC law. He gave an involuntary nod to the wall. With one sweep, he surveyed the office contents.

The week had not been kind to him. Jacqueline remembered those first days too well. As a disaster survivor herself, Jacqueline noticed the signs of despair. But unlike women who had their arsenal of makeup, he had dark bags under his puffy eyes and sagging skin that left him exposed, old instead of distinguished. Jacqueline was ultrasensitive to the telltale signs, having spent hours herself in front of the mirror trying to hide her pain.

Yet there were still hints of his sophisticated style. With well-cut gray hair and a matching trimmed beard and his expensive tailored suit and freshly polished wingtip shoes, he had a James Brolin feel. But no smile. No warmth. He was ready for battle. Old-school. Old-school men expected their attorneys to be men, with gray hair.

The air was thick, an awkwardness hanging in the air.

"Please, Mr. Hines, sit down and tell me what I can do for you."

"Is that your son?" Tyler pointed to a picture of Jack dressed as Green Arrow.

Jacqueline didn't look at the picture as she wanted him to stay focused. "Yes."

"Green Arrow. I didn't know kids today knew who he was."

Jacqueline smiled. "Very impressive."

Mr. Hines squirmed in his chair. "I loved comic books. Read them all. Do kids even read comic books today?"

"Mine did." Jacqueline shuffled some paper around. "Mr. Hines, how can I help you?"

"Well, Ms. Stone..."

"Please call me Jacqueline."

He didn't extend the same courtesy to her. He paused, debating. "Jacqueline..." He seemed to be searching for his words. Jacqueline waited.

"I am here on behalf of Ryan Mitchell," Tyler said.

There. It. Was. A paying client. Instead of feeling the elation she'd thought she would when given the chance to return to her old life, she wanted to throw up. Luckily for her, Mr. Hines wrung his hands in desperation, apparently too distraught to see her fear. He looked at everything and anything to avoid her eyes. His blatant desire for someone else was written all over his face.

That problem, a lack of confidence in female defense attorneys, fueled Jacqueline. She thrived on demonstrating the different, but just as valuable, assets of a female attorney. Most men wanted male lawyers. They equated brute, physical strength with legal armor in a courtroom battle. Jacqueline used this archetypal thinking to crush them in court. Despite her fear, Jacqueline felt something stir. That old desire to win. She didn't make idle chatter or small talk to make him feel comfortable. That's what he expected her to do. He was wrong. She was not what he expected.

They sat there, in a silent game of chicken. Tyler broke first. "Are you aware that his wife was murdered?"

"Yes."

"We're interviewing potential lawyers to represent him if the need arises. Mr. Mitchell hasn't made any determination as to his choice of firms, but we were hoping I could ask you a couple of questions."

"No."

"Excuse me?"

"Mr. Hines, the Ryan Mitchell I know is decisive. I don't appreciate this little game you're playing. As Mr. Mitchell's trusted advisor, you are aware of my trial successes and failures and what people say about me. Now let's get to the real reason you're here."

He didn't blink. He looked relieved. "Okay, Ms. Stone." Back to her surname. "You're right. Mr. Mitchell would like to retain you if he is accused of killing his wife. While we believe it will not come to that, we'd like to be prepared."

Mr. Hines paused, rubbing his forehead. "Please forgive me. I'm usually much better than this. It's just that it's…"

Jacqueline remained silent.

Mr. Hines raised his eyes to meet Jacqueline's. "I don't know much about you. But one thing seems evident. You're genuine. A good person."

"I'd like to think so."

"Mr. Mitchell isn't just a colleague. I don't say this to many people, but he is like the son I never had. He would never harm a hair on Tiffany's head. That's why this is so difficult. I need to make sure he's okay."

"Well, I can tell you if I take the case, and that's a big if, he will get the best representation."

Mr. Hines abandoned any sense of pretense. "What is the if? I can't let Mr. Mitchell down. He expects you to meet him at the hospital. This is the one thing I must do for him."

Jacqueline watched as the distinguished man's eyes started to tear. "Mr. Hines, there's nothing for you to do. I talk directly to my potential clients. If Mr. Mitchell wants to hire me, he'll have to ask. I sense there is more. What is it?"

Mr. Hines looked away. "It's just that I'm engaged to Victoria Westerfer."

"The victim's mother?"

"Yes."

Jacqueline knew the answer, but she asked anyway. "What's the issue?"

"I know she wants to find the person who did this to our family. But Victoria blames Mr. Mitchell. And that worries me. For that reason, I need to make sure Mr. Mitchell has the best representation."

"Regardless, Mr. Mitchell should retain counsel as soon as possible." It hadn't been that long ago that she was the best criminal defense attorney in the city. She slipped back into her skills as easily as into a conversation with a long-ago best friend. She knew her stuff. "The spouse is always the key suspect even if your name is Mitchell."

As much as her firm needed a client like Mitchell, she demanded one who trusted her abilities more. "And I agree with you. I am not sure I am the right attorney for this matter either."

Tyler looked at her. "Your bluntness is a welcome surprise. And people rarely surprise me. Maybe Mitch—sorry, I mean Mr. Mitchell—does know what he's doing. And I admire your frankness. It's refreshing. I am also impressed with your knowledge about me. It's just that Mitch...I hope you understand how distraught the whole family is. We have never experienced anything like this. But with everything going on, one thing has stayed constant. Mr. Mitchell always prepares for the worst. I don't know how he knows you, but he insists on you, and only you.

"And Ms. Stone, I truly fear for Mr. Mitchell. Victoria is out to see him pay. I love her dearly, but he didn't do this. He's a good man, husband, and father.

"I guess what I'm saying is, he didn't kill his wife, and I want, I want..." Tyler stopped himself mid-sentence. "Please understand. This is nothing personal. It's just that this is Mr. Mitchell we're talking about, and I need to make sure he has the best. Given the uh"—he seemed to be searching for the right word—"circumstances, I don't know if you're the right person."

"I said I agree."

"Well, I must admit that wasn't what I expected either. But then again, this week has been full of surprises. The reality is that Mr. Mitchell insists that you represent him."

Tyler ran his hand through his hair. He took a deep breath. "Would you please come see him and at least talk to him?"

Jacqueline hesitated. It was the case of a lifetime. It could make her career and keep her firm alive. She thought about Lisa. Her future. Lisa's young family would be secure, have health care. But Jacqueline's gut was telling her not to go. She felt the same strange sensation she'd felt only once before in her life. When they all got into the car. That fateful day. Could her body be trying to tell her something? Could it be trying to protect her once again? She didn't listen then, and it had cost her dearly.

She couldn't help herself. The thought of helping someone, of a real case, stirred something she'd thought had long ago died. "Mr. Hines, why don't we set something up?"

As Tyler agreed to set up a meeting, Jacqueline prayed. *Please let me be wrong.*

Chapter 9

DR. MARC FITZGERALD SAT IN THE GREAT ROOM OF his home, as his wife liked to call it, a plate of assorted cheeses, crackers, and grapes in front of him, as he scanned the *Philadelphia Inquirer*. Plaques of his awards and accomplishments lined the walls, and he filled with pride when people noticed. His achievements in the medical field exceeded his every dream. But now he'd replaced lively research debates with cocktail hour with his wife prior to going out to dinner. He no longer had to rush out the door to get to the hospital with a banana in his hand, trying to balance his travel mug. And he was miserable. He hated retirement.

His wife, Nora, rushed around the kitchen, cleaning up before she could sit and eat. When Marc first retired, he tried to wait for her, hating every minute as his food got cold. But she couldn't sit if there was any mess. To save themselves from divorce court, as a compromise, they made a pact that Marc could eat his food before his anal-retentive wife sat down. He enjoyed the quiet time to read anyway. But this evening he needed it. To think. CNBC played on the TV, and at least the market was up. His account had almost doubled since he'd been home. But for the first time in a while, he didn't care about the market. He needed to find out what they were saying about the murder of Tiffany Westerfer Mitchell. He switched to the local news. And there was the update.

His wife finally sat down to join him. Following his gaze, she looked at the screen. "Wow, is that who I think it is? *The* Tiffany Westerfer Mitchell? Somebody killed her?"

Marc hated how clueless his wife was. Life wasn't all about her book club and tennis. He reached for the remote. "Honey, shhhh. I'm trying to watch."

Marc rewound the DVR to hear the entire story from Jim Gardner of *Channel 6 Action News*. "Socialite heiress and philanthropist Tiffany Westerfer Mitchell, daughter of the late industrious magnate Preston Westerfer and wife of the enigmatic real estate investment guru Ryan Mitchell, was found dead in her Chestnut Hill mansion earlier this week. Chestnut Hill police are not sharing any details at this time but have now officially ruled her death a homicide. It is rumored that the only child of Ryan and Tiffany Mitchell was home at the time of the murder and may be a witness. Many people at Penn Central Hospital saw Mr. Mitchell run into the emergency room carrying his young son on the night of February 24. Both were reportedly covered in blood. We will keep you updated as developments come through."

A picture of Tiffany, taken at last year's hospital ball, appeared on the screen. Nora almost spilled her martini. "Oh my God. We know that woman. Wasn't she just here the other day?"

Marc regretted watching the news with his wife. He quickly shut off the TV. "Ahh, yes."

The story obviously had Nora's imaginative mind stirring as she almost put butter in her cocktail instead of on the bread. "Didn't you say she asked you if you would consider a position on the hospital board? Dear God, Marc, I wonder what happened! What if you can help? Do you think that board position had anything to do with her death? Maybe someone got mad that they were considering you?"

Marc cursed himself for coming up with that excuse. But when Tiffany Mitchell surprised him by just showing up at his doorstep after he refused her phone calls, he couldn't think of any other logical reason. And he sure as hell wasn't about to tell Nora the truth. "Oh, honey. You read too many mysteries for that book club. If I recall correctly, that woman had a lot of enemies. I bet with all those real estate deals, her husband is hooked up with some shady characters, and they killed her to get back at him."

Nora started eating. "Oh, I know. It's just that I have never known anyone, much less had any contact with anyone, who has been *murdered*. It's just so scary. We need to make sure we lock our doors."

Marc needed to allay his wife's fears. The last thing he needed was that damn book club coming up with theories. "Well, I can tell you it definitely wasn't about some hospital board. I bet you that hunk of a husband all you girls were raving about at the hospital ball did it. It's exactly what people say. It's always the spouse. I told you they seemed too perfect. I bet he beat her when no one was looking. And to think, you were so enamored with them."

Nora chewed on a piece of Brie. "Honey, it wasn't just me. They are a beautiful couple. Everyone was talking about how perfect and lovely they are. Were, I guess now. But as always, you were right. Can't judge a book by its cover. You just never know."

Yeah, lovely all right—until she threatens to destroy your life. To think of all I did for her family and then it backfires. Marc hated to even think of that day. The forced retirement. He wanted to fight it, but fighting the Harrisons was like taking on the Kennedys.

Nora's phone alarm went off. "Oh, honey, look at the time. We have to meet the Savadoves at the club in an hour, and I still have to clean up and get dressed."

As Nora grabbed the cocktail plates, she remembered. "But Marc. You never told me. Did you agree to accept the position?"

Marc kissed his wife on the cheek, buttering her up. "Of course I said no, Nora. I retired to spend time with you. I'm done." And he was. Done being the fall guy. He left his wife at the kitchen sink, happy in her own little world. Unfortunately for him, the real world was closing in. He was done taking chances. He needed a plan. As boring as life was, he wasn't spending his retirement in jail.

Chapter 10

PHILADELPHIA WAS STILL SLEEPING AS JACQUELINE headed to Penn Central Hospital. Unlike the day before, last night she had barely slept. Adrenaline pumped through her body as she looked out the window. Her driver, Bernie, had been with her so long he could read when she wanted to talk and when she needed silence. Bernie was a necessary, but costly, expense. Part of her wanted to push the gas pedal for Bernie, to fast-forward through the encounter. The other part of her was thankful the doors were locked because she imagined herself jumping out and running for the hills. But one thing was certain. She felt alive again. She was back in the game. Or at least a possibility existed. For whatever reason, Ryan Mitchell had asked for her. And until yesterday, she hadn't realized how desperately she needed to be needed.

"Jax, there's a lot of traffic up ahead. Do you want me to drop you off here so you're not late?" Bernie asked.

Emergency. One word. Stared back at her. And like a silent trigger, Jacqueline felt her heart begin to race. Not the emergency room entrance. Cars honked, but Bernie didn't move. "Jax?"

With shaking hands, Jacqueline grabbed her messenger bag. "Oh, sure. No problem. This is perfect. Thanks, Bernie."

Jacqueline froze as Bernie drove away. I can do this, Jacqueline decided as she walked through the doors of the hospital. But the moment the doors slid open, she returned to four years ago. And her mind flooded with memories of finding Jack here. Keep walking, she demanded. Take a step. Her feet moved, but her body reached for the walls. The hallway narrowed, and she could feel her heart beating faster. She leaned against a door. And she saw it. The light. Spinning in her eye. My aura. Dear God, not now. I can't have a seizure.

She reached for her pendant. Her hands knew the routine. She opened the cylinder quickly and popped her rescue pill in her mouth. She could hear sounds all around her, but she focused on her breathing. Please stop. Not now. As she took deep breaths, the spinning faded. The medicine was working.

"Ma'am, are you all right?" a young nurse asked, running by. Luckily, she didn't really have time to help and accepted Jacqueline's assurances that she normally rested against doors.

Keep walking. She brushed her hand along the rail and forced herself to walk. The bright, fluorescent lights exposed the fear on her face. She hoped the extra time she spent on her makeup had worked and that the expensive concealer would hide her emotions.

None of the precautions helped. Her panic rose. She instinctively tugged on her pendant. Breathe, she silently instructed herself. She could hear her therapist's advice. Focus on happy things. But as she passed through the corridors, the smell of disinfectant overwhelmed her senses. Each hallway seemed to stretch forever, each department flooding her with memories. Focus on the staff and the people. The stretchers and wheelchairs going by her increased her anxiety. She shouldn't have come. She grabbed the railing. She wanted to turn around and run. As she stood there, hands shaking, she found the sign for the Mitchell wing. Beautiful mahogany doors replaced the traditional white hospital doors. All she had to do was turn the corner and press the button.

Mr. Mitchell waited on the other side. He and his sick child needed her help. Images of her employees flashed in her mind: Lisa and Billy, her computer whiz investigator. She thought of their belief in her. And then out of the blue, a little boy appeared holding his mother's hand, his Spiderman backpack strapped securely on. Somehow she found the strength to move her feet. As she passed through the swinging doors, the Harrison-Mitchell wing achieved its goal. Gone were the muted, dull walls that blended seamlessly into the cold linoleum floors of the rest of the hospital. In contrast, the Harrison-Mitchell wing created a welcoming home where visitors felt like guests, with sparkling hardwood floors and beautiful grass-linen wallpaper. The stark difference overwhelmed Jacqueline. She turned to leave.

For some reason, she couldn't. Instead, her body moved forward, controlling this situation. Her need to see him overpowered her mind and almost immediately, she was standing in front of Patrick. She would have recognized him anywhere. His beautiful towhead ringlets were gone, replaced with the sandy blond hair of a now older boy. His eyes were closed as if he were the male version of Sleeping Beauty.

Patrick looked so much like Jack, and her mind flooded with memories. A longing to touch the boy propelled her into the room, and she laid her hand on his fingers. God, how she missed Jack's chubby hands, hands that created such mischief, painted on walls, climbed over furniture. She and John had to babyproof the entire house. The gates, the locks on cabinets. John joked that he was going to starve before he figured them out. They'd debated about taking the gates down because they desperately wanted another child. All gone. Never going to happen.

Jacqueline shut her eyes, and suddenly, she was in a different hospital room, hearing the dreaded words, "I'm sorry." It can't happen again. This child can't die like Jack. Just as she felt tears forming in her eyes, she heard her name.

"Jacqueline?"

She didn't need to turn around. She recognized the voice. She quickly dabbed her eyes and turned to face him. "Yes. Hello, Mr. Mitchell." When he saw her, his face relaxed. Jacqueline tried to ignore her racing heart.

"You came. I wasn't sure you would." Neither one approached. Mitch stayed in the doorway. "Thank you for coming."

"Of course." Mitch still possessed that regal, distinguished look despite his stubble and baggy eyes. Jacqueline felt even smaller as his six-foot-four frame towered over her. But the moment she walked in, she realized she had made a mistake. Patrick was lying there, wires attached to his tiny body. She could barely stand, feeling her legs go weak.

Mitch moved a chair closer to her. "Are you okay? Here, sit. I know it's difficult to see him like this. It breaks my heart."

She graciously accepted the chair he slid under her. "Sorry, I don't like hospitals." She knew he could see right through her and was thankful that he didn't press the issue. "I'm so sorry about everything. I can't imagine what you're going through." As she said the words, she hoped she fooled him. Her past contained the same unfathomable pain. She felt faint.

"Please. Not necessary. It won't help now. I didn't bring you here for your pity. I need your services." Mitch pointed to the hospital room. "And well, this wasn't exactly how I was hoping we'd meet again."

"That makes two of us."

Jacqueline looked at him. It was obvious that he hadn't slept. There were dark circles under his eyes. Her heart ached for him as he stared at her, seemingly unsure where to begin.

She handed him a package. "For Patrick. When he wakes up."

Mitch accepted the wrapped gift, covered with images of baseballs and mitts. "Wow. Wasn't expecting that. That's very kind of you."

As Mitch opened it, Jacqueline explained, "If I remember correctly, Jack—"

"Patrick," Mitch corrected.

Oh my God. Did I really call him Jack? "Forgive me. Patrick was obsessed with baseball. I heard"—Jacqueline paused—"that little boys love this story."

Well, at least mine did.

Mitch flipped through the book. "Thank you."

The sound of beeping interrupted her thought. "What's that? Is everything okay?"

Mitch quickly moved over and hit a button. "Oh, yes. These machines are ultrasensitive. He's fine. Or at least stable for now. They had to sedate him again." Mitch looked away. "I'm sorry for staring. Part of me was afraid you wouldn't come."

"To be honest, I was surprised when your friend showed up in my office and said you wanted me to handle your case. Nice man. But for the record, he wasn't impressed."

"Tyler is a great guy, but he's old-school."

"I got that impression." Jacqueline hesitated. As she watched Mitch stare at the monitors and check on Patrick, she decided she couldn't take this case. His life, and more importantly, little Patrick's, was on the line. She couldn't risk either of them just to see if she could stage a comeback. No matter how much her staff needed her to.

"But Mitch, unfortunately, I agree with him. You need someone else. Someone with a team of experts. That's not me. I came here as a friend, not as a lawyer. I can't take your case."

"Do you think that I killed her?"

The anger in his eyes scared Jacqueline. "It doesn't matter whether you did it or not. That has nothing to do with my decision."

He grabbed her arm, forcing her to look at him. To look at Patrick. "Someone did this to him. To me. I need you." She winced in pain, and he released his grip. "I'm sorry. Don't realize my own strength sometimes. But I need to know. Do you think I killed my wife?"

Jacqueline felt Mitch's eyes bore into her. She knew what it was like to be wrongly accused. "No, I don't."

Mitch leaned back in his chair as if the weight of the world was lifted. "Fine. That settles it. Now, what's the next step?"

Mitch seemed used to getting his way, but Jacqueline still wasn't convinced. "Hold it. It's not your decision."

"Please. I don't have time for this. I know that your father-in-law blames you for his son's death. He also kicked you out of his firm. To make matters worse, he has single-handedly used his own power and influence in the legal community to try to destroy you. Unfortunately for him, but I must add, luckily for me, his bullying tactics aren't working."

"Wow." Jacqueline's eyes widened, her posture stiffening as she gripped the arm of the chair.

Mitch continued. "Occupational hazard. I gather information and use it as I see fit. I hope my honesty isn't too off-putting. But the reality is I don't have time for games. I need you to represent me."

Jacqueline let the words sink in. Several well-known defense attorneys, both male and female, were dying to take this case. What was special about her? Jacqueline chalked it up to Mitch being unfamiliar with anyone else. She was determined to figure out what was in Mitch's best interest, even if he wasn't. "Mitch, I don't think you understand. I can't represent you."

"Then we have a real problem. Because you are."

Jacqueline hesitated.

He apparently interpreted her silence as a sign to plead his case. "See, when Patrick was born, I made him a promise. I told him that he would never know the kind of pain and humiliation that I knew. I promised him that he would never have to be a waiter, construction worker, or caddie. Please understand me—there is nothing wrong with those jobs. I did them all, and there is a lot to be said for hard work. But not my son. My boy wasn't going to know that type of hard work. No, my boy was going to hold his head high. He was going to have everything."

Jacqueline knew this was code for everything he didn't have. Despite the confidence he portrayed, she heard the pain and anguish between those lines. People had hurt Mitch badly, and that misunderstood little boy was still inside him. Now he was fighting to protect the little he had left.

As Mitch spoke, images of her father-in-law packing up her office and leaving it outside their house, of screaming at her after the accident, of holding Jack's lifeless body overwhelmed her. If she backed away now from this case, she would let her father-in-law win.

On the other hand, this case was going to be a media frenzy, and for once, the media could work in her favor. A judge would be less likely to push the envelope if the whole world was watching.

Mitch moved back over to Jacqueline. "That's why I need you. You're not a hired gun. People trust you. That's why I want you."

"Mitch, I really don't think you understand."

"No, Jacqueline, I'm not making myself clear. I need your services." And just like that, he transformed into the Iceman. Gone was the concerned, loving father she had met all those years ago. His broad, sculpted shoulders made him look like a giant stepping on the little people. He leaned toward her, his steely eyes boring into hers, forcing her to confront him. With his dark hair and chiseled features, he was a strikingly handsome yet mysterious opponent. But the way he spoke, that icy tone, sent chills up her spine. He could be very, very dangerous. The only question was, who was the enemy? Was he feeling threatened by the outside world or angered that he wasn't getting his way? Before Jacqueline could decide, he interrupted her thoughts.

His raging anger replaced the spark, the fire in his hypnotizing eyes. "Clearly you have never met my mother-in-law, Victoria Harrison Westerfer. She believes I killed her daughter, and she is determined to see me behind bars. It's just a matter of time. Hence, why I need you on retainer."

Mitch pushed his chair to face Jacqueline as if this were a typical negotiation. "Let me explain what I know. First, you are a brilliant attorney, but despite your attempts, your firm is failing financially. You need a high-paying client to save your firm. I need an attorney to win my case. We both have something the other needs. It's a win-win. I always like to expand the pie. Makes people amenable to my plans.

"But let me assure you. This is not a charity case. I'm talking about my life, my child's life. I have every intention of winning. And you fit my needs. You need money—I'm willing to pay top dollar. Don't ever discount the power of money. I learned its power when I was very young. Your firm will never have to worry. Plus, you accomplish your goal. You want to be back on top. You need it like I do. It's in our blood. You've just been hiding it for a while. This can catapult you right back to the top, where I believe you belong.

"I know you. You are not all about the money or the win. You need to believe in your cause. When you have something you believe in, then you, like me, won't quit until you win. If you don't believe in me, believe in Patrick. He doesn't deserve this.

"Finally, your skills are the antithesis of mine. Best case, I'm mysterious. Worst, they hate or fear me. And in business, that's fine. You, on the other hand, inspire compassion. You have a kindness and connection to people that I need if I'm going to convince a jury. Your petite size will make it impossible for the other side to bully you. If that's not sufficient, I know how you feel about Patrick. Do it for him. I'm the only parent he has left."

Jacqueline followed his gaze to Patrick. "Wow, you should be the attorney. That is a great argument. I can see why they call you the closer."

He was right though. She needed a purpose. She had been moving like a ghost for too long. Patrick and Mitch came into her life once before at a pivotal time. They saved her once. She believed in signs. "Okay, Mitch. You have a deal. But I have one condition."

Jacqueline paused to make sure she had his full attention. "I need complete honesty and transparency. You don't get any second chances. Fair warning, if you're lying to me, I won't hesitate to drop this case. And I promise you, if you think you have problems now, if I do drop you, your problems are only beginning."

Mitch raised his hand as if to accept her terms. "You have it. And I took the liberty of having my assistant get this from the house. It's Tiffany's datebook."

Jacqueline accepted it. "How did you know I'd take the case?"

"Jacqueline, you may not be convinced, but I am. I've spent too many years reading other people. I know you're right for the case. That's my secret weapon. I know people. I've studied them all my life. Plus, I believe I will be arrested any minute. If I know my mother-in-law, she's convincing them right now."

Jacqueline surveyed the room. "First things first. We need to protect Patrick. No one, and I mean no one, is allowed in here without your permission."

"Trust me. He's my only concern."

She looked at Mitch. In so many ways, their lives were on parallel tracks. They both had powerful enemies, people willing to do anything to destroy them. Jacqueline remembered the information Billy gathered in her preparation for this meeting. "What's bothering me is from everything I could read and learn from the news, you should have been arrested by now. You were found holding the body. You are certain you're not hiding anything from me?"

Mitch faced her. "No. I know of no reason why they believe I would want to murder my wife."

Patrick started to stir. Jacqueline watched as Mitch tended to his care. Father and son needing rescue. She knew her interview skills were rusty, but something didn't feel right. What was it?

Jacqueline nodded. The lawyer in her heard a lot of leeway in that answer. She knew what it was like to be wrongly accused, yet something about his cold, blank expression bothered her.

Chapter 11

MITCH RESUMED HIS VIGIL BESIDE HIS SON'S HOSPI-
tal bed after he was satisfied he'd accomplished his goal. He retained
Jacqueline Stone. She had the right mix of traits to beat this obstacle.
She softened his image, making him relatable to the jury if necessary.
He ignored the long-forgotten feeling of guilt rising in his gut. He
was, after all, the Iceman. The Iceman didn't feel anything. He destroyed and took what he wanted.

Tiffany's death caused his self-preservation to kick into gear. He
had learned over the years to camouflage his motives through observ-
ing the rich and powerful. No one used brute force or violence to
achieve their goals, but it was just as deadly. The key was to play on
people's needs and insecurities and find a way to match them with
your own if possible. He was no longer the eight-year-old little boy,
all alone in this world, but his fear this time was almost as great. The
difference was that this time, he was better equipped. He had spent
his life preparing so that he was never weak or exposed again, and
he wasn't about to let anyone stop him. He was on an island. And
his only focus was protecting Patrick and himself. He wasn't going
down. Not with breath still inside him.

If his muscles weren't so tense, he'd congratulate himself. His
legendary instinct of reading people didn't fail him. Like him, Jacqueline had an insatiable desire to win. Law was in her blood, and no
matter what she had been through, she couldn't refuse a chance to
redeem herself.

Despite his self-talk, the nagging feeling of dishonesty wouldn't
retreat. The way she looked at him. Her eyes imploring him to be
honest so that they could both be successful. He handicapped her,

holding the picture in his hands. But he also trusted his instinct that she could figure out how to win by herself.

He despised himself for questioning his actions. He hated indecision almost as much as weakness. She had saved Patrick once before. And if it were a different time, if the stakes weren't so high, he might have played it differently.

But they weren't.

And he didn't.

She didn't need to know about the picture. Or his past.

He had to make a call before he left.

Chapter 12

KATHERINE HARRISON CONCEILLO FLEW INTO A parking space at the offices of Harrison Investments, the tires screeching as she made the sharp turn, slamming to a stop only inches before the wall. Just a few more millimeters and her brand-new Mercedes 400 Coupe would have needed a facelift. The death of her sister Tiffany and her mother's belief that Mitch murdered her had destroyed Katherine's usual calm demeanor.

Despite her attempts at transformation by lightening her hair, hiring that stupid makeup consultant, and losing thirty pounds, Katherine remained in the background. After years of therapy, she accepted her role as the silent, smart sister that no one noticed, especially when Tiffany, the beautiful one, was around. And she would never be Tiffany. Tiffany, who shone in the spotlight, played the media—and even their mother—like a beautiful violin. Mitch knew the real her. Which worked for Katherine. She enjoyed her peaceful, uncomplicated life. But now she was bombarded with media and cameras everywhere she went. She needed to get inside. She grabbed her mobile from the console. It had been useless all morning. She must have called her husband Eric and left twenty messages with no response, and now she couldn't get in touch with her assistant, Ashley.

As Katherine entered the offices, she went directly in search of Ashley. Her worst nightmare was coming true. The family was using that anonymous text to bury Mitch. And it would bury him. And her. Despite her pleas to confirm the accuracy of the dates mentioned in the anonymous text, she didn't need it. That information was all true. She knew because she was there too. In those hotels. With Mitch.

She needed to warn Mitch. How did she let this happen? Just

when she thought she had gotten revenge on her sister, even in death, Tiffany was trying to ruin her from her grave. Katherine shook her head, attempting to dismiss the last real image of Tiffany. Tiffany laughing at her. The horrible, disgusting, *you're-so-ugly-and-will-never-be-me* laugh. Well, the game wasn't over.

Luckily, Katherine found Ashley in the file room, prepping for the day. "I'm so sorry, Kat, about Mrs. Mitchell. I can't believe she's gone."

Katherine smiled. Ashley knew her almost too well. They'd shared a special bond ever since Ashley started at Harrison Investments. Most of the other executives dismissed Ashley's application right away because she was shy and unpolished, despite doing well in high school. She had no experience or the corporate look their company required. Yet Katherine empathized with the awkward, pimply-faced graduate trying to better herself and hired her on the spot.

At first, Ashley was unsure of herself, constantly apologizing for her mistakes, so much so that even Katherine wondered if she should have hired her. Katherine stuck with her, encouraging her to have confidence in her abilities. Within three months, Ashley was employee of the month and was by far the best assistant at Harrison Investments. Katherine always made sure Ashley got the highest raises for all her hard work and overtime, and trusted her with the most sensitive materials. Ashley never let Katherine down. Katherine counted on that loyalty.

"Thank you, Ashley. I know you are. Would you please come in my office?" Katherine tried to hide the fear in her voice. She hoped she knew Ashley like she thought she did. It was one thing for a secretary to keep business information private; it was an entirely different matter to ask them to lie. Katherine had never so much as expensed a lunch that wasn't client related.

Katherine reached down in her desk drawer, grateful for her planning abilities. Ashley had been eyeing the newest Louis Vuitton bag, and Katherine had ordered one for her for her birthday. Her birthday wasn't until next month. "I know this is a little early, but this whole mess with Tiffany has made me realize that you never know..."

Katherine handed Ashley the present, wrapped Louis Vuitton style. Ashley couldn't hide her excitement. "Kat, this is so great. I've been wanting this bag. Thank you so much."

They hugged. "Enjoy it. You deserve it."

Ashley looked at Katherine. "Are you okay?"

"I'm as good as possible under the circumstances. I'm just so worried about Patrick."

"Of course. If there's anything I can do, please let me know."

"I will. Thanks, Ashley. I appreciate it."

Ashley stood to leave. "Is there anything else?"

Katherine hesitated. *Could she do this?* "No."

Ashley walked to the office door.

"Oh, by the way, Ashley, you remember that I was in my office all day on Friday when you came to tell me about Tiffany, remember?"

Ashley's eyes met Katherine's. She understood what Katherine was asking. "Yes, I remember."

Just then Katherine's phone rang. "Would you please tell the caller I am unavailable right now?"

Ashley answered the phone. "It's Mr. Mitchell."

Katherine grabbed the phone. "Mitch... Yes, I'll be right there."

Maybe her luck was changing. Mitch needed her to stay with Patrick. This was her chance.

Chapter 13

JACQUELINE FOUND LISA PACING THE LOBBY WHEN she returned from the hospital. "What are you doing? I don't need that baby falling out of you."

Lisa trailed behind Jacqueline. "Well, boss?"

Jacqueline smiled. She had asked Lisa to stop calling her boss a million times. Lisa never listened. "What?"

"Did we get it, boss?"

Jacqueline decided to have a little fun. "I don't know what you're talking about."

Fear crossed Lisa's face. "He hired us, right? Because I already have Billy working on it and..."

Jacqueline decided to come clean before Lisa went into premature labor. "Stop. Yes, we got the case."

Jacqueline and Lisa hugged. Winning the lottery probably didn't feel this good. Before Jacqueline could put her stuff down, her investigator, Billy Washington, walked in, followed by her receptionist, Claudia. "Please tell us we got it," he said.

Jacqueline stared at her group. Her family. Just yesterday she'd decided to give this all up. "Guys, we're back!"

Before cracking the proverbial champagne, Billy handed her the *Philadelphia Inquirer*. "No, boss, we're just ready to start. It seems like we have our work cut out for us."

Jacqueline examined her small team of four. To the outside world, they looked pathetic. Between her and Lisa, they only had about eighteen years of experience. Billy, her paralegal and investigator, was a former mailroom delivery person who toyed with technology on the side. Except working at the Stone Firm, he had no formal legal training. And Claudia was more of a makeshift office mom than receptionist, having been a good family friend of the Stones for years.

Yet, with all the best graduates in front of her, she wouldn't have chosen anyone else. Lisa never gave up. She worked and worked until she found the answer. And not just any answer—the right answer. Jacqueline often wondered if she made up the law as she went along.

Although Billy had no formal technology training, he'd probably mastered computers before he could crawl. If it existed, he would find it. He'd received a full ride to the Massachusetts Institute of Technology, as his mother would tell you in her first five minutes of talking to you, never using its common name of MIT, but he declined it to stay in the Philadelphia area to take care of her and pay for her medical bills. By day, he worked alongside Jacqueline as an investigator and by night, he attended school. If it was out there in the vast universe of the Net, Billy would find it. Couple all that with his street smarts and killer smile, and he was the best investigator out there. He was born with an innate ability to get the answer out of anybody.

As Jacqueline looked at her group, she knew that if anyone could defend Mitch, it was them. "Okay, then, what are we waiting for?"

In unison, the group said, "Coffee."

As she walked back to their brainstorming center, she felt the old Jacqueline emerging. The room gave birth to their theories and defenses, basically anything to make sure their clients never went to jail. She never banked on creating doubt; instead, she gave the jury an alternative. Her combination of hard work and legendary instincts made her one of the top criminal attorneys on the East Coast. Until.

Claudia emerged with coffee and bagels.

Billy looked around. "You know, Jacqueline, maybe we should change this place."

"Why?"

"Because it has no windows, and we are here so long, we don't even know if it is day or night."

Jacqueline surveyed the room. As a tech genius, Billy probably had a great design for the war room. But she was old-school. When Jacqueline used a paper and pen, something magical happened. Armed with the essentials, the large conference room had everything: room for everyone to spread out, lots of legal pads, and her board. Her beloved board survived the move from her old office. One section detailed the information they knew and the other, the questions they had. On the top, they wrote down the names of all the players, the evidence, and the motives as they were discovered. At the bottom was the time line, outlining where everyone was at the time of the murder. On the cork side of the board, they posted all relevant papers and pictures.

"No. It works just fine. Claudia, could you please make sure we order lunch? Our new client is happy to pay. Let's order something good because we have a lot of work to do."

Billy grabbed a blank legal pad and watched as Jacqueline wrote on the board, which no longer had any evidence of the Anderson trial.

Jacqueline tacked the photos of the murder scene on the board: Tiffany's body sprawled on the floor, blood draining from the gunshot wound. Then she looked in her bag. She had one more photo to add. She debated. But she needed to face it. She grabbed a tab and put up a photo of Patrick right underneath.

Jacqueline ignored the shocked faces of her team. She knew everyone saw the resemblance between Jack and Patrick. It was like seeing a ghost. No one said a word.

"Team, I want you to look at these photos. Study them. Commit them to memory. Put them somewhere where you will see them day and night. Look at how this woman was killed in her own home. This was a crime of passion. She did something, knew something that someone obviously didn't like."

For the next few hours, Jacqueline and her group divided up the tasks. "I want you to interview anyone you can. Talk to the neighbors and see if they saw anything, anyone out of the ordinary. It looks like she had an appointment last week with a Dr. Marc Fitzgerald. Start there. See if you can get ahold of him and find out what Tiffany wanted that day. We'll compare later."

As Jacqueline handed Lisa a copy of her notes, Lisa's growing stomach caught her attention. "But Lisa, please tell me if it's too much work for you. I don't want you overdoing it. Your first duty is to that baby. You hear me?"

"Yes, boss. But if I remember correctly, you were nine months pregnant and trying a case."

Jacqueline felt weak. The look of regret on Lisa's face. "Don't. We have work to do. Also, take these pictures—"

Lisa interjected. "I know. Make copies and have them sent to your house. Consider it done."

Jacqueline doled out more tasks. "Billy, Mrs. Mitchell was also apparently very involved with the hospital board. Start with that. Look into all claims against the hospital that appear suspicious. Also, we need to investigate Mr. Mitchell's company, Harrison Investments. See if there are any angry clients or opponents. Maybe someone is going after him."

Jacqueline turned back to the board and pointed to Patrick's smiling face. "Look at this little boy. Look at his smile. I promise you that he will never have that carefree smile again." Jacqueline moved to the picture of Tiffany's slain body. "Someone did this to her while he was watching."

The room was silent as the group took in the horror of what had happened. "You know what our job is. Mr. Mitchell and Patrick Mitchell are counting on us to find the person who did this. Now let's get to work."

Jacqueline checked her watch. "Okay, I have to run. Mitch promised to meet me at his house in an hour."

Lisa interjected. "So, it's Mitch? Jacqueline, you never told us how you met him."

Chapter 14

KATHERINE HARRISON CONCEILLO ENTERED PATrick's hospital room, every bone in her body shaking. Could she really do this? To her own nephew? She felt as if her life was spiraling out of control as much as Mitch's. Yet the fear of being exposed grew with each painstaking moment. Patrick must have heard her screaming at Tiffany. And then the vase. She had to follow through with her plan. For once in her life. She opened the door. Her heart stopped. "Oh, Marie."

Mitch's adoptive mother, Marie, jumped up at the intrusion. "Oh, thank God it's you. Katherine, my dear, I'm so sorry."

Katherine accepted the hug a little longer than she normally would have, giving herself a few extra seconds to hide her surprise. Unlike her own mother's slender, tall frame, Marie's round and portly build from years of homemade pasta felt like a safe haven. Katherine almost forgot how much she'd loved and needed those hugs during her lonely high school days. "Thank you, Marie."

Despite her puffy eyes and the clear exhaustion on her face, Marie grabbed a chair for Katherine. The consummate caregiver. "Katherine, sit. You're shaking. You poor thing. I can't imagine how difficult this has been on you."

They both looked at the fragile body in the bed. "It's just hard to imagine we were all at his baseball game the other day. I still can't believe..."

Taking the seat Marie offered, Katherine tried to comfort the woman who had treated her more like a daughter than her own mom. She never expected to face Marie. Her face warmed with guilt as the elderly lady broke down in her arms. She instantly regretted coming and wished she had the courage to talk to her husband. Eric could solve anything. Yet that insecure teenage girl petrified of rejection, still buried deep inside her, had won out. Again. Eric would never understand why she did it. No normal, loving person would.

Unable to do anything else, Katherine just let the tears stream down her face.

Marie put her wrinkled hand on Katherine's. "My dear, Patrick is going to be okay. He's a fighter."

Katherine's eyes turned to Patrick. "I agree. I just wish he would wake up. Has the doctor said anything? Do we know what Patrick saw?"

Marie blessed herself. "Oh, dear God. He better not have seen anything. I just can't even imagine it. I blame myself. I should have told Tiffany to bring him to my house. Did you know he was sick?"

Katherine searched the elderly woman's face. Until now, despite her age, Marie could outwork any teenager. No matter what the task, Marie could handle it. At fifty, she'd adopted Mitch. She called him her gift from heaven since she was never able to have children of her own. And then every year, on Mitch's birthday, Marie would retell the story of how she'd had to fight off all the young couples and convince the judge that "this old lady could handle an eight-year-old." They laughed as she retold stories of Mitch's active childhood. But Tyler had told Katherine the sad truth. No one wanted Mitch. If it wasn't for Marie, he would have ended up in the foster system.

Katherine responded almost too quickly. "No. I didn't talk to Tiffany at all."

Marie searched her bag of tricks for a tissue. "Well, it's all going to be okay. He must be. We can't take anymore. Mitch can't take anymore. So you haven't heard anything either?"

Katherine shook her head. "I haven't had a chance to really talk to Mitch yet."

Marie blew her nose. "All I know is the doctors said it's important that Patrick just rest. And we can't cry. Mitch needs us to be strong. Patrick will come out of this."

They sat in silence, watching Patrick breathe. "You know, Katherine, I always thought you would end up with Mitch. God, I wish you had. I know how much you loved him. I never thought your sister was right for him."

Katherine thought back to another time. "Well, I think you were the only one." Katherine debated. She always could talk to Marie. "It was hard living in Tiffany's shadow."

"Trust me, I know. I saw how hard it was on you."

"Please. Don't misunderstand. I would never *want* Tiffany dead." *Or at least when I am sane.* Katherine hoped Marie was too engulfed in her own pain to hear her fear. "It's just that she made it hard to love her. Did I ever tell you that I did work up the courage to tell Mitch how I felt?"

"No. You never told me."

Katherine looked at the elderly lady sitting beside her. God, she loved going to Mitchell's house, the smell of Marie's famous chocolate chip cookies hitting her as the door opened. Katherine imagined that was what a home should be. Although it lacked all the paintings, designer furniture, and fine china of the Westerfer home, and the entire house was the size of Katherine's bedroom suite, she would have switched places with Mitch in a heartbeat. The best part of high school was going to Mitch's house after school, even if he was still at practice. Katherine acted as if she was doing Mitch a favor driving him everywhere. *I'm helping Marie out so she doesn't worry*, she would tell everyone. But Mitch and Marie both knew it was because she was lonely. Her own mother was too busy to care. Yet they both played along, welcoming her. She and Marie would talk for hours as they waited for Mitch to get home. Marie always had homemade food waiting for their ravenous stomachs. And big bear hugs. It was love. True maternal love.

The opposite of the Westerfer home. Although Victoria was technically a stay-at-home mother too, she was never Mom. There were no bear hugs, just light taps on the cheeks. No homemade cookies. Ever. Only fancy desserts when company arrived. But never a treat just because. To make someone feel special. To say love. Instead, various nannies and cooks raised Katherine, Tiffany, and Harrison. No one truly cared about her day. Especially her mother. She was too busy with hosting affairs to care about the mean girls at Katherine's school or help with her damn curly hair. The few memories of her mother were of being reprimanded for how Katherine dressed or her posture, or nagged to do some stupid correspondence thanking someone for something.

"Katherine, it's me. Marie. You know you can always talk to me." Marie sat silently. Her dark eyes filled with love. "It might help both of us to talk. I can't stand the silence. You know Mitch. The Iceman. I hate that nickname, but you know what they say about truth hidden in jest. I've been trying to get him to talk. He must be in so much pain, but he just won't. Instead, in his usual fashion, he's trying to fix things. Get Patrick better."

Katherine studied Marie. Usually, nothing could faze the older woman sitting next to her. She had been so preoccupied with her own thoughts, she could only imagine how taxing the last few days had been on Marie. "Marie, are you okay?"

"I'm fine. I'm just worried about all of you. You know it's okay to have conflicted feelings. Your sister was an amazing person in her own right. And she had so many wonderful qualities. For one, she was an amazing mom. But I saw how hard she was on you. I know it must have been difficult living in her shadow. Please talk to me. Your secrets are safe with me. Promise."

Katherine thought back to that day when her world changed. And Marie, of all people, loved her probably more than her own mother. "I just can't believe this is happening. Tiffany was tough, but

I truly never wanted any harm to come to her. Please, you have to believe me."

Marie patted her hand. "My dear, everyone fights with their siblings. We all say things we don't mean. Everyone knows you loved her. Don't worry."

Katherine let the tears flow. "Oh, Marie. You don't understand. I never told you what happened."

Marie handed her a tissue. "Honey, you know you can always talk to me."

Katherine looked into the loving eyes. She needed to talk. To come clean. "Do you remember that day before the big football game when Mitch and I were at your house?"

"Yes. Mitchell went upstairs to get ready for football practice, and you and I talked. I told you to tell him how you felt."

"Well, when I went home that night, I decided I would tell him the next day. At the game."

Marie thought back. "Gosh, Katherine, it was so long ago. I just remember those games were a big deal. You girls would get all dressed up. Mitch, of course, was always stressed."

They laughed. "I can still see him studying that playbook. Well, anyway, I decided to take the plunge. Actually, two. First, I asked Tiffany for help. I just remember being so proud of myself. I was going to tell Mitch how I felt. And I confided in Tiffany. And to my surprise, she was so kind.

"She was excited that I wanted to get dressed up. That I would ask for her help. After all, as she explained, she was the queen of transformation. She didn't even realize what a backhanded compliment that was. She just kept telling me she was 'going to take me from the frog to the fairy princess.'

"I just remember it was one of the few times we were like sisters. Giggling, having fun. We had the flat iron out. She got all those damn curls out of my head. My hair was straight, just like hers. Of course, it wasn't as golden as hers. But it looked good. She put my makeup on. Did my hair. It was one of the happiest days of my life.

"I remember my mother came in and said, 'Wow, I never thought you two looked alike. But now I can see a resemblance.' What mother says that?"

Marie put her arm around her, like old times. "Oh, Katherine. I'm so sorry."

Katherine wiped her own tears. "Boy, do I feel like a horrible person. She's dead, and I'm still complaining. It's just been so emotional."

"Trust me, I understand. I think we all are overwhelmed." Marie rubbed Katherine's hand. "We all have a ton of anger and sadness. And death doesn't erase the past. You and Tiffany had a complicated relationship."

Katherine sat up. "I'm so sorry. I shouldn't be telling you all this."

"No, it's fine. To be honest, I always wondered what happened. I thought you were going to talk to Mitch, and then all of a sudden, after that game, all I heard was Tiffany."

Katherine laughed. "Trust me. Try being his best friend. I will never forget it. Tiffany claimed she wanted to just meet the guy I was interested in. She had heard about him, but they had never met since she was younger and new to the high school. And you know Mitch, if you weren't in his class or on the team, he had no time for you.

"She came down with me on the field for moral support, she claimed. But I should have known better. Tiffany wanted him. She always had to win at everything. And she did. I will never forget Mitch's face as we walked up. The smile he gave her. That look in his eyes. It was like something out of a movie, and I just melted into the background as they fell in love."

"Oh, I'm sorry." Marie paused. "Let me tell you something, Katherine, that I probably should have told you before. I believe Mitch fell so hard for Tiffany because she looked just like his biological mother.

She had the same long blond straight hair. I saw the resemblance the moment he brought her home. You know how everyone talks about Patrick's sky-blue eyes?"

They both looked at the little guy in bed. "Of course."

"Well, Mitch's mom had the same eyes. That crystal color of an island sea. I think he was trying to relive his days with his mom. I don't know if that helps."

A sad smile crossed Katherine's face. She shut her eyes. But then she remembered Tiffany mocking her. Tiffany after the game. That belly laugh that causes a person to bend over, holding their stomach. Tears were rolling down her face. And then Tiffany stopped. Actual shock came to her face as the thought hit her. Between laughs, she managed to say, *Seriously? You honestly thought he would choose you when he could have me? God, you are pathetic.* That same laugh Tiffany had given her...

Marie seemed to misunderstand Katherine's sadness. "Katherine, I'm so sorry. Are you okay?"

Katherine wiped her face as she remembered who got the last laugh. "Please. I'm acting like a child. It's me who should apologize. It's just been hellish."

Marie's phone rang. Katherine waited as she listened to one of the assistants panicking on the other end because of an irate client. "I'll be right there." Marie threw her phone in her pocketbook, which doubled as a catch-all bag. Katherine always wondered how Marie found anything in that bag. Clearly, she spent all her time taking care of Mitch and the workings of the office. As the former office manager of Harrison Investments, she still was a role model and a key figurehead there, keeping everything in order, down to the staples.

Marie looked at Katherine. "Never a dull moment. I need to get back to the office. Will you stay here with Patrick? Mitch should be back soon."

"Of course, go."

When Marie left, Katherine returned to her own thoughts. She watched her only nephew breathing. If he didn't have tubes hooked up to him, he'd look peaceful. His little chest rising rhythmically. She longed for his crystal eyes to dance with the mischief that constantly got him in trouble. But instead that little boy slept in the hospital bed, lost in his own terrifying world. She rubbed his hand.

Patrick was the last thread, the last hope of keeping the family together. *But if Patrick saw me...* The image of heaving the Baccarat vase at Tiffany's head invaded her mind. The blue glass pieces shattering everywhere as Tiffany swiftly moved out of the vase's path. The scared and angry look on Tiffany's face was priceless.

Patrick had to have heard me. Why did I do it? The memories motivated Katherine. She moved closer to the bed. Patrick's long eyelashes fluttered in sleep. Even he had the legendary long, graceful eyelashes that framed the blue irises of his eyes. Just like his mother, grandmother, great-grandmother. Everyone but her. She checked around the room. No one. She was alone. Alone with Patrick and her soul.

As much as she regretted Tiffany's death, Tiffany had spent her life making Katherine miserable. It wasn't supposed to end like this. But Katherine didn't have a choice now. She had to follow through. No one would ever understand. She wouldn't survive in jail.

She looked at his beautiful face, and out of habit twirled one of his long blond curls around her finger. She often wondered if God would grace her with a fair-haired boy like Patrick. Patrick with the legendary Harrison mane, soft to the touch, golden like the rays of the sun. She spent her whole life trying to prove herself worthy of the family name. She picked up the extra pillow.

She felt her heart breaking. *Why did you have to be home? Patrick, I'm so sorry.*

Chapter 15

DETECTIVE DAN O'NEILL WALKED INTO POLICE HEAD-quarters with a pounding headache. It had been a long week. He'd only gotten a few hours of sleep last night, and the captain wanted to see him ASAP. That called for another cup of joe.

"How did it go?" Dan's partner, Detective Grady, grabbed her own cup of coffee. Dan often had to remind himself of her real name, Grace Kelly, since she rarely used it. And she enjoyed being the antithesis of the beautiful actress turned princess. Hating it since she was young, she combined the two names to come up with Grady. Dan still enjoyed watching the shock on people's faces when they realized Grady was a kickass woman.

Dan put an extra packet of sugar in the cup to make it drinkable. "The guy's an asshole. He actually thinks he owns the hospital."

Grady put the carafe back in its holder. "Well, he may. He did donate that wing." Then she remembered. "Wait, I thought you were seeing your girl?"

Dan stared at his partner. She couldn't resist teasing him, especially when it came to his love life. Which was nonexistent. Not in the mood, he ignored the dig. "Funny. And cut it out. That's the last thing I need the captain to hear. And although it's none of your business, I heard she's really having a rough time."

They walked slowly to the captain's office, hoping to avoid the inevitable. "Are you saying that your classic Irish charm, and your Irish curse, didn't work on her? I'm beginning to like this mystery attorney."

By the time Grady had risen to detective and become Dan's partner, the only thing she knew of the mysterious Jacqueline Stone was her fast decline. Dan found it ironic that the two ethical minds he admired most seemed to be on separate roller-coaster tracks. He wished that Grady knew Jacqueline personally and not just by reputation. Then she'd understand.

"Come on, I was joking."

Dan gave her a murderous look. "Unfortunately, it's not a joke. I heard she's really in trouble. And I think that's what I hate the most. I think I'd rather her be angry or hysterical. Instead she's just there. I can't get through to her. It's been several years since the accident, and it is literally killing her. She's a shell of the attorney I knew. I feel horrible, but I don't know what to do. Can you believe she's doing insurance work?"

Grady took a sip of her coffee. "Dan, I don't know much about legal work, but a lot of lawyers make good money doing insurance work. Hell, I'm sure they make more than us. So don't feel that bad for her."

Dan took a sip of his coffee. "Maybe. But that's not it. She was never in it for the money. She cared about justice. Changing the world. You don't understand. You didn't know her. She used to be this beautiful, feisty bulldog. She could win you over with her smile, and if that didn't work, she could break your legs to get your full attention. She owned that courtroom. But last time I saw her, she looked like a rag doll that got the shit beat out of her."

Grady made a sad puppy face. "Dan, give the woman a break. She lost both her husband and son. That would destroy even the best of us. I'm surprised she's still working. And weren't you always complaining that defense work was too dirty for her?"

"No. Do you listen to me? I said I thought she was too trustworthy for criminal work. She just likes to see the good in people. And for the record, I agree with her. I'll never be convinced that her accident with her family was just that—an accident."

Grady swished her cup into the trash can, perfect shot. "We've been through this a hundred times. We can't find any foul play."

"No. Correction. We can't prove foul play. You will never convince me it was an accident. I just wish Jacqueline wouldn't think she always needs to do things by herself. I swear if—"

"Not doing this again," Grady mumbled.

"Come on, you know it too. Jacqueline was on to something. Something big. And proceeds to obtain evidence that would help bring them down. And then all of a sudden, it just happens to all go up in smoke, along with her family in the car? Tell me they weren't sending a message."

"Dan, I'm not doing this again. They had a witness. It's over, and you are in the hot seat about a real case. And you better get your head on straight. We need to have answers on the Mitchell murder. That's what you should be focusing on. Not your love life. Or, should we say, lack of one?"

"You're lucky you're a girl."

"Oh, please. We can decide this on the range whenever you're ready."

"No thanks." Since Grady was a marksman in the Army before joining the police department, that was the last thing Dan wanted. "Listen, I'm tired. Anyway, I went to see the husband at the hospital. I feel terrible about the kid, but we shouldn't have given the husband any special treatment. I don't care who he is or who he knows—he's a complete prick. If I was the mother-in-law, I'd think he did it too." Dan took a gulp of his coffee.

"She did find him holding the body. On that alone, we could get an arrest warrant," suggested Grady.

"Agreed. But, just being an asshole doesn't convince me he's a killer. This is going to be a high-profile case, and I'm not arresting the wrong person and having to explain that one on the stand."

"Well, I guess for once, the boss wants to weigh in on that decision."

"Thanks for the pep talk."

"All I know is we better work the case well. The rumor mill is saying that the boss is getting a lot of pressure from everybody to solve this case. And fast. And you know what happens when he gets pressure."

Dan tossed his cup in the can, missing the basket. "Have I ever cared about politics? I don't care what they want. I never have and never will play those games. I'm not living my life knowing I put an innocent man behind bars, if I can help it. Even if he's a rich asshole."

Before they could debate the issue, Captain Janson opened his office door. "O'Neill, Grady, get in here."

As he walked into his boss's office, Dan's only thought was that this was the type of case the old Jacqueline would love. But thankfully, she wasn't the old Jacqueline, and no way Mitchell would choose her for this.

Dan and Grady knew it was useless to interrupt their captain and just sat there until he exhausted himself from yelling. Captain Janson was a real trip, a stanch Catholic who attended five a.m. mass daily before work, but liked to curse like a sailor. "I've been bombarded with calls all day about this fucking case. Three calls alone from the DA, two from the commissioner, and just now, one from the mayor, who said he has gotten at least five calls from that damn mother, Victoria, with all the last names. So where are you with the evidence? Are you ready to charge him? And what the fuck happened at the murder scene? Who's responsible for that colossal screwup?"

Dan didn't want to go there. He was just as mad at his people, but he wasn't about to throw any of them under the bus. "Listen, it's over. I assure you that my men got the message. They know they made a mistake. They're not idiots, Cap. They know procedure—they know that the person who finds the victim can't leave the scene before I arrive, but come on, we are talking about Ryan Mitchell and the whole Harrison Westerfer clan. Someone just brutally murdered his wife.

And the kid was covered in blood, freaking out. Mitchell didn't run away. He just took his son to the hospital. That guy wouldn't have stayed if my men pulled out their guns. There were extenuating circumstances."

"It's a murder scene, for fuck's sake. There are always extenuating circumstances."

Dan read from his notes, trying to salvage the situation, his reputation and that of his team. "Look, it was a chaotic scene, and admittedly mistakes were made, but we did follow him to the hospital. And once the kid received medical attention, they did take the clothes from the kid and the husband, along with blood and DNA tests and pictures of both witnesses."

"The DA is going to have your head," Cap said, pointing at Dan.

Dan refused to take the bait. He knew the lack of sleep was getting to the captain and the first thing to go was his patience. "Cap, you've met Mitchell and his mother-in-law, right?"

Captain Janson threw down his pen. "What kinda question is that? Of course. Who do you think paid for the police rec center and the baseball equipment? And trust me, if she reminds me of that again, I'm going to throw a baseball bat at someone's head. So I'm repeating to you what I've heard constantly since this happened. Victoria Harrison Westerfer has been a pillar in the community forever. And like Salome, she wants the head of her John the Baptist on a platter, and that head is Ryan Mitchell's."

Dan understood. "Are you done? I'm tired of hearing about what that woman wants. I heard it all yesterday. Now can we talk about the evidence we gathered to determine if it's enough? Get some balls, or do you want to continue worrying about what that fucking woman wants?" Dan thought maybe using the language Janson seemed to enjoy would get his attention. *Ouch.* He may have gone a little too far. Especially since the captain got up and was already pacing his office, his telltale nervous sign.

"Really, O'Neill," he said as he turned and leaned on his desk, looking at Dan. "I'm going to let that one go because I know you're under a ton of pressure, but don't give me lip, or you'll find yourself back walking a beat till your balls are frozen and your feet are bleeding."

"Cap, got it, loud and clear. But I draw the line at doing what they want me to do. Plus, until we decide what we are going to do, I think it was good that we didn't piss Mitchell off either."

His boss sighed. "Trust me, I know. That guy has a lot of people in his corner. Or at least for a little while longer. But bottom line, O'Neill, we just can't afford any more screwups. The DA is about to have a heart attack or my balls. I'm not sure which will be first."

Dan understood. Ever since Ryan Mitchell made a ton of money in real estate investments and started spreading it around to all the right people in city politics, both the Westerfers and Mitchells were powerhouses. "Talk about being stuck between a rock and a hard place."

"You ain't kidding. Everyone is pressuring the DA to make an arrest, but he's scared shitless. He knows once he picks a side, he better be right, or the payback is going to be a bitch. And you know, O'Neill, shit only runs one way. That's why you're in the hot seat."

"Tell me something I don't know. It's just that my name and reputation are also on the line, and I am not going to jeopardize that to appease that blockhead."

By habit, the captain scanned the police room. Even though they all agreed that DA Cunningham's head was shaped like a block, the captain had to enforce the guidelines. No nicknames. Period. On the other hand, Dan needed some humor to keep him sane.

"Please, O'Neill. Keep it aboveboard. I have enough issues."

"Okay, but don't ask me again. I'll give the go-ahead on arrest warrants when I'm ready."

In typical Captain Janson fashion, he pivoted without giving permission. "What's your thought on the husband?"

Dan had his own thoughts, but he kept his expression unreadable. "First off, I get bad vibes about all of them. I don't like that Harrison Westerfer, and Mitchell is one scary dude. But I just met with the family like you asked, and they handed over some interesting documents. We actually may have something on that husband, but we need to do our own research and confirmation. I am not taking anyone's word for it."

Dan looked over at Grady, who finally spoke up. "And while O'Neill was off hobnobbing with all those rich, crazy people, I was actually doing work. For starters, the son, Harrison Westerfer, has an airtight alibi. True to form, he was trapshooting at the country club all day and he has a million witnesses. There's a rumor he's got a gambling problem, but even so, he couldn't have done it."

"And, I did look over the papers the Westerfers gave you, Dan," Grady said, reviewing her notes. "There was some big election at Harrison Investments a few years back, and from everything I can gather, Preston Westerfer, the father of the murder victim Tiffany Westerfer Mitchell, who was the CEO then, was grooming his only son, Harrison Westerfer, for the job. The big joke was Preston always called his son Junior but he wasn't a Junior. Wife insisted he be called Harrison. Guess she does get what she wants. But, despite all of that, somehow Mr. Mitchell becomes CEO. Rumor has it that to say Victoria Harrison Westerfer was upset was an understatement."

Captain chewed on the pen. "What the fuck does that have to do with the price of bread in China?"

"Price of tea, I think you mean," Grady corrected the captain.

"Whatever. Get to the point."

Grady explained, "When Dan went to see the Westerfers, they also claimed that Mitchell may have had something to do with the death of Preston, the late CEO, since he conveniently died at the time of the election."

"Do we know anything about Preston's death? Could it have been a murder?" Dan asked.

Grady shrugged. "I have forensics going back to check, but I'm pretty sure there wasn't an investigation. Mr. Mitchell did luck out with Preston conveniently dying."

The captain shook his head. "Stop. We are not investigating any more deaths. We are not their personal avengers. What about the present case: Tiffany Westerfer Mitchell?"

Dan brought him up to speed. "It appears our perfect Mr. Mitchell wasn't so perfect. The Westerfers have evidence that Mitchell was having an affair. And according to the company documents, he would lose everything—his company, his son—if she left him. Good a reason as any to kill her."

Grady added, "We just don't know the identity of the lucky lady. An affair would explain the broken vase. Crime of passion."

Dan nodded. "I agree. That man is everything they say and more. He is one cold, calculating bastard. Rumor has it that he literally walks over anyone and everyone to get what he wants. And I will tell you that the stories the guys are telling are scary. My guys, who you know have seen a lot, said Mitchell didn't shed a tear when he found his wife dead in their mansion. When they got there, his hands and clothes were dripping in her blood, and he pointed to her body and told them he was taking his son to the hospital. Not one tear. What kind of man doesn't shed even one lousy tear when his wife is murdered?"

"Listen, with as many years as I have on the force, I will never understand half the shit I see," the captain said.

"Well, I guess that works in business deals, but not when your mother-in-law rushes in and finds you sitting there holding your wife's bloody head. I guess you can understand why she thinks he did it. He didn't even call 911. The mother had to. There is something not right about that guy, and I will find out what it is."

"That explains why she has her panties in a knot. We don't have a murder weapon?"

"No." Dan waited, but he knew what was coming next.

"Did I read your report right? No one searched Mitchell before he left the scene with his son?"

Dan knew he just had to accept the verbal beating. "Yes."

"Jesus, Dan. Really? How are we to explain that? The man could have just walked the hell out of the house with the gun and disposed of it anywhere! What the hell kind of a rookie mistake is that?"

Dan had no excuse. "We did get his clothes later, and there's no gunshot residue on them. And, like I said, once the boy was taken care of, they did frisk him and had him change his clothes. We also have the mother's and the kid's clothes as well. Also clean."

"Great, genius. And the tooth fairy could have killed her too! The DA is going to kill me. Anyone with half a brain—and do I need to remind you how much money Mitchell has?—can tear us apart."

The captain rubbed his forehead. "The shit is truly going to hit the fan. The media is going to have a field day. And we are stuck in the fucking middle, goddammit. We just honored the guy last fall."

Dan hadn't thought about that day in a while. But given the change of events, he searched his mind for details. It was a circus, and Mitchell was in the middle of it. Given his height, you couldn't miss him. Add movie star looks, a blond babe, and you had a crowd wherever they went. Mothers and grandmothers rushed over to thank them for this or that. A handicapped kid fought his way through the crowd so he could thank them for sending him to camp that summer.

"O'Neill?"

"Oh, I'm here. I was just thinking about that afternoon. He didn't seem real to me. Something just didn't seem right. It looked like it pained him to listen to the kids. Yet when he talked about helping them and that no child should be without a loving parent, he seemed so sincere, so determined."

"Let's focus. What do we know about his background?"

"Not much. His actual record was sealed. We are working on that. But we know his parents died when he was young. Got adopted by his neighbor. She raised him and must have done something right because he got a scholarship to one of the most exclusive prep schools, and then a scholarship to Penn. Then it gets even better. He marries the beautiful fair maiden and takes over one of the fastest-growing real estate companies in the world. The only blip is that he did spend a few weeks in foster care, waiting for his neighbor to adopt him. He's been with her ever since."

Grady volunteered, "I'm going to investigate his background. Who knows? Maybe it will tell us something about the mysterious Ryan Mitchell."

"It's going to look bad for the department if he's arrested," Cap said.

"You bet. But there's not much we can do about it now. Plus we put all that money to good use."

Dan had something else on his agenda. "I agree with Victoria Westerfer about one thing—that kid is in danger. It's a matter of when. As in when the killer learns that the kid was there when the murder took place, he may try to come back for him. Assuming she or he doesn't already know the kid was there."

Dan watched as the captain started pacing again. "Well, it's our job to keep his presence at the scene out of the press. And the sooner we find the killer, the sooner that kid will be safe."

Chapter 16

NOT SURPRISINGLY, THE HOME OF RYAN AND TIFFANY Mitchell was released by the Philadelphia Police Department in record time. After the initial debacle where the police allowed Mitchell to leave the scene with his injured son with only one police car following, the DA and chief of police both made sure it was documented and inspected by the book. They enlisted only the top investigators, medical examiners, forensic specialists, and crime photographers. And Jacqueline would get access to all of it. But right now, she needed to see the scene, feel the victim's pain, and, most importantly, gain insight into the monster that took Tiffany's life.

Remnants of the yellow tape still hung on the outside doorway into the home. Jacqueline carefully ducked underneath to enter. Having investigated too many murder scenes in the DA's office, she knew the routine and put on the booties and gloves for the utmost caution. She recognized the rooms from the police photos.

She checked her watch. Mitchell should be arriving any minute. She needed to get to work. To view the scene alone. The sweeping aerial shots she'd seen in the press reports did not do the spacious home justice. Despite its traditional exterior, the walls lined with crisp white linen combined beautifully with the white furniture to make a person feel at home. But as much as Jacqueline wanted to savor Tiffany's talent in design, her eye was drawn to the crude yellow tape and red stains in the great room.

She wandered around, trying to figure out what the lady of the house had been like. The bloodstain on the white carpet stood out as if someone had thrown red paint on a Monet masterpiece. It didn't belong, destroying something so beautiful. Jacqueline kneeled next to the spot, examining the location where the body had been. He shot her while she was walking away. *Why did she turn her back on him? Was she trying to run away? Get him to leave? Did she know he had a gun?* Jacqueline caught herself using the male pronoun for the killer and knew it was on purpose. Her instincts told her the attacker was male, but she didn't know why.

"Did you see it coming? Did you know? Talk to me, Tiffany. Tell me what happened." Jacqueline realized that she was talking to the carpet and pulled herself up. The stillness of the house ran a chill up her spine. At the same moment, Jacqueline felt a warm breeze cross her face. She turned around, expecting someone to be there, but no one was. *I'm going crazy. Look for real clues,* Jacqueline chided herself, *not some ghost.*

The breeze caused her to turn toward the winding staircase, and she remembered Patrick. As she stood near where the body was found, she looked up. Because of the openness of the foyer, she could see the top landing right outside the master bedroom. The police report said that they found the mother-in-law right outside the master suite, holding the grandson, rocking him back and forth.

Patrick saw the whole thing, Jacqueline realized. *He knows what happened.*

Jacqueline turned back. Patrick watched from the banister as Tiffany fought with her murderer. She and her attacker argued right here. Jacqueline looked around the room, knowing that it contained the secret to Tiffany's death. A marble fireplace was flanked by built-in bookcases that seemed to grow out of the wall.

Jacqueline examined the pictures of the Mitchell family, and of Tiffany and her mother, that lined the shelves. The resemblance between the two Westerfer women was uncanny. But it was what wasn't displayed that bothered Jacqueline. Mrs. Victoria Westerfer clearly favored her daughter Tiffany, as Katherine was notably absent from the pictures, with the exception of one picture of the five family members. Based on the photos displayed, a casual acquaintance would never know Tiffany had a sister.

Not surprisingly, the shelves also contained original classics, including Fitzgerald, Hemingway, and Austen. Then Jacqueline noticed a row of leather-bound books. To her surprise, they weren't books at all, but photo albums. Jacqueline picked up one that contained pictures of Patrick's birth. She flipped through the pages, confirming what she'd suspected. Every picture was meticulously arranged in chronological order. She grabbed another book. It was of photos of Tiffany's wedding to Mitch.

"Please be very careful with those." A powerful voice ran a chill up Jacqueline's spine. Mitch descended the marble staircase. In another world, he could double as the handsome prince. Freshly showered, he stopped her in her tracks with his regal presence.

Mitch grabbed the book and put it back in its place. "I would appreciate it if you asked before you go rooting through our things." The dark look in his eyes explained the Iceman nickname. Jacqueline made a mental note to tell him to lose that look at the trial, or they were doomed before they even got to jury selection.

Jacqueline moved out of his way. "I didn't realize you were home. I'm sorry. I didn't mean to offend you, but you better get used to people prying into your personal life. And I need to build our defense, which means getting into all the details, even those that seem unimportant at first blush."

He frowned as he turned to face her. "Let's get this over with. What do you need from me?"

Jacqueline stepped back. Despite his imposing physical stature, she refused to be intimidated. "Well, for starters, I expect you to lose the attitude. We're on the same team."

"Fine. If you follow my requests, that can be accomplished. I just don't understand why I need to help since I hired you to do the job."

"I don't think you understand. You're an integral part of your defense. I realize this is painful for you. But—"

"No. Luckily for you, you have no idea how painful it is." Turning his back on Jacqueline, Mitch moved towards the window.

"Well, if we want any shot of winning this, and I assume you do—"

Mitch interrupted, "Please, let's get on with it. I didn't come here for a lecture. What exactly do you need?"

Somewhat surprised, Jacqueline squared her shoulders, broadening her resolve to not be intimidated by his tone. "I need you to take your time. I need you to walk me through everything you can remember about that afternoon."

Mitch moved through the room robotically, his eyes distant. "I called her name, and then I saw her lying here. Blood was spewing from her head. I knelt down and grabbed her. All I could think about was stopping the bleeding. I didn't even check for a pulse. I just wanted the bleeding to stop. Then Victoria came in. She started screaming and asking for Patrick. I didn't even know Patrick was home. So then we both ran around looking for him. I checked the first floor, and Victoria ran upstairs. He was up there, in that back corner. "

Jacqueline's eyes followed his finger, pointing to the back corner of the upstairs landing. She envisioned the little boy standing there, frozen in horror, witnessing the nightmare unfold below in the open floor plan of the house. She could almost see him, wide-eyed and trembling, peering through the banister. Then, upon hearing the gunshot, retreating to the back corner, out of sight of the killer.

Mitch's face turned pale.

"Mitch, I'm sorry," Jacqueline said softly. He stood up. "Don't be. You are doing your job. What else?"

Pointing to the openness of the room, Jacqueline said, "It confirms what I suspected."

Mitch nodded, his face void of emotion. If Jacqueline didn't know better, she would have thought she was boring him. "What?" he asked in an exasperated tone.

"Patrick knows who did this to his mother. So that's why we need to protect him. We must keep his condition as private as possible and limit the people who can see him to a minimum. Don't trust anyone."

Mitch nodded slightly. "I agree. I have his security under control." Checking his watch, he asked, "Anything else?"

Jacqueline shuddered. She found his cold manner disturbing. Where was the panicked, loving dad she'd met years before? Mitch acted like they were conducting a business meeting, not discussing his child's safety. She made a mental note to learn more about his background.

She turned back to the books. "The books are a great idea and clearly very meticulously maintained."

Mitch ran his hands over the leather. "Thank you. But it was all Tiffany. She loved pictures. And she loved these books. She would spend hours organizing them. She used to say that someone could tell her life by reviewing them."

Jacqueline quickly surmised that there had to be at least two books for every year. "I think she was right. May I?"

For the first time since he came down, Mitch smiled. "Of course. Thank you for asking."

Jacqueline returned his smirk and opened a book to a picture of Tiffany at the beach with Patrick. "She was very beautiful, Mitch."

"Yes, she was. She loved to have her picture taken. I think she gets that from her mother. And her grandmother. They lived and breathed the society pages. I never knew the two of them to be without a camera."

"This is a nice idea," Jacqueline said, referring to the photo albums.

"Yes, apparently, Tiffany's grandmother started it when she got married, and then Victoria Harrison Westerfer continued it. And then Tiffany did it too." Mitch grabbed a book and started thumbing through the pages.

Jacqueline decided to change the subject. "Why do you call your mother-in-law by all three names?"

"Well, you see, it was Victoria's family, the Harrisons, that had the connections, the blue blood. Victoria will tell anyone who listens that they are a direct line from English royalty. The Westerfers, on the other hand, were just the worker bees. Rumor had it that Victoria married Preston Westerfer because his family had income. Old Man Bryon, Victoria's father, blew through his inheritance the usual way. Bored out of his mind, he gambled as a pastime. It was beneath Bryon, or any of them, to work. And, Harrison is just like Bryon. Here's a picture of the old man." Mitchell handed her a photo of the stereotypical blue-blooded patriarch, ascot and all.

"Anyway, as they say, it was the perfect blend of money and connections. Thus, Harrison Investments was established. Harrison was the right name in all the right circles, and it was those circles that held all the power and money." Mitch put the book back. "Makes it a lot easier to get contracts, permits, etcetera when you have the right name."

Jacqueline thought about the legal community. It too had its own set of unwritten rules. "Wow, what a story. Interesting family."

Mitch didn't say anything.

"Mitch, someone wanted her dead. There are just too many beautiful and expensive things in here for it to be anything but a crime of passion."

Mitch surveyed the room. "Jacqueline, that's just it. I don't know who could have done this. What could she have said or known that someone would kill her over it?"

"I don't know, but I promise you, I'll find out."

"I'm counting on it." His eyes bore into Jacqueline's, demanding her full attention. Their storminess made her wish someone else were in the room. "I will not go to jail or let anything happen to Patrick."

Jacqueline looked at her client. Something inside him was alive again. Determination. "Well, then, let's get started."

Another idea struck her. "Do you think I could borrow these albums? The pictures could help us."

Mitch looked at them. "Okay, but you have to promise me that you'll guard them with your life. They are basically a photo gallery of my life with Tiffany. And, more importantly, they're the only thing Patrick has left of his mother."

Just then, Mitch grabbed a book, as if an idea had come to him. "What is it?" Jacqueline asked. He ignored her, flipping through one, and then grabbing another. "Mitch, what? Please don't hold back. You need to trust me."

He dismissed her question. "It's nothing. Anything else I can help you with?"

Jacqueline decided to use the only card that would motivate her in a similar situation. "Mitch, I need you to be completely honest with me. You realize it's a pretty good chance that Patrick saw whoever did this to his mother. He may have some information that is key to the whole thing. Have you been able to get him to say anything, or did he have anything on him that could be helpful?"

Mitch had that same strange look on his face, but said nothing. Before Jacqueline could question him again, his phone rang.

"Oh my God. I'll be right there," Mitch said to the caller. He ran out of the house.

Chapter 17

LYDIA HASTINGS SHOOK HER HEAD IN DISBELIEF. There on the TV was her beautiful neighbor, murdered. "Oh my God, I can't believe it."

"What is it, Mrs. Hastings?" Betty rushed to her employer's side.

"Please, Betty, stop. I'm just watching the news. Stop hovering over me."

"It's just that I—"

Lydia didn't let her finish. "I don't want to hear it. I know it's your job to watch me, but it doesn't mean I have to like it." Why was everyone afraid that she would do something stupid? If she heard one more time about leaving the stove on, she was going to scream. It happened once. Apparently for her husband and daughter, that was enough. As much as she loved Betty, she didn't need a nurse or a babysitter. But when she saw the fear and sadness in their eyes, she relented. Could be worse. She was lucky to have two people who loved her so much. She gave in. After all, Betty kept her company.

Immediately after Lydia yelled, she felt horrible. "Betty, I'm sorry."

Betty started to leave. "Don't worry about it, Mrs. Hastings. It's just that we all care about you."

Hearing how much everyone loved her only made it worse. Lydia didn't want to take her frustration out on Betty, but she hated being "cared for." She felt old and helpless. She hated having anyone watch her like she was a child. She hated to see the fear in her husband's eyes when she wasn't right where she was supposed to be. And most of all, she hated losing her independence. "I know, I know."

"Is there anything I can get you?"

"Please stop, Betty. You are not here to wait on me. And thank you, but no, I don't need anything."

Betty hesitated.

"I'm fine. Scout's honor," Lydia said, holding up two fingers. "I promise I'll be a good girl."

"You better." Betty gave her a smile. "Mrs. H., I know how hard this is on you. But if anything happened to you, your husband and daughter would never forgive me."

Lydia knew Betty was right. She decided to change the subject. "Did you know about this?" she asked, pointing to the TV.

"Yes, can you believe she was murdered? Everyone is talking about it. Are there any new developments?" Betty loved gossiping as much as Lydia.

"No, not yet. But they just said my neighbor, her husband, is a person of interest. I can't believe it. I don't know him, but he just didn't seem the type. I remember when they moved in. They seemed like the perfect couple. But boy, did they make the neighbors mad."

"What happened?"

"Well, the Mitchells bought that property across the street and wanted to knock down the Weston house to build something new. You must understand, Betty, I've lived in Chestnut Hill all my life. The people of Chestnut Hill love old homes with character. No Mc-Mansions ever.

"So when the Mitchells were going to build new construction, the neighbors were outraged. Chestnut Hillers don't like anything new, and they let the Mitchells know it. Personally, I thought they were all jealous.

"But the Mitchells were so gracious about it, explaining to any-one who would listen their plan for their home. And it was more beautiful than the drawings. When it finally went up, people were in awe. It didn't look like new construction. Instead, they nestled the house among those beautiful huge oaks. Doesn't it look like those trees grew up around the house?"

Betty looked across the street. "Yes. It's the prettiest house I've ever seen. Next to yours, of course."

"Oh Betty, please. You don't have to pretend with me. I love that house too."

They looked out the window together. "So did your neighbors finally come around?" Betty asked.

"What do you think?" They both laughed. "Of course they did. If you ask anyone today, they would all talk about how excited they were when the house was going up." Lydia was lost in another time. "People around here change history to meet their needs."

"You don't get involved in all that stuff, do you?"

"I try not to. Even with the Mitchells, I wasn't like the rest of them. I just wanted them to be good, kind neighbors. And up until a week ago, they were the perfect neighbors. They always made a point to say hello when they saw me outside, tending to my babies." Betty laughed at the reference to Lydia's flowers. "They kept to themselves, but they were always considerate."

She looked at the newspaper on the coffee table. "It's just so horrible. I remember when this top picture was taken. It was at the Make-a-Wish Foundation ball. We were there. That was before..." Lydia stopped. She rarely talked about her memory problem with anyone. "Anyway, I remember how beautiful they looked. Tiffany in the Vera Wang pink chiffon ball gown. Him in his signature Ralph Lauren tuxedo."

"You loved those parties."

"*Loved* being the operative word. I just can't stand the way people look at me now. I would just die if I couldn't remember someone's name."

Betty looked over Lydia's shoulder at the photo. "They do look beautiful. Strange, isn't it? You just don't know people anymore."

"Yeah, I guess."

Once Betty left, Lydia returned to the article. Tiffany was shot Friday in the early evening. Friday. Lydia shook her head. Where was she Friday? *Why doesn't that sound right?*

Focus. Think. She opened her eyes to look at the picture. Above the society picture was a picture of the murder scene.

Something about that day bothered her. Damn. She just couldn't remember. She tried to follow her doctor's instructions. *Relax, and the memories would come back.* But that was easy for him to say. He could remember what he had for breakfast.

She put the paper down and shut her eyes. *Breathe.* She could feel the wetness around her eyes. She wanted to cry. *No, you are not going to cry.* She forced her mind to concentrate. She used to be such an outgoing, fun person, but her loss of short-term memory was making her feel stupid and insecure. She was afraid to even chat with anyone now because she couldn't remember what she'd talked to them about yesterday, or if she'd even talked to them at all. Why was it that she could remember a stupid dispute among jealous neighbors years ago, but she couldn't remember where her husband went today?

She tried to tell herself that there were worse problems in the world. She was learning to cope, to make notes to herself that she could review. But it just made her feel old. At sixty-seven, she didn't want to be old. She wanted to be independent. She had earned the right.

Lydia continued to read the rest of the article. According to the datebook Betty kept for her, Lydia was working in her garden that day. She remembered that she saw something odd. That Mercedes. That was it. It came flying out of the driveway. Did anybody say anything about that car? It looked familiar, but for some reason she didn't think it belonged to the Mitchells. But what if she could help? What if he didn't do it? She hoped with all her heart that he didn't.

He seemed like such a nice fella, and he adored that child. They were always together.

In her dressing room, Lydia looked for a piece of paper to jot down a note about the Mercedes. She knew Betty left notepads all over for her, but of course, there wasn't one handy, despite the size of her closet. As she searched, her eyes settled on a picture of her and her husband on their last trip to Florida. Her husband held his pride and joy, a four-hundred-pound marlin he caught off the coast of the Bahamas. He beamed with pride. She found a pad, but before she could find a pen, she saw the note Howard left her. "Pack for Florida, honey." *Oh, I should start packing*, she thought.

As she grabbed her travel bag, she got that sickening feeling that she'd forgotten to do something. *Was I supposed to make a note about something?* Lydia wondered as she opened her luggage.

Chapter 18

THE POLICE ESCORT MET MITCH AND JACQUELINE AS they raced to the hospital. Despite numerous calls, no one would tell them anything about Patrick's condition. Mitch's mind raced incessantly as he swerved through traffic. He couldn't, wouldn't lose Patrick. *Did someone try to kill him? Or was it another panic attack? And where the hell was Katherine?*

The image from the photograph flashed before his eyes. *Stop*, he ordered himself. He needed to focus. He glanced at his phone. Several missed calls from Katherine. But he couldn't risk it. Not in front of Jacqueline. *Katherine, what did you do?* He should confide in Jacqueline. She was sitting right next to him. It was his chance to come clean. As his attorney, Jacqueline was obligated by attorney–client privilege to help him. Yet he couldn't. Not with Patrick's life on the line and too many questions in his own head. He had to go it alone.

They parked at the hospital entrance and raced to Patrick's hospital room. "Katherine, what happened?" Mitchell demanded when he saw her and Eric sitting outside Patrick's room surrounded by guards.

Katherine stood as he approached. "Mitch, I'm so sorry."

Mitchell rushed past her, barging into the room. "Is he alive?"

Dr. Vassallo looked up from the chart. "Mr. Mitchell, don't worry. He's okay. We finally got him back to sleep."

Mitchell ran over to his little boy and kissed his head. Just a few days ago, he was fine, at least physically. "Doctor, what the hell happened?"

She signaled for him to keep his voice down. "Please. Let's discuss this in private."

As they entered the consultation room, Eric and Katherine

followed like two lost puppies. "Mitch, I think this should be a private conversation," Jacqueline said.

The doctor waited, her expression steady but patient. Mitch's eyes flickered to Katherine's tear-stained face. "They can stay because I want them to know what happened. Please tell us."

The doctor's eyes filled with compassion. "This afternoon, your son had another episode and had to be sedated."

Katherine broke down in sobs. "I'm so sorry…I don't know what to do."

As they all turned to Katherine, Eric instinctively moved between his wife and Mitchell. "Mitch, please. Katherine has been here with him all day."

Mitch turned back to the doctor, his voice edged with desperation. "Continue."

The doctor nodded, choosing her words carefully. "Patrick had been showing signs of normalcy. His vitals were stable, though his breathing remained shallow and uneven, as if his lungs were unsure whether to fully relax. He has also been crying out for his mom during fitful periods of sleep. It's clear your son has witnessed something deeply traumatic. That trauma has sent his mind and body into a kind of shock, a protective mechanism to block out the memory. It's hard to determine exactly what he saw, but it was too much for his young mind to process. The pain and fear were overwhelming. His brain is trying to shut out the memory entirely, but the subconscious can't fully erase it."

Mitch's jaw tightened, his voice barely a whisper. "Cut to the chase. What caused another episode? How the hell can he go from stable to having one of these panic attacks? Are you saying Patrick saw his mother die?"

"No one knows for sure what Patrick saw. We won't until he is able to talk about it. But something triggered this episode, and the duty nurse described it as an almost reliving of events."

"What do you mean?"

"Something triggered Patrick's vitals to spike. His oxygen levels shallowed and his heart rate raced like a panic attack in adults. It could be anything. It could be as simple as a smell or a sound from that event or something more relevant like a person."

Jacqueline clarified, "You mean something or someone relating to the murder?"

"Yes."

"Just so I'm clear, Doctor," Mitch said, trying to stay calm, "if someone says something that is related to that day, or if he sees something or someone from that event, his body will act out even if he can't explain it to us?"

Everyone looked at Katherine. "But I was the only one here."

The doctor broke the awkward silence. "I'll give you a few minutes. I need to check on my other patients. Mr. Mitchell, you have my number if you have any other questions."

Once the doctor left, Jacqueline demanded answers. "I presume you are Tiffany's sister, correct?" she asked Katherine.

Katherine managed a slow nod.

"What happened?"

Katherine fell into the chair, wringing her hands. She refused to make eye contact. "I don't know. I honestly don't."

"Well, let's rule some things out. Where were you on the day Tiffany was murdered?"

"Ms. Stone," Eric interceded on his wife's behalf. "It is Ms. Stone, correct?"

"Yes."

Eric moved between Katherine and Jacqueline, creating a physical barrier to protect his wife. "Please leave my wife alone."

Katherine turned to Mitch. "You have to believe me. I don't know what happened."

Mitch put his hand up. "That's enough, Jacqueline. We are done.

Now, I think we can all use a break. It's been a long and emotional few days, and I need to just be with my son. Alone."

"Mr. Mitchell, please. I would still like to ask Mrs. Conceillo a few questions," Jacqueline said.

Mitch looked at Katherine. "Jacqueline, we are done."

Katherine's eyes glistened. Mitch pulled her close and hugged her, ignoring Eric and Jacqueline.

Chapter 19

"THANKS A LOT," BILLY MUTTERED AS THE DOOR OF Silverman and Keane LLP closed in his face. Another dead end. They had been working on the Mitchell case for a week now and they were still no closer to proving his innocence. Despite the frustration, he loved doing investigative work for Jacqueline. He viewed it as a game, a complex puzzle to be solved. One crucial piece was missing, and he was determined to find it. The fact that Tiffany Mitchell had been embroiled in some legal issue related to the hospital could be that missing piece.

But walking down Chestnut Street, where all the top Philadelphia law firms were, Billy felt the weight of each step. He moved from law firm to law firm, relentless in his quest for answers, but received none. Usually the thrill of discovery drove him to keep moving. But right now, his feet ached, and he felt like giving up. Tiffany Westerfer Mitchell appeared to be a member of the hospital board for glory only, a figurehead the hospital used for her name and wealth. Her expertise seemed to be fundraising and organizing galas—not exactly work that would motivate a murder.

Since most of the claims against the hospital were medical malpractice and had nothing to do with board members, his trip down Chestnut Street was almost over. Billy still didn't understand why the firms were located so close to one another in town. Maybe so they could all have lunches together—he frequently saw attorneys from opposing firms going into the Four Seasons. His high-powered lunch, however, was a quick stop at Five Guys.

He ordered a Coke and fell into the booth, exhausted from interviewing what felt like a million people. He grabbed a handful of the free peanuts and started cracking the shells open. Jacqueline needed him to keep going, so he pulled out his list and crossed off several more law firms. Most lawyers he met couldn't speak to specifics due to confidentiality provisions in the settlements. Hospitals and their lawyers were savvy enough to require such clauses so they didn't end up on some lawyer's website. But from the documents filed with the court, like the complaint, answers, and various motions, Billy was able to cross off many of the cases as having nothing to do with Tiffany.

Billy laughed to himself. He crossed off about a third of his list by talking to one firm. No wonder that attorney drove a Bentley around town. The millions the lawyer got from that hospital alone explained the expensive suit, the penthouse offices, and, of course, the car. Billy had to admit personal injury law had its perks.

As he left Five Guys, he realized he only had one firm left. Dread filled him as he contemplated telling Jacqueline it was a bust. He glanced at his watch and calculated that he had an hour before the Sixers game started. Enough time to shower and change. Personal injury law made him feel dirty. Sure, they helped a lot of people. Some of them at least. The majority, however, just seemed to be out to make a quick buck. Some of the lawyers didn't even try to hide their excitement over the severity of a client's injury. The worse the injury, the bigger the payout. Paralysis equals big bucks.

As he walked past a few homeless people, he hoped this last attorney held the key they needed. He crossed Chestnut Street to Ninth Street, feeling he was close. Yet, his enthusiasm waned when he arrived to find the place rundown and seemingly out of business. Even more discouraging was that the plaintiffs had only filed a writ of summons and then taken no further action, leading to the case being dismissed ten months later. Billy assumed that the lawyer was looking for a quick kill, and when the hospital didn't bite, he decided the case was too expensive to pursue, so he dropped it. Given what little there was to know about this lawyer and the few documents that were filed, Billy didn't have much hope.

His tenacity required he at least ask the guy. Jacqueline would kill him if he didn't overturn every stone. As he walked down Chestnut Street, he almost missed the office. Unlike the more successful plaintiff's firms, this office wasn't in a high-rise building or a beautiful renovated brownstone. There was no security desk. Just a red row home converted into offices. The small sign on the outside told Billy he had found the right place.

Billy knocked. No answer.

He knocked again. Just as he turned to walk away, a man answered the door. "Can I help you?" he asked, tucking his shirt into his pants. His disheveled appearance evidence of an afternoon nap.

"I'm looking for Kevin Handsman."

"That's me. Please come in. How can I help you?" The man brushed away old fast-food wrappers. He gave Billy the once-over, as if looking for obvious injury.

"Were you the attorney who filed this matter?" Billy handed him a copy of the writ. The copy Billy had didn't list all the defendants. Instead, the hospital was listed first as the deep pocket, a lawyer term for the defendant with the most money to pay.

The man looked at the writ. "Who's asking?"

"I'm investigating claims against the hospital. I was just hoping you could tell me what this case was about."

"Hold on, buddy. I did nothing wrong."

"I'm not accusing you of anything. I'm just trying to find out what it was about."

Billy got out his wallet. "Listen, I only want the facts. The only court document you filed was the writ. I need all the names." Billy flashed a hundred-dollar bill. "Will this help jog your memory?"

The man grabbed the bill and slumped down behind his desk. "To be honest, I don't remember much." He rummaged through what Billy suspected the man considered his filing system. He pulled out a thin file and placed it unopened on the desk. "A guy from Alabama called and asked if I would act as local counsel. I don't know what the case was about. I don't even do malpractice law."

"What was the guy's name?"

"Something Scaggs. I remember because I thought that was a horrible last name." He looked in the folder. "Yep, here it is...Frank Scaggs."

"How did Mr. Scaggs get your name?"

"I have no idea. I asked him, and he just said that he was a sole practitioner and that we should stick together. I told him I liked his thinking, especially when he sent me the three-thousand-dollar retainer up front."

"Did you ask any questions?"

"Well, no. He just needed a paper pusher, and I was happy to help. I do remember that he was very happy that he didn't have to file a complaint. He kept asking me if I was sure you can file just a writ." He laughed at his own joke. "Then one day he called and said that the case was over. He said to file the Motion to Dismiss and that I could keep the retainer. He said he got everything he needed. And that was it."

Billy paid handsomely for the file. Something told him there was more to this case.

Chapter 20

"DAMN HIM," JACQUELINE SAID, SLAMMING HER phone down.

"Someone's in a good mood," Lisa said as she peered into Jacqueline's office.

Jacqueline looked up. "Sorry about that. Did you hear me?"

"Well, not exactly. But I heard you stomping down the hall and then attacking the phone. What did it do to you?"

Jacqueline paced back and forth in a lame attempt to blow off some steam. "That man is just the most exasperating man I know. He wants me to solve this case and protect his son, but I'm not allowed to question anyone. Including him."

"Just so we are clear. We are talking about Mr. Mitchell?" Lisa asked.

"Yes. God, I just don't know what I am going to do about him." Jacqueline looked at her associate, hearing the desperation in her own voice. "What are you smiling about?"

"It's just that it's good to hear some passion in your voice, even if you are mad."

Jacqueline collapsed next to her associate. "Well, I'm not so sure. I just hope tomorrow is a more productive day. I can't let Mitch dictate the terms of the investigation."

Lisa handed Jacqueline a glass of water. "Why? What happened?"

Relief swept over Jacqueline as she continued. She slipped by calling Mitch by his nickname. And for once, Lisa didn't ask her about her relationship with her newest client. Instead, Lisa focused on their case, and Jacqueline filled Lisa in on Patrick's condition and Katherine's involvement. "I know both of them are hiding something. I just know it. Mr. Mitchell won't let me question her. He just protects her. And I can't help but wonder why. And I wish you could have seen the exchange between Katherine and him. I could tell her husband was not happy about it. And to be honest, I wouldn't be either. If Mr. Mitchell hadn't assured me how close he and Eric were, I would have sworn Eric was jealous."

Lisa took notes. "Well, that is interesting. I agree with you regarding the murder scene. It was definitely a crime of passion. Jealousy is as good a reason as any. Boss, are you sure Mr. Mitchell didn't do it? I have been doing some background checks on him, and he's not perfect."

Jacqueline took a sip of her water. "I read your report. Keep digging. We can't rule anything out, but I trust Mr. Mitchell. I do." She continued before Lisa could ask why. "And another thing. Mitchell's son, Patrick, holds the key. He is trying to tell us all something. I just don't know what."

"You think he saw the whole thing, don't you? That poor little boy. I can't even imagine. Are you concerned about his safety? And more importantly, do you think there could be something going on between Mitchell and Katherine?"

Jacqueline stood up and returned to her desk. "Yes. And no. I'm very concerned about Patrick. That child is in danger. And we need to find out why suddenly Patrick had another panic attack when Katherine was alone with him. Even if Mr. Mitchell doesn't want us to. But no, I don't think there is, or was, anything going on between them."

"Are you concerned that Mr. Mitchell seems to defend her?" Lisa asked.

Just then, Billy returned. "Guys, do you have a minute?"

Saved by the interruption, Jacqueline ignored the concern, and the group headed toward their war room.

"Give me some good news. Did anyone see anything?" Jacqueline asked. She had a laundry list of things for them to do, but she wanted to know if he made any progress. After her meeting with Mitch, she had more questions than answers.

Billy started, "You are not going to be happy."

"Okay, hit me with it."

"I interviewed everyone I could. Unfortunately, their next-door neighbors, an elderly couple named Howard and Lydia Hastings, just left for vacation to Florida. They won't be back for two weeks. The woman has some sort of short-term memory loss, so I'm not sure she'll be of any help anyway, but she was home the afternoon of the murder.

"Other than that, the only person who saw anything was the gardener at another neighbor's house, but he helps the prosecution. He was outside when, according to him, Mr. Mitchell came screeching into the driveway. He remembers thinking how lucky he was that no one was walking around. He saw Mr. Mitchell fly out of his Rover and rush into the house. About fifteen minutes later, a Bentley drove up, and that's when he heard all kinds of yelling."

Jacqueline played with her pen. "Well, Mr. Mitchell basically confirms that. He said that he couldn't reach his wife on her cell phone, and so he got nervous when she wasn't answering. And the Bentley probably belonged to the victim's mother, Victoria Westerfer."

"It also possibly supports the prosecution's rage theory," Lisa said. "Jacqueline, are we concerned with the time discrepancy? Do we know why Mr. Mitchell didn't call 911 if he was the first one on the scene?"

Good question. She needed to make Mitch focus, but her concern for Mitch's son made her ignore her own protocol. She needed her firm to work on Mitch's defense, not the prosecution's case. "As you know, Mr. Mitchell has been focused solely on getting his son well. But I'll talk to him about that. Next, Lisa?"

"I reviewed the social pages. Tiffany is—I mean, was—everything they say. Beautiful and perfect. Constantly in the papers heading this charity or that, but not one mention of any kind of enemy or even a mean word, for that matter.

"Also, I tried that Dr. Marc Fitzgerald. He wasn't home, but I got his chatty wife. She explained that he was on a fishing trip but should be back in a few days. According to her, Tiffany did stop by, apparently asking the husband to return to the board of the hospital, but he declined. They are enjoying retirement. Wife said she will try to reach him to see if we can interview him."

Lisa glanced at her notes. "I also talked to an Ashley Cox, Ms. Conceillo's secretary. She confirms that Katherine was in her office when Tiffany died. She said she told Katherine the news that day."

Jacqueline got up and put an X next to Katherine's name. She didn't like it. Though Katherine had an airtight alibi, she and her husband sure looked like they were hiding something. "Great job, Lisa," Jacqueline said. "But please stay on top of Katherine. Look into her past. Her relationship with Mr. Mitchell. Also, the doctor's wife. That doctor is the only lead we have, and I want to talk to him. See how Tiffany was, if she acted nervous, said anything, etcetera. Billy, information regarding the company, Harrison Investments?"

Billy had the financial documents in front of him, but he didn't look at them. "Not much, but I'll look into them. Mr. Mitchell did take over the company, basically when the old man died. From every source I could find, that wasn't the plan. Apparently, a Mr. Wallingford changed his vote at the last minute. It doesn't make any sense because up until the day of the election, he swore he would vote like Preston requested. They were the best of friends. Needless to say, the golden son, Harrison, was furious."

Jacqueline mulled it over. "Okay, keep checking. Find out what you can. It may be nothing, but I don't like the smell of it. I want to know why that person would turn unexpectedly on the favored son. Any news on hospital claims?"

Billy didn't need any notes on this issue either. "I found something that has some potential. Some attorney in Alabama filed a writ against the hospital a few years back, and guess whose name is on it?"

Everyone spoke in unison. "Fitzgerald?"

Billy clapped and pointed at them as if they had just figured out the final clue in a game of charades. "You guessed it."

Jacqueline smiled. They finally had a lead. "Excellent work. Was it a big or small firm in Alabama?"

Billy shrugged. "Haven't had a chance to research. But filed by an attorney named Frank Scaggs."

Jacqueline grabbed the datebooks. "Wait. That sounds familiar. I read that name in one of Tiffany's books last night. Mr. Mitchell was saying that at the time of the Harrison Investments election, Tiffany was involved in some major hospital board issue. And I could have sworn I saw a name like that."

She scanned the datebook. "Here it is. Meeting with Scaggs. That can't be a coincidence. Billy, find out whatever you can about this case. Lisa, you work on that Dr. Fitzgerald. Finally, gang, we need to find out everything we can about Katherine Westerfer Conceillo, Tiffany's sister. I got the sense at the hospital that she was hiding something.

"Billy, you oversee all the hospital claims. Also, see what you can find out about Harrison Westerfer. Start with the board members."

Jacqueline reviewed her agenda. "Anything else?" She looked at her group. They suddenly all seemed very interested in the papers in front of them. "What is it?"

Lisa and Billy exchanged looks. Jacqueline's heart raced since she knew they were silently debating which one would break the news to her.

"Boss, we looked into Mr. Mitchell's background too," Lisa said.

Jacqueline felt like a storm was coming. "Okay?"

"Did you know that his biological father was an alcoholic with a record and apparently abusive?"

Jacqueline remembered Mitch saying his parents died, but she didn't know the circumstances. "Spill it."

"They apparently both died when Mr. Mitchell was little. And he spent a while in foster care. There's not much on how they died."

Jacqueline had been so busy working on his defense that she skipped her normal number one task, a background check on her client. Before she could process the information, Claudia beeped in. Claudia only interrupted if it was urgent.

"Yes?"

"Mr. Mitchell's mother is on the line. You need to take this call."

It was difficult, but through the sobs, Jacqueline deciphered the gist of the message. Mitch had been arrested. "Mrs. Mitchell, calm down. I will get him out. I promise. But, if you want to help, and I know you do, can you think of any reason why the police would arrest Mitch? The more information we have, the better defense I can provide."

Mitch's mother continued to sob. "No, I can't. Mitch is a good man. He would never hurt Tiffany. He's not like his father. I tried, I really tried to make it right."

His father? "What do you mean? What about his father?" The floodgates opened. "Mrs. Mitchell, please stop crying. Mr. Mitchell wouldn't want you to worry." Jacqueline sat in silence, giving her time to grieve. The walls of protection she'd built for Mitch all these years were crumbling.

"You don't understand. It was my fault. I should never have let Mitch get involved with her. With that family. You need to help him. You need to protect him. They are going after him. He won't survive."

"Mrs. Mitchell, please calm down. We can't have anything happen to you. Who is with Patrick? Are you with him?"

"Yes, I'm in the hospital with him. But Ms. Stone, you need to get Mitch out of there. He won't survive again. You don't know him as well as I do."

Jacqueline tried to read between the lines, but the woman wasn't making any sense. "What do you mean 'again'? Mrs. Mitchell, did something happen to Mr. Mitchell when he was little that you think is important? Please, I'm his lawyer. I can help him."

Suddenly, Jacqueline could hear the anger in her voice. "Leave his past alone. Now do your job and just get him out. Now." The phone went dead.

Her associates stared at her. "Jacqueline, what's wrong? You're white as a ghost," Billy said.

The time had come. She was going back in. To a world that had kicked her out, literally. She tugged on her pendant.

Jacqueline looked up. "I'm okay, but Mr. Mitchell was just arrested. I need to go to the police station. Lisa, start the bail papers. I want him out yesterday."

Chapter 21

MARIE CREPT OVER TO THE WINDOW OF THE HOSPI-tal, watching as the cops escorted Mitch into the police car. Bystanders gathered outside to witness her baby's humiliation. Anger swelled up inside of her as people gawked, enjoying this humiliating moment. Mitch would survive. He always did.

He's too smart for all of them. He always has a plan, she reminded herself. She could still see him with those scholarship forms, telling her how important it was that he get into that stupid prep school. *Mom, if I'm going to be the best, I have to go to the best schools*, he'd explained. And Tyler was only too willing to help him with the paperwork. She smiled as she thought of how the two of them, both lonely souls with no children of their own, coparented Mitch. *We were doing coparenting before they even coined the phrase.*

But they had fought over his schooling. *I should have insisted more,* Marie chided herself. She never did like the idea, but Mitch needed to escape from his past. He always wanted more. And Tyler was there, willing to oblige. She had marveled at how comfortable and poised Mitch looked in his role as CEO. He entered the world of not only the rich, but the elite. She knew there was a difference. A big difference. Marie truly believed that. Only a few, those select precious few, could be in the elite, the blue bloods. Marie had seen enough episodes of *Dynasty* and *Lifestyles of the Rich and Famous* to know what the life of those people was like. She wasn't sure she wanted that for her Mitch. She wanted him to find true love. She worried about him fitting in with the free ride to Episcopal Academy. It would change his life, but it meant sacrifice. It wasn't easy for either of them. Being called the scholarship kid. Somehow, her Mitch broke through that glass ceiling.

It had been decades, but Marie remembered the day she adopted the boy with long dirty curls in need of a good bath and haircut. Him looking up at her. Lost in this world, with no one. How her heart broke, looking into that fearful but determined I'm-not-gonna-cry face. He was only eight, but he was trying to convince the judge he could take care of himself. After all, he could make scrambled eggs and mac and cheese and a hot dog. What else did a boy need? And he even had a job delivering newspapers. She knew he would be successful. His accomplishments blew everyone away, even Marie. But she feared their good fortune couldn't last forever. And it didn't.

They would solve this, Marie convinced herself. She had always protected Mitch and she would do it again. She would never let anyone, especially those Westerfers, harm her baby. The three of them had solved every problem they'd had in the past, and they could do it again. From the bullies at school to the snobs in business. Somehow Mitch found the will to not only survive but thrive. She counted on his strength. She wanted to swear, but then she would have to go to confession again.

Instead, she sat back down next to Patrick, trying to calm her racing heart. What did Tiffany do with those boxes? Asking all those questions. Why couldn't she have left Mitch's past alone? Well, she couldn't think about it. She had to save her strength to protect Patrick and Mitch. She hadn't told Tiffany about Mitch's past. And she sure wasn't telling that lawyer. She couldn't risk losing Mitch. Not again.

Her mind transformed into a photo album, flipping through pictures of Mitch as a little boy. She flashed back thirty years.

She was sitting in her row home, enjoying a hot cup of tea, when that busybody Viola banged on her screen door as cop cars flooded the street. Viola crying that their awful neighbor, that brute drunk, had murdered his sweet young wife. "Where's Ryan? Where's her son?" Marie demanded as Viola looked perplexed. Marie running over. She fought with the officers to let her in. Mitch sitting there, that blank stare. He was all alone in the world.

Lost, just like Patrick...No, Marie, she told herself. *Stop it, this isn't the same.*

The past was over. She believed that. Almost.

Yet her mind couldn't help but go there. *Stop this blubbering right now,* Marie chided herself. Mitch needed her to be strong, just like him. She could almost hear him now: *Only fools waste time crying.* She brushed her tears away and focused. All she had to do was keep everything in order until he came back. That's it. She could do that.

She wanted to curse, to damn God for what He was doing to her little boy. *Hasn't he had enough heartbreak, God?* She looked up at the sky, waiting for a reply. Frustrated, she turned her attention back to the window. God wasn't answering her, and at the moment, she didn't want to speak to Him either.

"It's my fault," Marie muttered. She never should have allowed Mitch to get mixed up with those people. She'd feared in her heart they would never truly accept him. Never. He wasn't one of them, and despite their smiles—those gorgeous pearly whites, they did all have gorgeous teeth—he didn't belong. Especially if they knew. She had spent the second part of her life, the one with Mitch, consumed with hiding his secret. Protecting him. And she feared it was about to come crashing down. *That Tiffany! I should have been more insistent.*

Between tears, Marie laughed. She had never been able to stop Mitch from doing anything. But she should have at least protected him. She should have told Tiffany to give him a break. Tiffany seemed to truly love Mitch, but who knows? Who ever knew what that girl was thinking? She kept everything to herself, all formal and perfect. "Oh God, I'm so sorry," Marie said, looking up at the sky. *Tiffany, I'm sorry. I just wish I knew you like Mitch did. You never had time for little old me. I hope you find your peace in heaven.* Marie blessed herself. *But that evil mother of yours. Now she's another story.*

Marie thought back over the last few weeks. Tiffany asking all those questions. About Mitch. His past. What was she supposed to do? She'd warned Tiffany to drop it.

She remembered that day like yesterday. Her heart had stopped as she pulled up to her house. Tiffany's car sitting in the driveway. The driver's door open. Marie jumped out so fast she almost forgot to put her car in park. "What are you doing? Why the change in schedule?"

Patrick was so surprised to see his mom he jumped out of the car too. "Mommy."

"How's my soccer star?" Tiffany said. As they hugged, Marie took the second to get her nerves under control. She would never get tired of seeing Patrick happy with his mom. "Oh, hi, Marie. Thanks for getting Patrick. Patrick, can you run inside and grab your backpack? I need to talk to Mom-Mom."

They both watched as Patrick ran into his second home, and Marie waited for the axe to fall. Tiffany always had an agenda. "Marie, I need to know about Natalie."

Marie could feel the panic rising in her chest at the mention of Natalie. She needed to stay calm. "What are you talking about?"

"Don't play dumb with me, Marie. You are his mother. You must know something."

Marie had learned well from Mitch that if you didn't want to answer a question, you asked another question. "Why are you asking me?"

Marie noticed the boxes in Tiffany's car. "Are those my boxes? I told you I'd bring over the stuff when I had time to go through it. Why didn't you tell me you were coming?"

Tiffany stared at her. "Why do you care? Are you hiding something?"

The Hail Mary was going through her head as Marie tried to stay calm. "What? I'm sorry. I don't know what you're talking about."

Before Tiffany could argue, Patrick returned with a cookie in hand. "Mom-Mom said I could have this because I played so well."

"It's okay, Patrick. You can have the cookie. Now please get in the car." As Patrick climbed in the backseat, Tiffany had whispered, "I know you know more. I need to know."

Stop this, Marie told herself as Patrick stirred in his hospital bed. *Oh, what did I do? Dear God, why didn't Tiffany listen?*

Marie remembered that she wasn't talking to God right now. And their secret was safe. Fresh tears fell down her face, making it almost impossible to see. She reached for another tissue. Box empty. *Great*, she thought as she wiped her eyes with the sleeve of her shirt. She tried to push the images out of her mind—Tiffany gone, the hospital room, the steady beeping of the monitors—but it was impossible. Watching Patrick's tiny body, hooked up to all those wires, haunted her. The fear that gripped him, even in sleep, was written all over his little face. And then, that blank stare. It was as if she was looking into the past and future at the same time. She wasn't sure how much more she could take.

She shook her head, refusing to go where her mind wanted her to go. *How could this be happening?* she asked God. She really didn't want to talk to Him. But she didn't know who else to turn to. Prayer had been her saving grace over the years, and her faith had protected Mitch. Her Mitch. It had always been just the two of them. Mitch was always so strong, so determined to take care of everything.

She would die before she told anyone. Not that nosy detective who kept asking her questions about Mitch. And not that lawyer. She would be damned before she said anything to hurt her Mitch.

She turned on the television in Patrick's room to distract herself. *Patrick will come out of it*, she told herself as she watched him breathe. *Mitch did, and so will Patrick.* She remembered how the hospital wanted her to get all these fancy doctors for Mitch, but she just didn't have the money. She couldn't afford it. So she just prayed and prayed. Then one day, he snapped out of it. Woke up like nothing had happened. She remembered how the doctors had warned her not to speak of the incident for fear that he would have another panic at-tack. The doctors told her that if he had another attack, she could lose him inside his mind forever. Marie took their instructions to heart, and she never spoke of the incident again.

Never. Not with Tiffany. Not with anyone.

Mitch's arrest was all over the television. Before she could turn it off, the headline flashed: "Murderer or Widower?" A picture of Mitch, arm in arm with Tiffany at the Make-A-Wish Foundation ball. Unable to resist, Marie admired their beautiful faces. Then, with no warning, Marie's mind flashed to another image. An unexpected one. That of Tiffany brutally murdered. *Oh my God* was Marie's last thought as she fainted to the ground.

Chapter 22

SCAGGS SAT IN HIS COMFY LEATHER SOFA AS HE watched the Crimson Tide score another touchdown against the Tigers on his big-screen television. This was living. He knew all that time in law school would pay off. A Corona in one hand. His new plasma TV hanging on the porch. Correction: his outdoor living room, as that fancy blond designer had explained. He was glad he'd chosen the bigger model. Everything looked better on it. And he knew he was the envy of all his softball buddies. He thought about inviting them over for the game, but he was tired of them drinking him out of house and home. Just because he came into some money didn't mean he had to pay for everything.

The Tigers took a time-out, so it flashed to a commercial. Scaggs thought about getting another beer, but he was too tired. Instead, he flipped through the channels. He refused to watch commercials. Nothing else was on. Reruns, movies, and news. He was about to flip back to the game when a picture on the news caught his eye. And then he saw her. He would never forget that look.

He turned the volume up. "Now we turn to an update on the death of Tiffany Westerfer Mitchell. The coroner has ruled her death a homicide. Mrs. Westerfer Mitchell was found shot dead in her Chestnut Hill mansion. Her husband, real estate mogul and philanthropist Ryan Mitchell, has just been charged in connection with her death."

Scaggs was no longer listening. He was staring at the picture. This wasn't good. Shit. He knew messing around with her could be trouble. But that case was too good. He picked up his phone to check on his accounts. It was time to take that trip to Mexico he'd been thinking about.

Chapter 23

SITTING IN THE POLICE DEPARTMENT'S PRIVATE IN-
terview room, Jacqueline observed Mitchell's legendary dark, piercing gaze, described in a *Forbes* article years ago. His stormy eyes held
a mysterious intensity that she, and apparently others, found both
captivating and intimidating. This aura of power and enigma drew
investors and helped him close deals that others couldn't, earning
him the title of America's Rising Star.

His rapid ascent was shrouded in rumors, with some attributing
it to sheer determination and others whispering about darker methods. Regardless of the truth, one thing was certain—no one dared to
cross Ryan Mitchell. Until now.

He remained motionless as she approached the table, his eyes fixed
on the wall in front of him. She noted with relief that the captain had
honored her request: this visit was free of handcuffs. Her long-stand-
ing history with the DA's office had its perks, and since Mitchell had
been formally charged with Tiffany's murder, she had been granted
the initial discovery. However, she hadn't had the chance to review it
yet. Her primary concern was his welfare.

"Anybody home?"

"Well, I guess part of me knew this was coming, but I can't believe
it. I know my mother-in-law hates me, but she has gone too far."

Jacqueline sat down across from him, noting the dark circles
and his growing stubble. "We don't know she's the reason you're
here."

Mitch put his hand up. "Enough. This has Victoria's name all
over it. That mastermind has declared war. Without Tiffany, battle
lines have been drawn. And now we need to destroy."

It was Jacqueline's turn to put her hand up. "Hold it. I'm not destroying anyone."

Mitch turned his anger on her. "I don't think you understand how—"

Jacqueline had heard enough. "Stop. You hired me to do a job. And you asked me to trust you. Now I need you to trust me. I know what I'm doing. Either I do it my way, or I'm out of here."

Mitch stared at her. She could almost see the wheels spinning. "Fine. Tell me your plan."

Jacqueline hoped her bravado masked her fear. She was back in the game, and the stakes were higher than ever. "Well first, I filed the paperwork. It's official. I'm representing you. My plan is to find the real killer. That should be simple."

She watched as the anger left his face as he smiled. "I like simple. But how the hell do you propose we do that?"

They stared at each other. Jacqueline had that uneasy feeling again. He was hiding something.

Mitch broke the silence. "Well? Listen, I know you saved Patrick once. And I always trust my instincts. You are the right person for this. But I need to know you understand the stakes."

"Of course I do. But, Mitch, what happened in the past is completely different. This is your freedom."

"Not really."

She filled him in on the next steps. "You're confident that you told me everything you can think of?"

"Positive."

"We're working on your bail papers right now. But an issue came up this morning that you may be able to shed some light on."

"Ask. I have nothing to hide. And presently nothing to do."

"What happened with the election? How did you become CEO?"

Mitchell's legendary darkness returned. "I don't know what you want to know. I earned that job. It was mine through hard work, long hours, and tough negotiations. I don't know who you are talking to or what investigation you're wasting your time on, but I will not have my integrity questioned."

Jacqueline braced herself against the verbal assault. "Hold it right there. We are on the same team, but I need to know what I'm up against."

"My company is not an issue. My liberty, however"—he pointed to the four walls—"clearly is."

She wanted to press him. But before she could, the door opened and Detective Dan O'Neill walked into the room.

Chapter 24

JACQUELINE FROZE. SHE WAS NOT SURPRISED THE captain had put Dan on a high-profile case that demanded only the best. Yet she wasn't prepared for the shock and betrayal written all over his face. She stood up and walked toward him.

Dan broke the awkward silence. "Ms. Stone, I'm surprised to see you here."

"Did I miss something?" Mitch asked, reading the tension. "Detective O'Neill, when did my counsel become your concern?"

Jacqueline faced Dan. "Yes, Mr. Mitchell is correct. I am representing him against these ridiculous charges. And you are violating my client's civil rights by interrupting an important attorney–client meeting."

Dan raised his eyebrow. Jacqueline ignored the silent question in his eyes. She didn't need his protectiveness. Not now. Not in the middle of the biggest case of her career. "Detective, I think there are more important issues here. Mr. Mitchell is instructed not to talk to you. If your office needs anything, you can go through the proper channels."

Dan continued to stare. Jacqueline had never seen him speechless.

It appeared only Mitch could find the words. "Is there a reason for your visit?"

Dan ignored Mitch's question. He directed his words to Jacqueline. "That's fine. I'm not interested in asking him any questions. I have his statement."

Dan turned to face Mitchell. "I'm just here to advise you, as Patrick Mitchell's legal guardian, that we intend to interview him as soon as we get medical clearance."

No one saw it coming. The room burst alive. Mitch flipped the table, lunging at Dan at the sound of Patrick's name. Almost instantly, blue invaded the small space. It seemed like every policeman in the city barged in to protect Dan. Despite her valiant efforts, Jacqueline failed as the neutral buffer, and the cops tossed her aside like a rag doll. Mitch went into attack dog mode, forcing a sea of blue to pull him from Dan. They pulled him off Dan, slapping the restraints on Mitchell's wrists.

"You leave my son alone. I swear to God if you touch him, I'll kill you," Mitchell screamed as the cops led him away.

Dan turned to Jacqueline. "You can't represent that man. He's dangerous."

Jacqueline felt a flare of anger as she locked eyes with him. "That is none of your business, Detective O'Neill."

Dan glared at Jacqueline. "Don't give me that detective crap. Tell me you are not going to do this. I forbid you from representing Mitchell. Didn't you see that temper? Are you going to stand there and tell me he didn't kill his wife?"

Jacqueline refused to give into her anger. She smoothed down her skirt. Composing herself. "I'm sorry, but I cannot discuss that with you."

Jacqueline started to exit. The transformation had started. The divide widening. Dan was no longer her friend. As a cop and obviously the arresting officer, he'd become the enemy. And Jacqueline always destroyed the enemy.

"Fine, Counselor, have it your way. But Mitchell's going down. I don't know what you're thinking, but he's a dangerous son of a bitch."

She didn't respond.

Chapter 25

"ARE YOU LISTENING TO ME? YOU NEED TO DROP THIS case."

Jacqueline shook her head in disbelief. "Dan, you need to stop. I will be forever grateful for your help when my family died," she said, her tone softening, remembering how Dan risked his career to unofficially investigate the car accident despite strict instructions from above to drop it. "But you have no right to demand anything. I've appreciated your concern over the past few years. I truly have. But this is what I do. This is who I am. I need you to do your job and let me do mine. Okay?"

"You're not taking on this case."

"Dan, I won't argue with you. I've already entered my appearance. The real question is, how could you have arrested him?"

Dan stared at her with admiration in his eyes. "Jacqueline, did you see the body? He shot her in the back of the head. In front of their son, I might add. Don't let that pretty face charm you."

"I'm not having this conversation with you, *Detective*," Jacqueline said. "But here's some free advice. You have the wrong guy. Mr. Mitchell had no reason to kill her. She had a vote on the board, and he needed her for the upcoming election. He may be a lot of things, but I think we can agree he is brilliant. This murder was messy and unplanned, completely out of character for someone as meticulous as Mitchell. He wouldn't have risked everything on such a reckless act."

"That's exactly my point. He needed her."

Jacqueline stuffed the discovery file in her bag, refusing to look at Dan. "Isn't that what I just said?"

"God, you make this so hard. The old Jacqueline would never

have asked that question. Please tell me you know about your client? You did your research like you used to?"

Jacqueline ignored the reference to her past reputation. "I don't appreciate your insults."

Dan pointed to her briefcase. "Did you even read the information you just stuffed in there? I'm not trying to insult you, but you do realize there is a good twenty-minute delay from when the gardener saw him pull up to his home and his mother-in-law got there, right? *Twenty minutes.* How did your client explain that? What took him so long to find the body? It was in the front room, for God's sake. Why didn't he call 911? His mother-in-law had to do that. Which forces any normal person to ask, what was he doing all that time? That answer is simple. Killing her."

As Dan outlined the case, Jacqueline felt her façade breaking. Since Mitch hadn't been arrested until today, she didn't have privilege to the official reports until now. And, while she would never admit it to Dan, she hadn't done her usual examination and question of her own client like before. Or she would have known it was a full twenty minutes. *What was Mitch doing?*

Jacqueline pointed to the door. "I'm going to leave. You know as well as I do that everyone acts differently. Dan, you may be used to homicides, but not all of us are as cold as you."

Dan shook his head. "Me, cold? This guy wrote the book on ice. Jax, watch him. He's not like John, he's not a good guy. He's a money-hungry thug who took advantage of a pretty girl with his charms and football skills. My understanding is that Tiffany liked the bad boys. She was something of a rebel. Liked to push her mother's buttons. So she married him to prove she could turn an asshole like Mitchell around."

Dan grabbed her arm, forcing her to look at him. "Jacqueline, you know me. I don't just go around arresting people."

"I know all that. But it's all circumstantial. It doesn't prove anything."

Dan shook his head. "Jacqueline, you don't get it. She wasn't going to cooperate."

"What are you talking about?"

Dan handed her a piece of paper with the transcription of an anonymous text. "Read it. You better go back and talk to your client. He was having an affair. The victim knew about it, and she was going to ask for a divorce."

Jacqueline refused to digest this information in front of Dan. She couldn't let him read her expression. "Detective, I want every bit of evidence you claim to have. This dog and pony show may work on other counsel, but not me. If you want to talk, call my office."

Dan continued as Jacqueline gathered her things. "Ah, Pretty Boy didn't tell you about the affair, did he? Was he too busy playing the grieving widower? Just remember, Jacqueline, this isn't someone from your neck of the woods. According to everything I read, Ryan Mitchell struggled and scraped his way to the top. Talk about bottom shelf. Our case is airtight. Everyone in the office knew exactly when he left the day of the murder because he walked out of an important closing as soon as his wife called.

"Yet there is twenty minutes unaccounted for. We have evidence that he was having an affair and that Tiffany had the means to ruin it all for him. Plus, her mother walks in, and he's holding her head, Jax. Holding her *head*. Not on the phone, not screaming for help, but leaning over her body. Add to that his well-known temper, and you're lucky if he doesn't get the death penalty."

Jacqueline didn't answer, so Dan continued. "Think about it. Now don't take this the wrong way, but don't you wonder why *you*? Mitchell is one of the richest people in town. Of all the defense counsel he could choose, why would he pick you?"

Jacqueline felt her face heat up. She had to get out of there.

Dan stood between her and the door. "Mitchell is using you. You can't represent him, Jax, he's the worst kind. Because behind all that charm and beauty, he's master manipulator. He killed his wife. He's a user. You do know that, right?"

Dan appeared to read from his notes, but Jacqueline knew better. "Counselor, I'm sure you're aware, as it's part of the public record, that Preston Westerfer, the former CEO of Harrison Investments, conveniently died in the middle of a huge family feud. And Mitchell walked away with the CEO position. Finally, it's also public record that Harrison Investments is facing some serious financial problems. With all this in the open, is this really the case you want to mark your return to criminal defense, your big comeback?"

"I'm leaving."

Dan moved back. "Fine. Don't listen to me. But think of all the evidence we have against him. There's proof of the affair. You're good at what you do, or at least the Jacqueline I knew was. Follow the evidence."

Before Jacqueline could leave, Dan grabbed the door. "We are also analyzing the vase and their home computer. It's only a matter of time before we know who he was having the affair with. When we have the results, I'll call you. If his mistress is around, the prosecution will find her. And we know she'll cave. The threat of accessory to murder gets them every time. These socialites want nothing to do with a mess like this one. Trust me. This is one calculating operator. He's always three steps ahead. Please—don't get involved with him."

"Please let me leave."

Dan opened the door for her. "Jacqueline, check the medical records. His own son screamed in the hospital, 'Daddy, don't hurt Mommy.' His son saw him do it. And I will get that kid to talk. I won't let Mitchell get away with it or hurt you, Jax, I promise."

And Jacqueline never knew Dan to break a promise.

Chapter 26

VICTORIA SLAMMED THE DOOR. "HE'LL PAY FOR THIS."

Tyler rubbed his forehead. He didn't know how much more his heart could take. He'd just hung up with Marie. The family he cherished was slipping through his fingers. "Victoria, please calm down. What happened?"

"Do you believe that nurse wouldn't tell me?" She mimicked the nurse. "'For privacy reasons, Mrs. Westerfer, we are not allowed to give out that information. You'll have to talk to Mr. Mitchell.'"

Tyler guided Victoria over to a chair. "Please, honey, sit down."

Victoria pushed Tyler away. "Stop it. I don't want to sit down. I want that nurse fired."

"She's only doing her job. You need to calm down."

"Calm down? He won't let me see my own grandson. But of course, his mother is sitting with Patrick. What right does Marie have to be there? Her and those damn chocolate chip cookies. If Marie has her way, Patrick is going to be a three-hundred-pound roly-poly."

Tyler was worried about Patrick too, but he couldn't tell Victoria that. "Victoria, he's just trying to protect Patrick."

"Protect him? From me? That boy needs to be protected from him." Victoria paced around the library. "Tyler, I'm afraid. We both know Mitch's rage. What are my options?"

Tyler refused to remember Mitch's rage. Over the years, Tyler had worked with him to get it under control. And they did. "What?"

Victoria glared at him. She switched seamlessly back into client mode, treating Tyler as her employee, not her fiancé. "You're the best attorney in Philadelphia. Use your connections. Get me custody. We both know Mitch did this. You of all people know what he's capable of."

Tyler gently rested his hands on Victoria's shoulders. "Please, Victoria. You can't believe that. Mitch loved Tiffany. And we both know he loves Patrick. He would never hurt them."

Victoria pulled away. "You and I both know that isn't true. We've seen what he's capable of. He almost killed that football player. And God knows how many other people he's destroyed. Both literally and figuratively. It's only because of your assurances and Tiffany that I kept quiet. Well, I'm done. I can't let anything happen to Patrick."

Tyler stood there. "Victoria, we can't go for custody. That will kill Mitch."

"Good," Victoria said. She turned to leave.

Tyler tried to stop her. "Victoria, let me talk to him. He'll listen to me."

Victoria slapped Tyler. His face stung, but her eyes scared him most. In her eyes, he saw war. "You need to make a choice. Me or him. I will not risk Patrick's life too. Go file custody papers or pack your things. He's a monster, and I'm not going to sit here while he can harm a hair on my grandson's head. That animal killed my little girl. Either get him out of our lives for good or don't come back."

There it was. The ultimatum. She was asking him to choose sides. Tyler peered into the face he'd loved since he could remember. All he'd ever wanted was her happiness. He'd never been able to say no to her. Never. His eyes caught a glimpse of her engagement ring. Besides his real estate dealings, it was the single most expensive purchase he'd ever made. And the most precious. It had to be the biggest ring she'd ever had. Better than any ring Preston had given her. Tyler was weeks away from the life he'd always wanted.

But this was Mitch. The boy he loved like a son. His mind flashed to Mitch's rage. The rage Tyler had long ago thought was buried.

Victoria pleaded. "We need to do this. We need to protect Patrick. You know how manipulative Mitchell is. You remember how he turned Tiffany against me. You witnessed it. He knows my secret, and he made my own daughter use it against me to get what he wants. He's pure evil, and he will harm Patrick and destroy me!"

Victoria was right. As much as he loved Mitch, Tyler would always choose her. Tyler had to make sure her secret was protected. Tyler wouldn't let anyone hurt her.

Victoria looked at Tyler with that bewitching face. "We need to protect Patrick. He's all I have left of my precious daughter."

He no longer protested. He always did whatever Victoria needed. Tyler didn't think matters could get worse until Harrison walked in.

The huge grin on Harrison's face confirmed that he hadn't overheard the conversation with Victoria. For once, Victoria said what Tyler wanted her to. "Harrison, not now."

But Harrison's grin only got larger. "Mother dear. I have just the news for celebration."

Tyler realized the one thing that could cause them to rejoice. His heart broke as Harrison relayed the information. "I just heard that bastard has been arrested. Mother, we are bringing Patrick home."

Chapter 27

LISA CHECKED HER WATCH. SHE HAD A LOT OF WORK to do, but her ultrasound appointment was in thirty minutes. Jacqueline was right. As much as Lisa loved law, she loved her baby more.

She printed out everything she could find about Dr. Fitzgerald and hopped in an Uber. She would just make it. She had purposely taken the latest appointment of the day so that both she and Jacqueline could attend. Not surprisingly, she rushed all the way to Penn only to sit. And wait.

No Jacqueline yet. Lisa couldn't blame her; no one could anticipate Mr. Mitchell's arrest. But really? Today of all days? With her husband traveling and no one else here, Lisa faced the reality of doing this alone. She checked her watch: five minutes until her appointment. Her heart raced with anticipation to see her baby, praying everything would be fine.

Read, she commanded herself, trying to calm her nerves. She checked her phone. No messages.

She picked up her research. Dr. Fitzgerald had an incredible career. Not only did he practice, but he also devoted his life to research. And development. It appeared Dr. Fitzgerald did very well for himself. He apparently held a bunch of patents. But research requires money. Big money.

There was an article about the dedication of the new hospital wing. Lisa was so engrossed in reading it that she didn't hear Jacqueline come in. "I didn't miss it, did I?"

Lisa looked up. Jacqueline seemed drained. "Are you okay?"

Jacqueline waved her hand. "I'm fine. In fact, I'm more than fine. I can't wait to see the newest member of our family."

Lisa rubbed her tummy. "I know, me too. I'm so sad that Conor is going to miss this, but between the doctor's schedule, Conor's, and now ours"—she gave Jacqueline a conspiratorial bump on the arm—"I couldn't reschedule. It means a lot to me that you could come with me."

"Please. I'm honored to be here. And I wouldn't miss it for the world." Jacqueline looked around the office. "Wow, this place is gorgeous. Feels like I'm going in for a spa treatment."

Lisa handed her a brochure. "I know. Isn't it amazing? It has all the latest technology. Look at these ultrasound pictures."

Jacqueline took the book and flipped through the pictures.

Lisa noticed her lack of enthusiasm. "Oh, Jacqueline. I'm so sorry." She tried to take the booklet back.

"Please stop. Trust me, it has nothing to do with you. I ran into Dan at the police station, and he is really riding me about the Mitchell case."

"What did he say now?"

Jacqueline shook her head. "We are not talking about work. This is all about you and that beautiful baby." Jacqueline touched Lisa's belly as she looked at the history of the practice. "This is impressive. This practice has been here for years."

A nurse came out. "Ms. Matherson?"

Lisa raised her hand. "Yes, here."

Jacqueline put the brochure in her bag. Once again, she felt like she was missing something.

Chapter 28

JACQUELINE FINALLY MADE IT HOME. SHE QUICKLY shut the door behind her, resting against it. The rescue pill worked. She had made it through the appointment, the day. Despite her honest attempts to be happy for Lisa, the loss of her own child overshadowed the appointment. Exhaustion weighed heavily on her, making the journey to her bedroom seem insurmountable. She desperately needed to lie down, but the dining room table haunted her with pictures and reports of the Mitchell case. Tiffany's bloody head glowered at her. Patrick's sweet face stared, pleading for her to solve the puzzle.

She threw her briefcase down. The anonymous text Dan had given her still echoed in her mind. Thank God she hadn't read it there. Mitch's lie was clear in black and white, confirming her suspicions and revealing his deceit. Dan was right. Her old self would have trusted her instincts, interrogated Mitchell until he confessed. The Quiet Queen, who turned over every stone, was officially gone. She took out her pill case and popped her nightly prescription, steeling herself for the trek to the bedroom.

Feeling lightheaded, she clung to each dining room chair, and then the walls, inching her way forward. Her bedroom seemed miles away, and the room began to spin. Images of the murder scene darted in front of her, mocking her. Patrick's pleas mingled with Jack's pale ocean eyes. Dan's voice laughing, *Why you?*

She made it to the bedroom, grabbing her bureau for support. Was Mitch exploiting her family tragedy? Was this all a setup? *Could he have killed his wife and asked me to represent him, knowing I would do anything to save Jack, I mean, Patrick? Or banking on some type of malpractice or mistrial claim?* Thoughts swirled around her. She heard Mitch's outrage as he denied any alleged motive, masterfully playing the loving husband and concerned father. All an act? Had her skills, her legendary ability to read people, failed her?

The images flashed relentlessly—John, Jack, Patrick, Mitch. Her head felt like it was going to explode. She stumbled to her bed. She put her hands over her eyes, begging the images to stop. Mitch and his denials. His protests. *Jacqueline, I don't know why they would think I could possibly do this to her.*

An image of Jack's smile was the last thing Jacqueline remembered as she fainted.

———————

"GET OUT OF THIS FIRM. WHAT ARE YOU DOING HERE? Do you honestly think that you could kill my son and my grandson and I could look at your face?" her father-in-law, John Bodworth Stone Sr., had shouted at her when she returned to the office for the first time after the accident.

Darkness had fallen, and she never expected anyone to still be there. Her own grief and pain made it unbearable to sleep, so she went to the office to see if... "Dad, I only came to—"

With tears streaming down his face, he snapped, "Don't ever call me that again. Get out."

Jacqueline could still see the venom in his eyes, and it only matched her own self-loathing. The accident never made sense to her. John was an excellent driver and had witnessed her seizures before. Whenever she had a seizure, she got an aura, a signal, in her right eye. A tiny little light showed up in the right corner and started to spin, then would spin a little faster for about ten minutes. She would have had time to warn him to pull over like she always did. She always remembered getting her aura when she woke after a seizure. But not that day. She didn't remember getting one. Yet a witness claimed he saw her having one, and that's why John lost control of the car. Killing him and Jack.

It didn't make any sense to her. So she had gone back to the office for the case file she'd been working on. The car fire destroyed the relevant documents she had with her that day, but she should have had some of the documents on the system. She needed to reconstruct what happened. Yet her respect for her grieving father-in-law forced her to leave it all behind. Thank God for Lisa. Lisa, who had witnessed her seizures before, didn't believe the story either. Before she left the firm, Lisa gathered all the documents on the accident and had brought them to Jacqueline at her shore house.

Jacqueline arrived at her beach home, her dream home. The salty breeze did little to ease the weight of her grief. After the funeral, she couldn't bring herself to return to the Philadelphia home she'd shared with John and Jack. The beach house would offer a change of scenery and perhaps some solace. She and John used to joke that Stone Harbor was their island even though the name was a complete coincidence. But the pain and the memories followed her, relentless and loyal as a well-trained dog. Her boys were in every inch of the beach house too.

She shed her black dress and threw it into the fire, watching the flames consume it. She never wanted to see that dress again. With trembling hands, she opened a bottle of cabernet. She then turned to the box of documents, desperate to uncover something that might explain the tragedy that had shattered her life.

She fell asleep and woke to the sound of seagulls outside. Hugging herself, she felt the sleeves of John's faded gray Boston College hoodie and wished his arms were wrapped around her. His scent still lingered on the fabric, a bittersweet reminder of her loss. The weight of her grief almost paralyzed her, but she had to move. With the little energy she had left, she forced open the sliding glass door, smelling the salt air. She welcomed the cool April breeze. As the sun started to rise, she spotted him, a little boy playing with his toy boat near the shore. Jacqueline closed her eyes, attributing the vision to last night's alcohol and the fatigue that had haunted her over the last few days. She took a deep breath, just as her doctor had advised, trying to steady her mind. How could she explain to her family that she was on the brink of madness?

Determined to snap out of it, she focused her gaze. Then her heart almost stopped. Oh no. A little boy with blond curls. With a Phillies cap on. Just like Jack. Panic surged through her. This was no illusion. A little boy was in the ocean, and he was about to drown.

When Jacqueline finally realized the ocean had engulfed a real little boy, she tore down the beach after him. She swam around the water, sure that he had gone under in this spot. She saw his head bob up a few feet away, only to disappear as quickly. Another wave hit her, pulling him just out of her reach. In the distance, she heard someone shouting, but she couldn't make out what he was saying. Nor did she care. Despite her eyes stinging from the salt water, she had to find the child.

She grabbed his little hand above the water and pulled him close to her. "It's okay. It's okay, I have you," Jacqueline said. "I'll take you in." The wave crashed over them, but her years as a lifeguard had trained her well. She rode the wave in, pulling the little boy to safety. The little boy resembled Jack, but he wasn't Jack. She let him catch his breath.

As they got out of the water, she saw a man running toward her. Only one other time had she seen so much pain on a person's face. "Patrick, Patrick, are you okay?" the man shouted as he grabbed the boy from Jacqueline. Jacqueline didn't have to ask. The boy's father. The little boy started to cry. "Daddy, I lost the boat. I lost the boat you gave me."

The father burst out laughing, hugging Patrick. "Haven't I told you never to go in the ocean by yourself? Don't you know what could have happened? I can buy you a million boats, but I could never replace you. Don't ever do that again! Promise me you will never do that again."

The idea of getting a million boats seemed to get Patrick's attention. "I promise, Daddy, I promise. You're the best!" Patrick gave the father a huge hug. Jacqueline moved away, afraid she was going to cry herself.

The man turned to Jacqueline. "How can I ever thank you? I ran so fast, but I knew I wouldn't be able to reach him. I'm just so glad you got to him when you did. I don't normally let my son go to the beach by himself. You must think I'm a horrible father."

Their eyes locked. For some reason, Jacqueline wanted to tell this total stranger about her own loss of John and Jack, but she couldn't. She realized that she was standing in soaking wet clothes.

"I'm just so happy you got him. Thank you. I'm Ryan Mitchell. And this is my son, Patrick."

Patrick was now playing in the sand. He seemed to already have forgotten his near-death experience. Grateful she didn't need to explain, Jacqueline took the father's hand. "Jacqueline Stone."

"Jacqueline, what can I ever do to repay you?"

"Do you have a towel?" The request broke the seriousness.

Ryan Mitchell looked at his watch. It was only six in the morning. "I thought I was the only one to get up this early. Do you normally go swimming at sunrise, or was it our lucky day?"

JACQUELINE TOSSED AROUND. HER MIND PLACED HER back in the ocean. The wave looming over his tiny body, his blond hair barely peeking above the water. She jumped over the waves, but she was too far. Another wave entangled her. She thrashed her hand to reach him, but she missed him. She paddled through the waves again. The wave crashed, taking Patrick under. His blond hair disappeared below the deep green-blue of the ocean. She dove, searching

142 · MARY V. SLINKARD

the murky water for Patrick. She couldn't find him. Then his hand popped up. She grabbed it, but it was too wet. He slipped through her fingers.

"No, no, I can't lose him. Patrick, Patrick, Jack..." Jacqueline screamed. The waves wrapped around her, tighter and tighter. She couldn't break through. She couldn't free her hands to reach him.

"No!" Jacqueline heard the sirens in the background. Help was on its way. It wasn't going to be there in time. No one was going to be able to save him. She couldn't break through the waves. The sirens were getting louder. They were closer. It didn't sound like sirens. It sounded more like...

Jacqueline sat up. Her bedsheets were wrapped around her like a cocoon. Sweat soaked her clothes. The ringing. It was her phone.

"Hello?"

"Jacqueline, where have you been?" Lisa said.

Jacqueline cleared her throat. "I'm home. What's wrong?"

"We've been worried sick about you. I was on my way to your apartment. Mr. Mitchell's bail hearing was this morning."

This morning? Had she been asleep since yesterday? "Oh my God, call the court!" Even on her worst days when she was drowning in her own sorrow, Jacqueline had never missed a court appointment.

"Relax, Jacqueline. When you didn't answer, I took care of it. But we have even bigger problems. Mr. Mitchell has been trying to reach you. His mother-in-law is suing for custody. There's an emergency custody hearing about to start."

Custody? Then it hit her. She remembered. They must be using the anonymous text and the arrest to support their motion for custody. "Send the papers to me and meet me at the courthouse. Have Claudia call Mitchell and tell him I'm on my way."

As Jacqueline dressed, she didn't know how she would withdraw as his attorney, but her sanity depended on it. Mitchell would have to deal with his own custody issues.

Chapter 29

HARRISON WESTERFER COULD TASTE VICTORY OVER Ryan Mitchell as he entered the elevator of Harrison Investments. *You should have never come after me, dear brother-in-law. Stealing my rightful place as CEO of this company was a brilliant move, but as Grandfather Harrison warned, if you go to battle, you kill. Leaving someone maimed is recipe for suicide.* In the years since Mitchell stole the election, Harrison planned his revenge, hiring the best investigators into Mitchell's past. He put all that information about Mitchell in a package for that stupid detective, O'Neill. Another nail in that coffin.

Harrison had planned to murder Mitchell slowly, but he never expected Tiffany's death. Still he improvised perfectly, protecting his own secret. With Mitchell out of the way, Harrison's future, the future he'd always assumed was his, was secure. Mother was attacking Mitchell's most vulnerable spot—Patrick. Harrison would enjoy the next move. The true brilliance, however, was the plan itself. While Mitchell struggled to hold on, he'd have nothing left to protect his kryptonite. And then he'd lose his freedom and his empire. Then, and only then, would Harrison celebrate.

Harrison knew the perfect person to help him achieve his dream. Eric Conceillo was sitting right where Harrison expected him to be. Buried under mounds of paperwork. "Harrison, not now."

Harrison ignored him, shutting his office door. "Hello to you, dear brother-in-law."

Eric didn't look up. "What do you want?"

Harrison knew how to get his attention. "Question. Who do you think I should tell first? The police or that hot little defense counsel?"

"Harrison, I don't have time for games. Not everyone gets paid for nothing—some of us actually earn it."

Ignoring Eric's insult, Harrison searched the air as if debating with himself. "I think I'll start with the police. They would definitely be interested in what I know about my sister, or should I say your wife, killing Tiffany."

Eric's face flushed the color of his red pen. "You bastard. Are you that selfish you would bury your own sister with lies?"

Now that Harrison had his attention, he smiled. "Relax, little man. Relax. I don't want my big sis mixed up with any of this either."

Eric stood up. "Harrison, I don't know what you are up to, but I'm not buying. Now get out."

Harrison decided to play his trump card. "Eric, I know your little secret."

Eric wavered. "I don't know what you're talking about."

Harrison moved closer, whispering. "Tiffany told me everything. I would never betray her confidence. But now that she's dead, I bet she won't mind. How do you think Mitchell would feel if he knew you made a play for his wife?"

Eric moved toward the door. "Get out and take your fake news with you."

Instead of leaving, Harrison sat on the edge of the desk, removing Eric's Montblanc fountain pen from its holder. "Really, bro? You do realize everyone knows that you and your buddy Mitchell don't have an ounce of blue blood in your bodies, right? That no number of fancy things are going to fool anyone?"

Eric grabbed the pen out of Harrison's hand. "What do you want?"

Harrison jumped off the desk. "Now there's a good question. I'm glad you're more agreeable. See, to make it crystal clear why you are going to give me what I want, I'm going to give you all the facts. I know you're the fact man. So here's the scoop."

Harrison deliberately paused for effect. He enjoyed watching beads of sweat form on the nerd's brow. Images of Eric and Tiffany flashed in Harrison's mind. If his investigator hadn't recorded the two of them leaving the Union League together, he wouldn't have believed it himself. The nerd actually made a move. How he'd enjoyed showing the pictures to Katherine. "I know about you and Tiffany. It was obvious to everyone how in love with her you were. You used to follow her around like a little puppy dog."

"Give it a break, Harrison. That was years ago. How old were we? Three? Get out of this office."

Eric's performance was almost convincing enough to make Harrison doubt himself. Almost. "Please, if I was a betting a man..." He laughed at himself. Everyone, especially Eric, who paid his gaming debts through the family fund, knew Harrison was a betting man. "Well, maybe I should say if I was a better man, I would tell the cops what I know about you and my perfect sister Katherine. Personally, I think Kat killed Tiffany. Makes sense, given it must have been impossible being the sister of the beautiful, perfect Tiffany Westerfer Mitchell. The cops said it was an act of passion. And who hated Tiffany more than dear old sis?"

Eric's face had gone white. Harrison continued walking around the office, debating the issue out loud as if the two of them would solve the mystery. "On the other hand, there's you. You loved Tiffany, and I do think you also love Katherine. Although I can't understand why."

With a dismissive wave, Harrison continued. "Look, it doesn't matter to me if you or Katherine did it. Mitchell going away for it is even better. To think of him rotting in jail and me taking over his life. Works for me."

Eric's voice cracked. "What the hell are you talking about?"

Harrison pressed on, relishing the opportunity to torment Eric. "I just never thought you would act on it, considering Mitchell being your best friend, not to mention your boss, and all. But don't worry, you're not alone. Tiffany captivated every man on the Main Line— that was her power. I just never imagined she'd let you touch her. I'm not surprised the Iceman bored her with his obsession with money. But that's beside the point. You, however, are going to help me get what is rightfully mine. And here's why."

Harrison looked straight into the little man's face. Eric's brow was creased. He probably had his own suspicions about his wife. Harrison moved in for the kill. "See, I was on the phone with Tiffany moments before she died. She had called looking for our mother. Did you know that?"

Harrison bowed his head, taking a moment of silence. Extending the excruciating pain for the nerd. He whispered, "It will always haunt me that I never helped Tiffany. I could have done something, don't you think?"

Eric's fearful eyes gave him away. "Get to the point before I kill you."

Harrison raised a brow and laughed. "Wow. Clearly you learned nothing from Mitchell. You really should learn to hide your fear better. Should we add you as a suspect?"

Eric opened the door. "Get out."

Harrison shut it. "All right, hold your horses. Anyway, Tiffany wouldn't tell me why she needed Mother. But you know what I did catch? I heard Tiffany say, 'Katherine, what are you doing here?' right before she hung up with me." Harrison watched as Eric's face went pale.

"But don't worry," Harrison assured, lowering his voice conspiratorially. "I'm keeping it under wraps. Mother and I even told the police that Mitchell was having an affair because someone sent Tiffany an anonymous text."

Eric's lips twitched, as if he wanted to interject, but he remained silent.

Harrison debated about boasting how they sealed the deal with the lie that Tiffany had talked to the family estate lawyer about drawing up divorce papers. In truth, Tiffany never believed Mitchell would cheat. Harrison itched to spill the truth but knew it would jeopardize everything if Eric ran to the police.

Harrison continued. "That scenario suits me just fine. I want Mitchell behind bars. But do you want to know what I think?" He leaned in, watching Eric closely. Eric stayed silent, tension radiating off him, and Harrison half expected to see a puddle of pee at his feet.

"I think Katherine sent that anonymous text about Mitchell having an affair. I think she wanted to get back at Tiffany. Personally, I can't see Mitchell and Katherine together. But they do work all those late hours." Harrison made a disgusted face as if he had eaten a lemon. "Ugh. But I'll take it." Harrison tilted his head, as if a thought has just occurred to him. "Or is that a set arrangement, trading sisters?"

"You bastard." Eric lunged at Harrison, but Harrison easily dodged his feeble attempt at attack. Unlike Eric, who spent his days crunching numbers, Harrison was obsessed with the gym, and it paid off. He easily pinned Eric against the desk like a small child, planting his face down on Eric's beloved signature blotter.

"I wouldn't try that again if I were you." Harrison twisted Eric's arm behind his back. "I would love to snap your arm in two. Don't tempt me. I want nothing more than to destroy you and Mitchell. Make no mistake, I'm going to destroy Mitchell. You, on the other hand, have a choice. So listen."

Not expecting a response, Harrison continued. "I think Katherine was mad at dear little sister and finally got fed up." Harrison released his hold so Eric could focus. "You didn't think I knew, did you?"

Eric's face flushed. "Harrison, you have no idea what you're talking about. Now either get out or get to the point."

Harrison lowered his face next to Eric's, leaving inches between them. "I'll tell you when I'm finished. Now if I were you, I'd shut up.

Did you really think I'd let you and that low-life Mitchell steal my family's company and walk away? Do you think I learned nothing from my grandfather? I know my dear sisters were always competing with each other."

Eric gritted his teeth. "You're a loser. You know it, and everyone else knows it too. You couldn't run this company if your life depended on it."

Harrison felt the rage build inside of him, but he could hear his therapist telling him to *channel that energy to get what you want*. He couldn't lose it again, he reminded himself. He'd been lucky before with his father, but he didn't want to push it. He had too much to lose. "Listen, you little shit, your only option is to do what I say," Harrison whispered. "They say you're so smart. Then act like it. Don't decide to grow a conscience now. You'll regret it. Just get me CEO, and maybe I'll keep your secret. Hell, you make me CEO, and you can keep your job *and* your wife's secret."

Harrison checked his watch. "Oh, dear brother-in-law, I think we still have time to make the custody hearing. You know what that means, right? Today is the day that Patrick becomes a true Harrison Westerfer. Should we tell Mitchell before or after court that he's losing not only his child, but his business too? I wonder what will be more devastating to the Iceman?"

Chapter 30

DESPITE THE INTENSELY HOT SHOWER IN HIS MULTI-million-dollar home and the impeccably tailored navy suit, Mitchell couldn't shake the grim feeling of the holding cell and the acrid scent of confinement. Freedom, he reminded himself, was his, even though it came with the indignity of an ankle monitor. He had to admit, the intrusive band was better than that suffocating box. The worst part had been the gnawing sensation of déjà vu, the haunting recollection of the bars slamming shut, his desperate attempts to get out. But what were these memories?

Mitchell jumped when Marie walked in the courtroom. "Mitch, my baby. How are you? All I've been doing is praying. This isn't your fault. We will get through this. God will take care of all of this for us."

Those words. He'd heard them before too. Marie pulled him into her, like she always did when he was a boy, trying to shield him from all the ugliness.

Mitch broke free. "Mom, we need to talk."

She inspected his face. "Are you okay?"

"What do you think? I just got out of jail, and they are trying to take my son away." As Mitch turned to face her, he saw the tears filling her concerned eyes. "Mom, please don't cry. I don't have time for this."

Mitch put his arm around his mom, physically shielding her. He needed something else. Answers. Being the good son only resulted in nightmares. Nightmares that haunted him day and night. He knew Marie could help make sense of it. But he questioned whether the process would kill her. She kept blubbering in his arms. "Mom, come on. I need you to be strong."

Her puppy dog eyes rose to meet his. "I am. Anything for my boy."

Mitch smiled. She had sacrificed so much for him. Could he ask more? Patrick's life was on the line. He looked around the courtroom to make sure he couldn't be overheard. "Mom, did I visit my mother's grave?"

"Why?"

Mitch didn't have the time or patience to explain. "Mom, I keep having these recurring dreams, or nightmares really. At first I thought the little boy was Patrick. But I think it's me. I'm standing at a gravesite. And there's a playground next to it. I don't want to be there. I want to play on the jungle gym with the other kids. I want to leave. But you are there. You're holding me. I feel smothered. I don't want a hug. I want to get away. And the ground is red. It's soaked red. I want to know where the grass is, and you keep saying, 'It's not your fault. It's my fault.' Just like now. Why?"

Mitch waited for Marie to answer. Instead, she let the floodgates open. Tears streamed down her face. When Jacqueline walked over to the table, Mitch transferred his anger to Jacqueline. "Where the hell have you been?"

She refused to look at him. "Not now, Mitch."

Mitch watched as Marie walked out of the courtroom.

"All rise, the Honorable Judge Barrett presiding," the bailiff called. Mitch hid his frustration by focusing on the judge as he entered the courtroom.

Chapter 31

JACQUELINE HAD TO GIVE THE WESTERFERS CREDIT. They knew when to go for the kill. Standing next to opposing counsel were Victoria Westerfer and Tyler Hines, looking more regal than any royal family. Victoria's golden hair was swept up into a chignon bun, revealing her china doll face, which looked like a rare gem against her dark navy suit. With her pencil-thin, statuesque figure, anyone would swear she was a runway model. Tyler Hines, with his gray hair and broad build, stood protectively on guard next to her. Jacqueline noticed that Katherine and Eric sat directly behind them. Next to them stood another man, whom Jacqueline knew from pictures was Harrison Westerfer. His attempt to look like a concerned uncle failed. Instead, the corners of his lips turned up, exposing the carefree attitude of someone who had never worked a day in his life. He might as well have been licking his lips at the thought of Mitch's destruction.

"Good afternoon, everyone. Please take your seats," Judge Barrett said to the courtroom. "It is my understanding that we are here to address the custody of a Patrick Harrison Mitchell."

Jacqueline grabbed Mitch's elbow to keep him in place. She knew he wanted to jump up and scream, but she needed to keep him calm. Since she hadn't been addressed by the court, she shot Mitch a look. *Let me do my job.*

Counsel at opposing table stood to address the court. Jacqueline knew her by reputation only. A University of Pennsylvania professor, Ms. Chun was the leading child advocacy attorney in Pennsylvania, if not the country. *The Westerfers don't mess around.* "Yes, Your Honor. If it would please the court, my name is Ms. Lois Chun, and

I represent Mrs. Victoria Harrison Westerfer, the maternal grand-mother of the child of issue. Under Pennsylvania statute, title 23, section 2511(a), Circumstances That Are Grounds for Termination of Parental Rights, we move to terminate the parental rights of the biological father, Ryan Mitchell, to Patrick Mitchell."

Jacqueline jumped up. "Your Honor, if I may—"

The judge thumped his gavel. "Counselor, sit down. You will have your turn."

As Jacqueline returned to her seat, Ms. Chun continued. "We move for young Master Mitchell to be placed with his maternal grandmother since Mr. Ryan Mitchell has been charged with homicide. Of the boy's mother, I might add."

Jacqueline had enough. "Your Honor, move to strike that from the record. May I please be heard so that we don't waste any more of the court's time?"

The judge waved to Jacqueline to continue. "Your Honor, first, this statute may only be invoked when, and I quote, 'The parent has been *convicted* of criminal homicide.' There has been no conviction in any matter, and to the contrary, we are confident that the charges against Mr. Mitchell will be dropped soon. Furthermore, Patrick Mitchell is presently at Children's Hospital, where he should remain—"

Ms. Chun rose from her seat. "Objection, Your Honor. There is no evidence of—"

It was the judge's turn to interject. "Hold it, Counselors."

"Your Honor, if we may," Jacqueline said. "What I wanted to say was I believe the parties can reach a mutual arrangement until the criminal matter can be resolved. May we have a few moments among counsel to see if a settlement can be reached?"

"You have fifteen minutes."

"All rise." As the judge left the courtroom, Jacqueline knew the real work was just beginning.

Chapter 32

"WHAT THE HELL WAS THAT?" MITCHELL DEMANDED as he slammed the door to the counsel room. He lowered his face inches from hers.

It had taken them hours. Hours of Mitchell throwing papers, punching walls, yelling at her, screaming about the Westerfers—basically melting his Iceman image—to achieve this deal. And it was a good deal. Mitchell had retained custody of Patrick, but he had to share Patrick's medical condition with the Westerfers and give them visitation rights to Patrick in the hospital.

"How dare you!" Jacqueline spat back, meeting his gaze. "Sit the hell down. You should be *thanking* me. By a miracle of miracles, you somehow retained custody of your child. So you're welcome. And now I'm done being your counsel. Here." Jacqueline thrust the withdrawal papers at him.

Mitchell barely glanced at the document before throwing it on the floor. "You're joking, right? What are you talking about? What are you doing?"

Jacqueline stood erect. The years of insecurities, sadness, loss built up inside her, giving her strength she never knew she had. "What am *I* doing? Really? I was very clear with you from the beginning. I will not represent anyone who cannot be honest with me." Jacqueline paused, making sure she had his full attention. "I warned you, Mitchell. I would not and will not put up with your antics. You've been lying to me, and I won't stand for it. You have that beautiful child in the hospital fighting for his life. And what do you do? Lie to me."

Jacqueline feared her voice could be overheard outside and willed herself to stay calm. Despite the hell she was in, she could feel herself

154 · MARY V. SLINKARD

growing stronger, finding the will to fight. Years of competitive sports had given her the strength to say to hell with him and his money. She'd rather starve than be bullied by any man, especially a client.

"I don't lie."

Jacqueline stretched her small frame to stand eye to eye with him. "Really? Are you honestly going to stand there and tell me you aren't keeping something from me?"

Silence.

Mitchell broke first. "You said don't lie."

Now Jacqueline wanted to punch a wall. "Goddammit, Mitchell. Do you honestly want to play games with your life? With me? With Patrick's life?"

Jacqueline feared he would strike her. His eyes blazed with anger. "Don't you ever say that again. I would kill for my son. Don't you know I'm doing everything to protect him?"

"Does that mean lying to me? Tell me, Mitch. Because for some crazy reason I thought you needed me. You have thirty seconds before I walk out that door. What are you so afraid of? You still have a son. A beautiful son. I know you're hiding something from me. Why? What are you not telling me?"

Mitch turned and rested his arms against the wall, silent. Jacqueline witnessed his internal struggle. He was probably struggling with the fear of losing a child. Despite Mitch's notorious and well-crafted reputation, his façade was slowly crumbling.

It pained Jacqueline, but her own sanity demanded her withdrawal. She picked up the signed custody deal the two of them had just spent the last few hours negotiating. And her withdrawal papers. "Mitch, I'm sorry. I truly hope you find someone to help you."

She turned to leave.

From the corner of the room, his arms still on the wall, he said something she never expected.

"I killed her."

Chapter 33

JACQUELINE DOUBLE-CHECKED THE DOOR. CLOSED.

She tried to think. And not panic. She'd never had a client outright confess.

Mitchell, still facing the wall, broke down. "God, it's good to say it."

Jacqueline led him to the chair. This conversation could not be a screaming match. "Mitchell, we can work out a deal. But you need to talk to me. Tell me everything. Did she confront you about the affair? Is that what happened?"

Confusion showed on Mitchell's face. "What are you talking about?"

Jacqueline felt just as confused. "What are *you* talking about?"

Mitchell turned, his mind beginning to work. "Well, I guess, first things first. Are you still my lawyer?"

Jacqueline looked at Mitchell. Little by little, layers of the protective shield she'd built since John and Jack's deaths peeled off to reveal her old self. The lawyer. The brilliant gamesman slowly returning. She would never be the Jacqueline from before the accident, but key parts of her old self were slowing emerging. Just in time. "Mitchell, I'm still your attorney for the purposes of this discussion. But we need to get something straight. I can't help you if you hide things from me. I never expected a confession. I thought it was the affair."

Mitchell shook his head. "What affair are you talking about?"

Jacqueline filled Mitchell in on what she knew, handing him a printed copy of the anonymous text.

Mitch threw the paper on the table as if it was poison. "What is this? Who sent this?"

"That's what I'd like to know. According to Victoria, Tiffany received this anonymous text a few days before she was murdered. Apparently there's a website where a person can send an anonymous text, and it can't be traced back to the sender. Someone sent this to Tiffany. Mitch, it has dates and places, outlining the specifics of the affair. Do you recognize any of this?

"Of course I do. These are the hotels I use, places I had major deals." Mitch paced the room. "No. Tiffany wouldn't have believed this. No way." He appeared to be talking to himself. "She couldn't have died thinking I *cheated* on her," Mitch spat out.

Confusion consumed Jacqueline. Either Mitch was an amazing actor, or...

Mitch faced her. "You think someone sent this to her?"

Jacqueline nodded. "Yes. And so does the Philadelphia police force after your mother-in-law explained to them that Tiffany received it just days before her murder. Victoria, with Katherine's help, confirmed the dates and places with your calendar. According to her family, Tiffany was planning to divorce you."

Mitch prowled around the room as if planning an attack.

Finally, he turned to her. "Jacqueline, listen. When I think back to that week, Tiffany was angry, and I assumed it was because I was working so hard. She was giving me the cold shoulder, and I just blew it off. She knew I was in the middle of the biggest deal of our lives, and I needed to concentrate. She knew how I operated when it came to that. And all she would say is, 'when it's over, we need to talk.'"

Jacqueline wished she could read Mitch's mind. "Talk about what?"

"I don't know. But something was definitely bothering her. I thought it was because I wasn't spending time with her and Patrick. I can't believe that she thought... Oh God, Tiffany. No, I don't think she would believe this."

"Mitch, if you weren't having an affair, who wrote this and why?"

"Jacqueline, you have to believe me. I wasn't having an affair, and I have no idea who sent this. I swear."

Jacqueline hadn't forgotten what started this conversation. "If you didn't know about the affair and weren't hiding that from me, what are you hiding? And why did you kill Tiffany?"

Mitch reached into his pocket. "I was hiding this."

Chapter 34

HARRISON RECLINED IN HIS LEATHER OFFICE CHAIR, staring at the city. The custody hearing didn't go as planned, but it was a step in the right direction. *Patience*, he reminded himself as he admired the view. He'd never really noticed how beautiful the city was. Then again, he never had any reason to be in the office. All of that was about to change. He reminded himself not to celebrate too soon. He'd made that mistake before, and he wouldn't do that again. Mitchell proved his adversarial skills, but Harrison had spent the last four years sharpening his. This time he was going for the kill.

Harrison shuffled the financial papers on his antique cherrywood Louis XIV desk and stared at all the beautiful things in his office. It sure did show well. Hell, it should, for all that money he paid that fancy designer. It didn't matter. Nothing mattered once Mitchell stripped him of his rightful title. No amount of rare furniture, paintings, or—to Harrison's surprise—even money could remove the sting of rejection. No, that pain stayed, and it wasn't until Mitchell paid with everything dear to him that Harrison would have exacted the perfect revenge.

He had to hand it to Mitchell—he played his hand magnificently. He'd only seen Mitchell as a welcome diversion for his father. At first, Harrison just assumed his father humored Mitchell since Mitchell was equally fixated on stocks and strategies. The two of them could debate strategies for hours. That suited Harrison just fine. He was more than happy to let someone else endure his old man's boring stories of conquests and rise to the power table. He'd rather blow his brains out than waste an evening in that suffocating library, feigning interest in deal structures. He had parties to attend, cocaine to snort, and admirers eager for his attention.

But then Mitchell had swooped in and grabbed Harrison's crown. *Well, you should have killed me, brother, because I've had nothing to do but plan my revenge all these years.* Harrison puffed on his cigar despite the clear no-smoking policy in the building, staring at the portrait of his old man. He should put a picture of Mitchell next to him. They'd both done him a favor. *Ironic, really,* Harrison said to the portrait of Preston. *You fueled me to finally want to work, describing me as a "spoiled, no-good brat" who hadn't earned the right to your company. Well, I taught you. And it was never your company. It was my grandfather's. Big mistake.* Harrison laughed, remembering how his father literally choked on those words as he held Preston's medicine just out of reach, inducing a heart attack. To this day, Harrison still wondered if his mother knew he killed his father, but her anger at dear old dad for picking Mitchell was just as palpable. Harrison did her a favor.

Well, dear old man, I hope you are finally proud. Harrison laughed at the portrait the designer had convinced him—over sex, of course—to hang. He could still hear her shrill, high-pitched voice explaining that the picture of his late father would give him the appearance of the respectful son. Harrison smiled every time he looked at it, not because of happier times with his father but because he knew he'd win in the end.

Your boy Mitchell may have borrowed the CEO position, Pop, but he'll pay. He gave birth to the new me. I'm no longer the no-good playboy. I finally have a mission. Now, it's no longer a game, but my life. You messed with the wrong Westerfer.

Harrison reminded himself to be careful. The heart attack for his father had worked. But Tiffany's death changed the rules. No, Mitchell was going to lose everything he loved, bit by bit. A fate worse than death.

Harrison checked his list:

Wife. Gone. As unfortunate as it was.

Reputation. Gone.

Status. Gone.

Freedom. Gone.

Company. Gone.

Harrison smiled. It felt good.

Next, Patrick. Harrison did enjoy the little guy occasionally. But taking him from Mitchell would be the icing on the cake. Harrison also needed to make sure that lady lawyer didn't interfere.

He only had one more thing to do, then he had it all.

Chapter 35

JACQUELINE STARED AT THE PICTURE, HER MIND RAC-
ing. It was Mitchell's face in a softer, female version: his birth mother.
"Patrick had this picture the night of Tiffany's murder?"

Mitch's jaw clenched as he glared at the photo, his frustration
radiating from him like heat. His hands shook, but not from fear—
there was anger in the way he dragged his hand through his hair.
"Yes," he confessed, his voice sharp. "That night. Victoria was holding Patrick, and that picture fell out of Patrick's bear. I grabbed it
before she even noticed."

Jacqueline's mind snapped to attention. "The stuffed animal Patrick's been holding?"

Mitch nodded. "Yes. Bear has a secret compartment. I didn't have
time to think. The cops were about to show up, everything was chaos.
I just stuffed it back in there."

He was pacing now, running his hands through his hair in frustration. "It was instinct. I don't even remember the exact moment I
did it, it all happened so fast. But the whole thing... it's been haunting
me since."

Jacqueline felt the tension in the room thicken. Mitch rubbed his
temples, clearly exhausted, but his anger was palpable. "When it was
safe," he explained, "I took it from the hospital. I put it in the house
safe because I wasn't about to let anyone else get their hands on it
until I could figure out what the hell it meant."

He shot Jacqueline a look, his eyes burning with frustration. "Do
you get it now? I've been going out of my mind over this. It's been
driving me insane, trying to piece this all together while everything
is falling apart."

Jacqueline tried to steady her own racing thoughts. The photo, the bear, Tiffany's murder—it was too much. She looked down at the picture, feeling its weight. What if this was more than just some old photograph?

"I brought it today to show it to Marie," Mitch said, his voice tight with controlled anger. "Because I'm done sitting on this. I need answers."

Jacqueline wished Mitchell had felt comfortable enough to share this with her, but it confirmed her feelings. Her instincts were still working, and this gave her hope. "Mitch, can you think of any reason why Tiffany had this picture? Why she put it in Bear?"

Mitchell shook his head. "That's the problem. I don't remember anything about that night. I just remember coming in the door. The next thing I know, I'm holding Tiffany's dead body, and Victoria is screaming at me."

"Did you ever black out like that before?"

"No. Never. That's what's so strange. Then I found the picture of my birth mother. Nothing made sense."

"I know this is tough, but you need to trust me. You need to tell me what's going on."

"Jacqueline, that's just it. Don't you get it? I don't trust anyone. I'm just so angry. Always have been. You don't understand."

"Make me understand. For Patrick's sake."

Mitchell sat down next to Jacqueline. "I don't remember my birth parents very well. And I forbid Tiffany or anyone from talking about them. The last thing I remember about them is my dad telling me that everything was going to be great. Things were changing, and we were going to have an amazing life. He always called me Champ. 'Champ, you can do anything. Be anything.' That's the last thing I remember him saying.

"My next memory is waking up in a hospital bed. And everything was far from great. Basically the exact opposite. Marie was sitting there. She had always been so kind to Mom and me. When my parents worked late, she would always check on me, bring us baked goods. She told me that they were gone. Killed in a car accident. I never believed her, though. One time, I heard her talking to Tyler, saying something about my dad and being drunk. I think my dad's drinking may have caused the accident.

"But it didn't matter. I never returned to my house. In fact, I went to foster care until Tyler did the paperwork for Marie to adopt me. They apparently took me to the hospital after the car accident, and I was some charity case. Tyler was an attorney on the hospital board and heard about my situation. Marie, in Marie fashion, begged him to help us. He did all the paperwork for free. I've been lost and angry ever since." Mitchell told Jacqueline about the rage he had as a young kid and how his coach helped him channel it. Or so he'd thought.

"Well, your blackout explains the delay in calling 911." But Jacqueline didn't like it. It wasn't going to sit well with a jury. At all. She looked over at Mitchell. He refused to make eye contact. "What is it?"

"You are not saying the obvious answer."

"What is that?"

Mitchell turned to face her. "What if Tiffany confronted me about my past, and I flipped out? It makes sense. I forbid her from ever talking about my birth parents. Patrick had the photo when I found him. He must have gotten it from Tiffany. She must have confronted me about my past, and I killed her. What else makes sense?"

Jacqueline shook her head. "No, I don't believe that. You are not a murderer. Plus, everything you've explained is circumstantial. Mitch, you weren't holding the picture. Patrick was. Tiffany hid it because she was trying to tell us something. Where's the gun? Do you even own one?"

"No, I don't. I can't imagine what Tiffany knows about my mother that anyone, other than me, would kill her over."

It confirmed Jacqueline's fears. "Mitch, I believe Patrick is in danger. He knows who killed Tiffany. But just so we are clear—you don't remember what happened? Including Tiffany's murder?"

Jacqueline saw fear in Mitch's eyes. He whispered, shaking his head. "I don't know. What if I killed her?"

It was Jacqueline's turn to be convincing. "But if you didn't have an affair, then why would you kill her? And Mitch, the little I know of you, you would remember something like that. Look how you acted when I confronted you."

Mitchell nodded. "I agree. But Jacqueline, I want you to understand. If I did this, I promise you that I will turn myself in. I won't keep Patrick in this hell. I love him too much."

Finally. Jacqueline felt like he was telling the truth. "That's why it was so important to the custody deal that we keep Patrick in the hospital. Mitch, can you use your influence with the doctors? I know you trust Katherine, but I don't. At this point, I don't trust anyone. Someone is setting you up, and they are doing one hell of a job. He's safe there." There was still another matter that needed to be resolved. "I need to know something though. Why me? Why do you need me?"

Mitch looked confused. "I told you. I trust you. I don't trust many people, especially lawyers."

"Then Jack has nothing to do with this?" Jacqueline could barely say his name. The pain was still so raw after all these years.

Mitchell sat down next to Jacqueline. He looked as emotionally and physically drained as she felt. "Jack is your son?"

Jacqueline nodded.

"Wow. You really don't know how talented you are." Mitchell handed her his handkerchief. "I'm so sorry for everything you've been through. And I'm sure your son was amazing. But trust me, he has nothing to do with this. I only wanted you to represent me because I thought you believed in me. I thought you knew I could never kill my wife."

Jacqueline cast her eyes away. "You know about the accident?"

Mitchell voice softened. "Of course I do. Jacqueline, I can't imagine...I haven't even had time to process my own loss. But I can't even imagine if I lost them both. I'm so crazy with guilt and sadness."

"Here." Jacqueline showed Mitchell a picture of Jack on her phone.

Mitchell looked at the photo. "Wow. They could have been brothers. He and Patrick look so much alike."

"I know. It's uncanny. Hence the problem. For some reason, everyone I care about has the warped idea that somehow you hired me because of Jack."

Mitchell looked confused. "Listen. After you saved Patrick's life, I couldn't just let you walk out of our lives without trying to repay you. So I researched you. I found out what an amazing defense attorney you were and how the legal community, especially your father-in-law, treated you after the loss of your family.

"I have ears all over this town. Your father-in-law made your life a living hell. I know about the pressure to quit. And, as I'm sure you are aware, I have some connections. I wanted to intervene and help. But everyone I know that knows you told me not to. That you wouldn't accept my help. Trust me. I gave it a lot of thought.

"Let's be clear, though. I didn't hire you out of some warped sense of pity or gratitude. I will be forever grateful for that day on the beach, but I would never risk the success of this case for anyone, including you. I have too much riding on this. As much as I appreciate what you did for me, my son will always come first."

Mitchell looked at Jacqueline. "Do you really not know your own reputation? Before the accident, you were hailed as the leading defense attorney in the state. Hell, I heard about how you won the most unwinnable cases in Philadelphia.

"Everyone in the courtroom can see it. You believe in your clients, in proving their innocence. You defend your clients with your heart and soul, not with fancy lawyer tricks. You're the real thing. You're genuine. People want to trust you. That's what makes you win."

Mitchell's eyes met hers. "I need a lawyer who believes I couldn't have done this."

Jacqueline needed to come clean. "Well, you're not the only one with secrets. I need to tell you mine." Mitch deserved the whole truth. "I'm an epileptic."

Mitch laughed. "What kind of research team do you think I have? I know that."

Jacqueline held up her hand. "That's not it. A few years ago, I was representing a defendant that was going to bring down a major crime syndicate. I'd been working like a dog. John insisted we take a break and get some fresh air. He said it would clear my head. We were headed to the park. John said I could even bring my trial brief. I sat on a bench and worked, and on occasion I looked up to see him and Jack playing. God, I didn't realize it then, but I'm so grateful I had that afternoon.

"The accident happened on the way home. I don't remember it. They say I had a seizure. A witness saw me convulsing. But I don't remember ever getting my aura. And I always get it before a seizure. John was used to them and was a great driver. He would never have jeopardized us. But they claim that John was allegedly trying to help me when he lost control of the car. He died instantly. Jack was rushed to the hospital. He was in a coma. He lasted three days."

"What do you think happened?"

"All the evidence points to simple negligence. But I don't believe that. Never will. The car went up in smoke, along with my trial brief, and the accident basically scared my client from testifying. I honestly don't know if it had anything to do with the case, but it left an indelible scar." Jacqueline toyed with her pendant, thinking back to another time. "The weirdest part was I had this feeling come over me that something was wrong that day when he asked me to go to the park. I knew we shouldn't go. But I ignored it."

Mitchell interjected. "That day on the beach. That was shortly after the accident?"

Jacqueline nodded.

"Geez, Jacqueline, I'm so sorry."

Jacqueline reached for her necklace. "I thought I was hallucinating, seeing Jack in the ocean."

"And that thing you do. Where you pull on that necklace. What's in there?"

Jacqueline looked down. "Bad habit. It's an emergency pill. If I feel another seizure coming on, I take one."

Jacqueline waited for the next question that she knew was coming. "Do you still have them?"

"I haven't in a long time, but I still carry it. It's like a security blanket. That's why I never drive. I'm allowed to by law because I get the aura. I just don't want to risk it. Crazy, right?"

"The aura...it's a signal of some sort?"

"Yes. Different people get different ones. Mine is a spinning light in my right eye. As the seizure approaches, the light spins faster and faster until I'm unconscious."

"Oh my God, Jacqueline. This must be so hard for you."

"It's not bad. I deal with it. But I'm sorry. I should have told you from the beginning." Jacqueline paused. She had to say it. "I couldn't save my Jack, and I am so afraid I can't save Patrick."

Mitchell forced her to look at him. "I saw you at the Murphy trial."

Jacqueline remembered it well. It was the last case she tried before the accident. The courtroom was packed. "You did?"

"Yes. I snuck in the back. I left the office to listen to closing arguments. You were brilliant."

Jacqueline looked at Mitchell. "Thank you. But Mitch, we have some real issues here. And they are not going away."

"Is this about that cop? Did he say something to you?"

"Dan has nothing to do with this."

"Who is he to you anyway? Your boyfriend or something?" Jacqueline tried to move away. "I have a right to know. Especially if he's influencing my lawyer. Who is he?"

Jacqueline felt her face growing red. "Stop it."

Mitchell refused. "Since this is the honesty conversation, I think we should talk about it. I saw the two of you the other day. He may not be important to you, but you sure are important to him. He would have killed me the other day if he could."

"He's just a friend."

"Well, in case you didn't know, he'd sure as hell like to be more."

Jacqueline refused to be interrogated. Her love life, or lack of one, was not the issue. "Dan has nothing to do with this. Right now, every piece of circumstantial evidence points to you. Even if someone else had motive, no one else had opportunity. You had both. Of course, there's still the matter of means, and since they can't even find the gun, they can't tie that to you."

Jacqueline explained what Mitchell was up against. "The prosecution's theory is that you killed her in a fit of rage. That she found out about the affair and wanted a divorce."

Mitchell shook his head. "That doesn't make sense. Tiffany would never confront me like that. If what you are telling me is true, and she believed I had an affair, Tiffany would never have interrupted that deal. Why would she interrupt me to accuse me of an affair she'd supposedly known about for days? No. That is wrong. She would never be part of a scandal. She wouldn't pull me out to threaten me.

"And the more I think about it, I'll tell you something else. I may not win any awards for the best husband or father, but I know my wife. She was scared on the phone, not mad."

"Okay, but obviously something changed. That's what we need to find out."

"Jacqueline, I'm truly scared. What if I did do it? Do you believe that I killed my wife?"

Jacqueline looked into Mitch's piercing eyes. She searched his face for the answer. She quieted her mind and listened to her soul. And then she decided to do what she had always done—trust her instincts. "No, I don't. But I'm not going to be on your jury, and the evidence is mounting up against you. That note is convincing. We know you didn't have an affair—that you would remember. But, to the jury, it's your word against the family and the note. But, to me, it proves someone is setting you up. And they're doing a damn good job."

Jacqueline placed her hand on his. "We need someone to help us. Someone who knew your biological mother."

Mitch had a thought. "I don't remember much about her. But I know someone who might."

Chapter 36

DR. MARC FITZGERALD OPENED THE DOOR TO HIS fishing cabin in the Poconos and let out a sigh of relief. It had been a long, overdue, rewarding day of just fishing. He loved his wife Nora, but she was killing him. He never realized how much she liked to talk and clean. If she wasn't peppering him with questions, she was cleaning right behind him. *Honey, did you like Patty's dress? You played tennis great today. When should I set up the next match? What do you want for dinner?* He barely got in the door after fishing all day when he started a fire. A blazing fire and strong drink were what he needed.

But before he could relax, he needed to make a call. He looked around his cabin. It was much smaller than his permanent residence, but he loved it up here. So basic, peaceful, and rustic. Nora hated fishing. She just didn't have the constitution to sit quietly for any period, especially hours. And cooking the fish? The first time she came with him she almost passed out watching him do it. Before, the cabin was a welcome break. Since retirement, it was a lifeline. Three whole days. All by himself. No Nora. No questions.

But despite the joy the cabin usually brought, this time he wasn't here for sport. He needed privacy. Time to think. He didn't know where it all went wrong. He looked over at his small desk under the window, facing the woods. His chair sat so close to the fireplace that despite the frigid weather outside, he often felt the fire's heat would cause him to burst into flames. How many days and nights had he sat in that chair poring over medical journals, doing his research, documenting his findings? He set out to change the world and help people.

But all that research cost money. And the Harrisons had it. God, what a fool he'd been. He could do all his research, make amazing strides, and they would fund it all. For a few simple favors. Favors.

Now he could go to jail. And despite all the success and money he'd accumulated, there was no comparison between a successful doctor and the true powerful and wealthy.

He wasn't going down without a fight. One thing he'd learned was to keep your friends close and your enemies even closer.

The call was answered on the first ring. "I was just thinking about you."

Marc wished he'd never had to make this call. "Well, trust me. I have no desire to talk to you, but I need to make myself clear. I'm not going down for this. You need to do something. I told you once, and I swear I'll do it. I'll go to the police and tell them everything. I am not going to jail for you. I don't care anymore about the money."

"Calm down. Give me a minute." Marc heard the slamming of a door and the background noise vanished. "Where the hell are you?"

Marc debated answering the question. "I'm at my cabin. Trust me. There's no one around here for miles to hear me."

"I have everything under control."

Marc looked in the kitchen for some bourbon. He needed a drink. "Great. That's what you said last time. I need to know. Did you kill Tiffany Westerfer?"

"Of course not. Why the hell would you think that?"

Marc found the bottle. "Because she came to see me a few weeks ago, asking a lot of questions. I told you to get her off my back. And a week later, she's dead. That's a strong coincidence."

"Listen to me. Stay calm and don't panic. Trust me when I say this. I had nothing to do with her death. What's the matter? Aren't you enjoying all the money I paid you? No one is even looking at the hospital. Let's keep it that way. Stay calm."

Marc took a swig of the bourbon. "Well, you better be right because what I do know is I'm not going to jail."

"Listen, you just stay up there for a few days, fish, relax, and I'll take care of everything here."

Chapter 37

AS JACQUELINE STEPPED INTO HER OFFICE BUILDING the next day, for the first time since the accident, she felt a flicker of her old self—at least the part of her that was an attorney. And even more importantly, she was on the right track. Tiffany put that picture in Patrick's bear to tell Mitch something. Jacqueline wished Mitch had trusted her earlier, but unfortunately, she could relate to his fear. But it no longer mattered. His mother held the key. Jacqueline forwarded the picture to Billy, asking him to investigate Mitch's parents, and she couldn't wait to find out what he learned.

As usual, Lou the doorman was there to greet her. "Good morning, beautiful. I mean, Miss Stone," Lou said, shaking his head with a smile. "Sorry. Couldn't help myself."

"Good morning, Lou," Jacqueline replied, half wanting to reprimand him, but instead giving him a big smile in return.

Lou looked at his watch. "Early even for you, isn't it?"

"I know, I know. Can't help myself," Jacqueline joked, pointing to her briefcase.

Lou shook his head as Jacqueline headed for the elevators. "I just don't know about you young folks anymore. Shouldn't you have some fun?"

Jacqueline smiled. "Someday, Lou. Someday, I promise."

Jacqueline felt safe just knowing he was in the building. Despite his white temples and beer gut, she knew he would never let anything happen to her on his watch.

As the elevator doors opened to her office, blackness hit her. Only the emergency lights were on. She bent down to pick up the mail and papers left by the building's super and put them on Claudia's desk. As

Jacqueline went through the rooms, turning on lights, she welcomed the quiet. After hashing it out with Mitch yesterday, she was more convinced than ever that he was being set up. But by whom? And why?

Armed with her coffee, she headed down the darkened hallway flipping on the lights with her briefcase. Distracted with all her to-do items, she congratulated herself on her instincts. She knew Mitch was holding back. And the picture made sense. Now she just had to put all the pieces together.

She turned the knob to her office and hit the lights. Then she saw it. She shook her head. It couldn't be. She squeezed her eyes shut, trying to delete the image from her mind, but the object came into focus. The red ugliness against all the white papers.

Right on the middle of her desk was a Green Arrow doll. Jack's favorite stuffed superhero. His protective persona was once so strong, reassuring, more valuable than any night-light in Jack's room. Today, it mocked her. The figure was propped up against the back of her computer screen. His own arrow pinned a bloody note to his chest. Blood-red paint dripped all over him and the desk, staining his green cape.

Jacqueline felt herself go numb. Her heart started beating uncontrollably fast. As her panic grew, her hands lost all grip. Her coffee cup hit the floor. She didn't want to get close to the doll. But her feet started moving, fear and curiosity propelling her closer. She read the note.

Drop the case.
You know what you do to children.

Jacqueline grabbed the desk for support. Images of Jack holding the Green Arrow and flying him around the apartment flooded her brain. Green Arrow traveling everywhere with them. Then the nurse in the hospital handing her the superhero, all covered with dirt and ash from the crash. Jack never let go of it even as he was pulled from the vehicle.

As Jacqueline refocused, she realized that next to the bloody toy, her desk was covered with pictures. The collage of her beautiful family that she usually kept in a drawer. Pictures of the case. Of Mitch, Tiffany, and Patrick. Close-ups of Patrick and Jack, both with bloody tears dripping from their beautiful faces. *Your Fault* painted all over their angelic faces.

Her breathing went from fast to racing in a split second, a trigger announcing the onset of a seizure. She saw a light in her right eye start to spin. She heard her doctor's voice warning her against shallow breathing or a sudden spike in heart rate. She tried to force it to stop, but her heartbeat fluttered wildly as memories flooded her brain. Holding little Jack's body in the hospital. Burying her boys. Her eye started to twitch.

Jacqueline gripped the chair, her hands turning white. She reached for her pendant, fumbling to get her rescue medicine out. The tiny pill fell through her trembling hands. As she dropped to the floor to find it, the light in the corner of her eye brightened and spun faster, signaling the impending seizure. There was no time. Her thoughts garbled. The hourglass started.

Jacqueline knew she only had seconds to find the pill. She searched the carpet, but the spinning light was causing everything to blur. *God damn it, where are you?* She glanced at the desk phone. She could call for help.

She rummaged on the floor again, desperately searching across the rug, knocking over the client chairs. Her doctor's warning screaming in her head, *Make sure you get yourself somewhere safe.* The sharp, protruding corners of her desk mocked her. Then she saw it. The tiny pill under the desk. If she walked around, she could easily reach it. But she didn't trust her legs anymore. She felt the loss of control flowing through her body. The light was spinning faster now. The hourglass was almost empty. She needed to get herself in a safe position. The pill could save her. She decided to reach for it.

Just as her fingers grazed the pill, Jacqueline fell back. The seizure started.

Chapter 38

"HELLO, LUCKY ONE," BILLY SAID AS JACQUELINE started to wake. He had been torn between calling the cops and protecting his boss. Clearly somebody was out to get her. After his internal struggle, his allegiance to her won out. He worked in a corner of her office, careful not to touch the crime scene, but staying close enough to keep watch over her. "You do that to me again, and I quit."

His lame joke failed to land as Jacqueline stirred and blinked. Once Billy learned of her epilepsy, he read everything about it he could get his hands on, especially how to protect someone during a seizure, when to call for medical help, and what to do after. Up until today, he'd never had to use it. He watched as Jacqueline slowly came to. He knew her mind was like a computer rebooting. It took several minutes for her to fully reorient herself even after she was conscious.

Given the importance of the case, Billy wasn't surprised to see the lights on in the office when he came in this morning. But he was pissed. As he walked down to her office, he decided to voice his concerns. Unlike the others, he wasn't going to walk on eggshells around Jacqueline. No one ever talked about her condition, but it was just foolish. They were a team, and she needed to act like it. She'd left him a message at midnight last night, and now she'd arrived at the office before dawn. And she'd been doing this for days. It was too risky. Either she listened or he was done.

His anger quickly turned to shock when he found her on the floor. She wasn't hurt, and her pulse was normal. The heavy sighs associated with someone coming out of a seizure were slowly disappearing as her breathing returned to normal. He decided to give her a few minutes before the lecture.

"Please tell me you didn't call anyone yet." Jacqueline attempted to sit up.

"Really? That's your first thought. Now I'm convinced I should call mental health services. Why are you taking these risks?"

"Billy, please. I don't need a lecture. I need my investigator. Do you have any idea who did this to my office?" Jacqueline pointed to the bloody pictures on her desk.

He shook his head. "Jax, this is not just threatening, it's sick. Someone got into our office and left that for you. Isn't that the superhero Jack always carried? Come on, Jacqueline, someone is trying to ruin you and drive you crazy. Only a crazy person would use your family's tragedy to prevent you from doing this case. We need to call the police. Someone is out to get you. We're in over our heads." Billy held the phone out toward her. "So am I calling, or should you?"

Jacqueline's hands trembled slightly as she reached for the phone. "Give me a minute." Billy stood by, watching with a mix of concern and admiration, as Jacqueline, with deliberate grace, transformed back into the consummate professional. She took a deep breath, smoothed down her hair, and squared her shoulders before dialing the police.

As they waited for the police, Jacqueline interrupted the silence. "What if I take you up on your deal? You've been trying to teach me how to protect myself. What if I promise to learn how to use that gun?"

Billy stared at his boss. Years ago, John had insisted she buy a gun for protection, especially given her foray into criminal law, with its unsavory characters. But Jacqueline had never taken the gun out of the safe, let alone learned how to use it.

Jacqueline met his eyes. "I'm a fast learner. Remember how I told you that John, Jack, and I used to go to those archery lessons with my father-in-law?"

"What? When Jack was into the Green Arrow?" Billy asked, pointing to the bloody doll.

"Yes. The Green Arrow. Don't you remember? John wanted us to learn because he wanted Jack to have the same great memories he had from his childhood hunting with his dad. He basically forced me to go with him and Jack up to the Poconos. John said I was a natural, a perfect shot."

Billy shook his head. "What are you talking about? You hate weapons. Didn't you get into a fight with John's dad over some expensive collector's bow and arrow he tried to give Jack for his birthday?"

"Damn. Your memory is good. Not the point, though. I'm a good shot."

Billy leaned against the desk, lost in thought. Since the inception of the Stone Firm, they'd only handled civil and insurance cases. He'd nearly forgotten the old Jacqueline. The fearless one who singlehandedly took on criminals and asshole opposing counsel without blinking, walked into the prisons to interrogate inmates and cops alike, and presented her case with unmatched ferocity in the courtroom. Despite the gravity of the current situation, a smile tugged at his lips.

"Jacqueline, a bow and arrow is completely different than a gun," he said.

"Then teach me," she countered, her tone challenging. "Listen, I agree with you that what this animal did was sick. I bet you a hundred bucks that it's that asshole father-in-law of mine. He's really just a distraught, grieving parent who can't bear the thought that I've moved on. That said, I need to be able to defend myself. Will you help me?"

Before Billy could respond, Detective O'Neill burst into the office, his eyes blazing. "Absolutely not," he thundered. "Ms. Stone, are you officially crazy? When will you learn to let the police do their job and you do yours?"

Billy watched the intense exchange between Jacqueline and the detective as O'Neill processed the scene and questioned her about what happened. Billy could see the concern etched in the detective's face, the tension in his posture. He knew the detective's feelings for Jacqueline went beyond professional duty. And as he observed Jacqueline standing her ground, he couldn't help wonder which version of her—Old Jacqueline or New Workaholic Jacqueline with a gun—was more dangerous.

Chapter 39

OUT OF HABIT, KATHERINE WAITED FOR THE KEURIG to fill her cup with much-needed coffee. Between Patrick's panic attack, accusations from that damn attorney, and the custody battle, her head ached. Katherine searched for her keys.

"Hey, you're up early," Eric said, as he walked into the kitchen, hair tousled. "I was surprised you weren't still awake when I got home last night." Eric moved closer, blocking the door to the garage. He forced her to face him.

"Oh, yes. I was exhausted." Katherine looked at her watch. "Honey, I really do have to run. Another emergency."

Katherine couldn't get to her briefcase. Eric stood directly in front of it. "Really? You're going to leave just like that?"

Katherine pointed at her phone. "I'm sorry, but things are crazy in the office."

"And they're not here? What the hell are you thinking? Do you understand who that defense attorney is? That she wants your head—or anyone's head, for that matter—on a platter to serve up for the jury? Where are you running off to? I'm the early bird, not you."

She moved around him and reached for her bags. "You're overreacting. I think she's just trying to do her job. You know, look good in front of Mitch."

"I don't think you understand." Eric barricaded the door with his body. "We need to talk. Stop protecting Mitch. When will it not be about Mitch?" Eric grabbed Katherine by the shoulders. "Do you want to go away for Tiffany's murder? Because I'm sure that damn lawyer can convince a jury that you killed her."

Katherine stared at her husband. *How much does he know?* She thought about that day—her rage at Tiffany. Tiffany laughing at her. "Affair with *you*?" like it was the funniest thing she'd ever heard. *Don't think about that now*, Katherine warned herself, feeling the heat drain from her face.

Eric looked at her. "You're a terrible liar. Please talk to me."

Katherine looked into his soft eyes. She once trusted those eyes.

Eric pleaded. "I know what Stone is like, or at least was. She's notorious for finding a scapegoat. Giving the jury someone else to blame. And I'll be damned if she is going to make you her plan B."

Katherine looked at her husband. She struggled with the need to confess and her own self-loathing. Could she admit to him what she did? He and Mitch were best friends. What kind of monster would he realize he married? She needed to escape his questioning eyes. She despised herself for accepting his protectiveness without question. But at what cost? The lawyer wasn't going to stop. She knew she should tell Eric, ask for his help. But she couldn't. Not yet. "I appreciate your concern, but I really do need to get to the office." As if on cue, her phone rang. "Yes, Ashley. I'll be right in."

Katherine put her phone in her bag. "I gotta run. Another investor is threatening to back out. Let's talk tonight."

Eric released his hold and stared at her. Genuine concern covered his entire face. He didn't even ask her where she was the afternoon of Tiffany's murder. *He thinks I killed her*, Katherine realized. Shame engulfed her whole body. She planted a kiss on his cheek. "Tonight, Eric, I promise."

She grabbed her keys and got into her Mercedes. He stood there watching her. Her smart, loving husband. Yet, he... She desperately wanted to erase what she'd seen. The betrayal. Eric's arms around Tiffany, the same way he held her. But her mind replayed every detail.

She thought again about confessing to that lawyer.

Eric stood by the steps. "Katherine, promise me you won't talk to Jacqueline Stone without me being present?"

Katherine nodded. "I promise."

Chapter 40

THE CATNAP ON THE COUCH IN HER OFFICE WORKED. Jacqueline kept the second part of the deal she'd made with Billy. If she recuperated, he'd work. She found him in the war room with the others. "What did you find?" she asked.

From the look on his face, it wasn't good. "I filled the group in on the photo. There isn't much about Mitchell's biological mother except this."

Lisa handed Jacqueline some pictures from an old newspaper article.

"Oh my God," Jacqueline said. "If it wasn't for the date, I'd think this was—"

Her employees spoke in unison. "The Mitchell murder."

Jacqueline sat down, shaking her head. "How could that be? Mitchell said his parents died in a car accident."

Billy explained. "Sorry, boss, but the murder was in the newspapers. Granted, it's a very small article. And since Marie adopted him, giving him her surname, I don't think anyone every made the connection. A regular investigator would never have found it. But lucky for you, I'm not a regular investigator.

"Back to his mother's death. It's all right there. Pretty cut and dry. Her name was Natalie Kluge. And according to my research, there was a struggle, bruises on her wrists. And then she was shot by her husband. The father was out of work. Got hurt on a construction job. There were several complaints of abuse and yelling. Their neighbors even called the police once. They were having money problems. The night of the murder, a neighbor heard a gunshot and called the cops. Husband was passed out and wife was dead. No one saw anyone else come in or out of the house other than the two of them. It was a slam dunk case. I'll keep digging. But as of now, I can't find any connection between Tiffany's death and Mitchell's mother's death except Mr. Mitchell."

Jacqueline perused the article. "But I don't get it. This is 1992. That would make Mitch only eight. No one can honestly think he had anything to do with her death?"

Billy nodded. "No. But read on. You're not going to believe who saw the murder."

Jacqueline was afraid where this was going. "Witnesses say their son was home at the time of the murder," she read aloud from the article.

"You got it. Just like his son," Billy added. "I couldn't learn anything else because Ryan Kluge's, aka Ryan Mitchell's, juvenile record is sealed. Including any medical records."

Jacqueline was lost in her own thoughts, trying to figure it out. "So, it may be possible that Mr. Mitchell doesn't even remember because he was so young at the time. Do we know if he went to the hospital?"

Billy shook his head. "No. Literally, there is no other information. It was barely a blip in the news."

Jacqueline slumped in her chair. "We have our work cut out for us, gang. Because I did some research on my own last night." She paused and passed out some papers to the group. "I looked into Mitchell. We may not have his records, but there was information on the football incident in college. Apparently, he got into a fight with a teammate at practice, and the rumor was the teammate almost died. I suspect the school did what it could to cover it up, but that rumor is out there. And I'm sure the prosecution is going to have a field day with it."

Billy said what the rest of the group was thinking. "I hate to say it, but how would the death of a young woman, who was clearly murdered by her husband thirty years ago, who lived across town and had absolutely no connection with the Westerfers ever, cause someone to murder Tiffany? I even searched catering companies, chauffeur companies, cleaning companies, domestic help, teachers at Patrick's school. Nothing. And the husband held none of those types of jobs, let alone with the Westerfers. I'm sorry, but the only connection is Mr. Mitchell."

"There's more. I know it. We just have to find it," Jacqueline said, turning to Lisa. "Anything to add that doesn't help the prosecution?"

Lisa gathered her notes. "Yes, actually. I'm still trying to reach Dr. Marc Fitzgerald. I did find something interesting. As we know, Dr. Fitzgerald was involved in a lot of research and development."

"And we also know research costs money," Jacqueline said.

Lisa nodded. "You're correct. Guess who not only funded the research, but made a lot of money from Fitzgerald's developments?"

Jacqueline and Billy said in unison, "Harrison Investments."

"You got it. And Dr. Fitzgerald did a lot of research on different medicines too."

Jacqueline had a thought. "If that case in Alabama involves malpractice, maybe Dr. Fitzgerald wanted Harrison Investments to come to his rescue."

"But how does that involve Tiffany and not Mitchell?"

Jacqueline looked at her white board. "Good question. What I do know is we aren't going to find the answers sitting here. Billy, get on the next flight to Alabama. Find out about that case. Both of you focus on Tiffany, her family, and her datebooks. Find out what you can about the anonymous text regarding the alleged affair and see if you can find anyone who supports Mitchell's position that this affair never happened. Look for anyone who would want to set Mitchell up. I'll focus on the death of his biological mother. My gut is telling me that someone may be using that murder to set him up for Tiffany's. There must be a reason why Patrick was holding that picture. I don't know what it is, but we are meeting with someone who might."

Chapter 41

HIS NIGHTMARE HAD COME TRUE, ERIC REALIZED. HE had to choose. Katherine or Mitch. When Marie called to tell him that Mitch had been arrested, he felt his world crumbling. All his hard work, all the energy he and Mitch had put into rebuilding the company, making every dream and more come true, vanished in an instant. His normal analytical thought process disappeared as well. He only had to deal with the present. And despite the prospect of his best friend heading to prison and the company he'd spent his career building vanishing, his only real concern was for Katherine. He had to protect her. At all costs.

And he would. He chose Katherine.

He knew that Stone woman's scapegoat was Katherine. Katherine's well-known sibling rivalry with Tiffany was a perfect motive for murder. Add Katherine's recent actions and behavior, and it was only a matter of time. Damn. If she had only come to him. He still didn't know what pushed her over the edge, but she'd failed miserably at covering her tracks. When he couldn't find her that day, Eric had tracked her to Tiffany's house. At the time of the murder. And that broken vase. It had Katherine written all over it.

Now he had to fix things. But the more he tried, the more impossible the options. With Tiffany gone, he didn't know what to do. His first thought was to confide in Mitch. But how could he face his best friend and tell him that they had betrayed him all these years? It wasn't related to any of this. They had covered their tracks. But Tiffany was upset about something recently and he clearly failed her. He had to protect Katherine now.

He searched his brain once again, desperate to decipher Harrison's riddles. *Damn you, Tiffany. Why wouldn't you tell me what you were afraid of? You knew I'd help—just like I helped you keep Harrison's gambling debts from Mitchell.* Something changed her. That he knew. Right after the election. She did something to help Mitch win the CEO spot. Eric would bet the farm on it, and unlike Harrison, he wasn't a betting person.

That strange meeting a few days ago gnawed at him. Tiffany had insisted on meeting away from the office—so unlike her. Damn it, he should've pushed her—forced her to talk. She'd started to open up; he'd seen it in her eyes. But at the last second, she changed course, shutting down and refusing to say what had her so terrified. She insisted it wasn't about their secret with Harrison's debts, but Eric couldn't believe that. What else could it be? He'd tried to console her, to pull the truth out of her, but all she left him with was a hollow promise: *I'll tell you in a few days.*

Eric's obsession with detail had uncovered her role years ago. Her confidence that Mitch would get the CEO position didn't match reality. They shouldn't have won. And then her change in demeanor. Talking about protecting her family. Helping Harrison. Something happened on the hospital board that forced her to change course. The fashion-and-party-obsessed Tiffany disappeared and a more focused investigator emerged. Mitch's past became her own obsession. Wanting to know anything and everything. Yet she refused to tell Eric anything, really, fearing he'd tell Mitch.

It was only a matter of time before Patrick could talk. Eric had to protect Katherine. Time was running out.

There was only one hope left.

Chapter 42

THE NEXT DAY, BILLY TOOK THE FIRST PLANE HE could to Birmingham, Alabama. He had nothing to go on but the name and address of the attorney's office that lawyer had given him. After an extensive search on the internet, he found nothing about a Mr. Frank Scaggs. Who doesn't have a Facebook page or website today? Yet Jacqueline insisted he follow up with this lead. Even Martindale-Hubbell, the trusted directory for attorneys, had the same address. From there, he learned what he already knew: that Scaggs was a jack-of-all-trades lawyer, otherwise known as a whatever-pays-the-bills lawyer.

After a long drive through several small towns, Billy stood in front of an empty office building. *Thank God Mr. Mitchell gave us a cash advance*, he thought. He checked the address for the third time. It was the right place. But whoever had been here was long gone.

Billy decided to knock on the attached buildings to see if anyone knew anything. On the third try, a man dressed in a white undershirt finally opened the door. "Excuse me, sir, I'm looking for a Mr. Scaggs. Do you know where I can find him?"

The man stared at Billy through the chain lock. "Nope."

Billy noticed the rent sign, which gave him an idea. "Do you know who owns the building? I'm looking to rent the office space."

Billy watched as the man's disinterest quickly disappeared. "I'm the super for that building. Just because it's vacant doesn't mean it's cheap. Let me find the rent information. Come on in."

Once Billy got inside, he decided to come clean, but continued with the universal language. Holding a twenty, he explained what he needed. "My name is Billy Washington. I'm not interested in renting, but I do need to ask the prior owner, Mr. Scaggs, a few questions about a case he handled."

The man was not happy with Billy's deceit, holding out his hand for more. Billy reached in his pocket and handed the man a fifty.

"Sure, I know him."

"Well do you know where I can reach him?"

"Maybe."

Billy counted the rest of his money. He only had two hundred dollars left, and he still needed to get back to the airport. He handed the man another hundred. "But that's it. What do you know?"

"Sorry, man. You missed him. He packed up his bags, paid the full month's rent, and left."

"Do you know what kind of law he practiced?"

The man looked at Billy like he was crazy. "Nah, I don't bother with my tenants. They pay the bills. I stay out of their way. We both like it that way."

Billy thought about strangling the guy.

Reading the anger in Billy's face, the man offered, "He did have a secretary. She came around the other day, complaining that she needs work and asking if I knew anyone who was looking." The man paused. "I know where she lives."

Billy knew the routine. He handed over his last hundred and got the secretary's address. He hoped she was more helpful because he was out of cash.

Although the woman didn't live too far away, it took Billy a long time to find it since many of the small houses weren't well marked. Unlike the outskirts of Philadelphia, which were lined with row houses, Birmingham had many small dilapidated houses lining the dirt roads. Like many towns, there were signs of investors, as some of the places looked renovated. Given how his day was going, Billy was not surprised that the one he needed was not one of them. It was much smaller than its neighbors. While the yard was freshly mowed and small flowerpots greeted visitors, the lawn was more weeds than grass, the small front porch was in desperate need of a new screen, and broken stones were used as the walkway. As Billy carefully navigated the broken steps leading to the porch, the Alabama sun beat down on him, making him thirsty for a cold glass of water. Since there was no doorbell, Billy tapped on the screen door, not wanting to disturb its delicate framework. No one apparently heard his knock over the baby crying. He yelled in. "Hello, is anyone home?"

A young woman came to the screen door with the crying baby in tow. "Can I help you, honey?"

"I'm looking for Mr. Scaggs's secretary."

The woman apparently mistook Billy for a future employer since she sat the baby on the floor and opened the door. "Well, that would be me, honey. I'm Georgeanna, but all my friends call me Annie. Would you like to come in?"

Billy took the invitation to come in the house and get out of the Alabama sun, even if the room didn't have air conditioning. "Thank you."

"How can I help you?" Georgeanna asked, grabbing the toys off the sofa.

"I need some information about Mr. Scaggs."

"Oh." Georgeanna couldn't hide her disappointment. "I thought you were looking for a new secretary. What did the scoundrel do now?"

"I'm not sure. That's what I'm hoping you can tell me." Billy watched as a little girl appeared and Georgeanna picked the baby back up. He needed to keep her interested, and from the looks of it, she could sure use some money. "I'm sorry to bother you, but if you can help me, I'll make it worth your time," he explained, holding up his checkbook.

The universal language of money worked. "Sure. Sorry about the kids. I'm watching my sister's baby to make some money since Scaggs left me high and dry. And this is my daughter, Clarabelle. What do you want to know?"

"Whatever you can tell me. I'm most interested in a case that he filed in Philadelphia."

"Oh, that case. Sure, I remember that one well. How could I forget? Never saw the man happier."

"What happened?"

Georgeanna sat down next to Billy, making sure she had his full attention. "Boy, it's nice to finally have another adult to talk to." She gave the baby a pacifier. "You see, Scaggs never did like to work. He would sit around the office all day basically doing nothing. But he was one of the only attorneys in town, so people would come in now and then with their problems.

"He paid me nothing, really. But we had this arrangement, ya see. He would let me bring my baby girl with me to work if I answered the phone without her crying. He only cared if someone came to visit. Then I would put her in the playpen in the back."

"Did someone from Philadelphia come to see him?" he asked, hoping to bring her to her point, if she had one.

Georgeanna got a good laugh out of that question. "No, no, no. You got it all wrong. Someone from here had a problem with a hospital in Philadelphia."

"Do you remember the name?"

Georgeanna looked like Billy had just asked her to recite the Declaration of Independence. "Honey, I don't remember names. I just remember a woman coming in hysterical. Scaggies took her into his office and talked to her forever. Then he walked her to the door, consoling her, telling her everything would be okay. I thought for a minute old Scaggs was going to cry himself.

"But then the minute the door shut, he started doing a jig. Picked up my baby and started dancing with her. I never saw him so happy. He just kept saying he hit a gold mine and singing some silly baby song."

"Do you remember anything about the woman?"

Georgeanna eyed Billy's checkbook. "Maybe." Billy started writing.

"I don't remember her name, but I do remember she lost her daughter. It was in the news."

Billy felt dejected. It was a good start, but he needed more.

As if reading his mind, she asked, "What's wrong?"

"I need more information. I need a name."

Georgeanna thought for a minute. "I can barely remember my own name. All I remember is about four years ago, Scaggies finally hit it big. Bought everything he could put his hands on. Fancy car, fancy clothes, the works. He actually gave me a big Christmas bonus.

"I asked him to tell me the details, but he wouldn't. He was all hush-hush about it. Like I cared or anything. I was just asking to be nice. Anyway, it was funny because he finally started paying attention to my baby. After that case, he'd always pinch her face. Oh, and if he sang that song one more time, I thought I'd kill him."

"What song?"

"Oh, you know the one, 'Thank God for babies, thank God for babies.' Something like that. He kept singing it wrong. I can't remember what it was. I kept correcting him, but he just kept on singing it his way."

"Can you think of anything else?"

"I'm sorry. I wish I could remember more." Georgeanna's face lit up. "I don't know if this would help, but I have his files."

Billy wanted to kiss Georgeanna. "You have Scaggs's files?"

Georgeanna smiled, missing teeth and all. "Sure do. The damn jerk just takes off and doesn't give me any warning. Elderly neighbor yells at me to pack up the place. What a mess. What the hell am I going to do with all this stuff? But stupid me, I didn't know what to do with all of it so I just brought the stuff here. I was afraid that he would blame me for something. It was just weird how he left so quickly. I

192 · MARY V. SLINKARD

got the sense something went wrong, really wrong. He knows I have a child to support by myself and how important the job was to me."

"Where are the files now?"

"In my basement."

"Georgeanna, this is your lucky day." Billy wrote a large check to Georgeanna Somers.

Chapter 43

COME ON GOD, GIVE US SOMETHING, JACQUELINE prayed as she worked in the back of the car.

"Almost there, Ms. Stone," Bernie said. "So you can stop tapping that pen of yours or at least learn a different tune."

"Sorry, Bernie. Ran out of lollipops." Jacqueline smiled as she needled him back, holding up the empty bag.

Bernie let out a belly laugh. When Bernie had started driving for Jacqueline, he surprised her one day with a bag of Dum-Dum lollipops since her fingers were constantly moving. Bernie said they served two purposes. First, they could help her take down bad guys, and second and more importantly, she could stop driving him crazy with her nervous tapping habit.

Jacqueline checked her watch out of habit, but she didn't need it to know she was running out of time. The case against Mitch was building, and she didn't have much in way of the defense. There were too many questions. Katherine was holding something back. Jacqueline knew it by how defensive her husband Eric acted. If he was Mitch's best friend and had nothing to hide, he should be helping more. Why isn't he? And the picture? Why did Patrick have that picture? What, if anything, did the murder of Mitch's mother, Natalie Kluge, have to do with Tiffany? Other than to help with the prosecution theory that it was the basis of Mitch's rage? Which then brings up the question of the affair. Is it all part of an elaborate setup?

Her gut told her Natalie's death was somehow related to Tiffany's murder, but she didn't know why. Did Tiffany stumble on this thirty-year-old murder, and someone killed her for it? Tiffany Westerfer and Natalie Kluge were worlds apart. But there was one person who could help her answer some of these questions. Mitch's adoptive mother. Lisa had tried to interview Marie, but Lisa felt like she was hiding something. Jacqueline decided to use the only card she had left to get Marie to talk. Mitch.

Bernie dropped her in front of Marie's home. It was exactly as Mitch described. He explained how he bought Marie the home with his first million. When Mitch was young, Marie would tell him stories about her dream of the two of them in their own home, with a big yard for him to play in and surrounded by a white picket fence. Jacqueline could only imagine Marie's joy when she saw her house for the first time. The front path was lined with bright sunflowers in an array of yellow and pink.

Mitch opened the door. "Jacqueline, please come in."

Jacqueline wasted no time. "How's Patrick? Any change?"

Mitch's expression brightened. "He's awake. Physically, he's better, but he doesn't appear to remember anything. We have strict instructions not to discuss anything until the specialist arrives, which should be soon."

"That's so exciting," Jacqueline replied, then shifted her attention to the next issue.

Marie reluctantly took a seat in the far corner. "I don't know why you need to talk to me."

Jacqueline turned to face her. "We need your help. Can you help us?"

Mitch jumped to her defense. "Marie is, for all purposes, my mom. She would do anything to help me."

Marie stood up and grabbed her rosary from the table. Jacqueline walked over to Marie. "He means 'anything to *protect* him,' doesn't he, Marie? Did Mitch tell you that a picture of Natalie Kluge, his birth mother, fell out of Patrick's bear after Tiffany's murder?"

"I don't know what you're talking about."

Mitch looked confused. "I feel like I'm watching a bad movie."

He handed Marie the photo. "This picture, Mom."

Marie didn't answer. Instead, she started mumbling, and Jacqueline realized she was saying the rosary.

"Marie, Mitch doesn't need prayers right now. We need information. My team found this article about Natalie's murder." Jacqueline showed Marie the newspaper clipping.

Mitch's face moved from Marie to Jacqueline and back again. Marie refused to look up. "Mom, what is it? Talk to us."

Marie was sobbing now. "Please, please, don't do this. He'll get sick again. The doctors couldn't guarantee me that he would be okay."

Before Jacqueline could react, Mitch grabbed the clippings. "Oh my God. No. This isn't true. My mother didn't die like this. You always said it was a car accident. That he didn't mean it. He had been drinking..."

Jacqueline watched the transformation in Mitch's face. He was no longer the Iceman but a scared eight-year-old boy.

"Mitch, I'm so sorry," Marie said. "I didn't know how to tell you. When your mother died, you went into shock, just like Patrick. You were just like Patrick. But I didn't have any money. I couldn't afford fancy doctors.

"You were touch-and-go. They didn't know if you were going to come out of it. Then one day, you woke up as if nothing happened. The doctors told me not to talk about it, that you could have a relapse. But you never did."

Mitch walked across the living room, far from Marie. Jacqueline could sense he was trying to reconcile the new information. When he spoke, it was a whisper and almost to himself. "I can't believe this. But it's beginning to make sense. The memories." He looked at the picture. The gravity of the implication resting on his face. "My mother's murder is exactly like Tiffany's. How could that be?"

"I don't know, son. I couldn't believe it. When I saw the article about Tiffany's murder in the paper, it was like I was back on

Thompson Street thirty years ago. Tiffany always looked so much like your mother, with her long blond hair. I always thought that was what attracted you to her in the first place."

Jacqueline needed something helpful. There had to be some connection they were missing. "Marie, why were you so upset that day they arrested Mitch? You were talking about him not being like his father."

Marie looked at Mitch. Tears flooded her eyes. "A few weeks before Tiffany's death, Tiffany called me and asked if she could come over.

"I thought it was a little odd because Tiffany rarely came over without Mitch. You must understand, Tiffany was always so busy, planning parties and going out and all. I was so excited to get a chance to visit with my daughter-in-law and grandson that I didn't give it any thought.

"Then she showed up and started talking about the new house and the fact that Mitch would be forty soon. I didn't understand where she was going with all that. She said she would like to have some pictures of Mitch when he was a baby, of his birth mom and all."

Marie looked at Mitch, wringing her rosary. "I'm so sorry. I should have never let her drive away with those boxes."

Mitch sat down next to Marie. "Mom, it's okay. Just tell us what happened."

Marie seemed to gain strength as Mitch held her hands. "You should have told me she was coming."

Mitch shook his head, not understanding.

"A few weeks before her death, I picked up Patrick from soccer practice and brought him here, like I always do. When we arrived, Tiffany was here with the boxes from the attic already in her car," Marie explained, looking only at Mitch.

Mitch interjected. "I remember Tiffany was going on about how we didn't have anything in the house from my childhood. We were talking about it one night, and I said that my mom always had pretty books, and she would read to me at night. She would always write in the book and put the date on them. She said she bought the best hardback versions of Dr. Seuss so that one day she could pass them on to her grandkids."

Marie let out a sigh. "Well, I wish you would have told me she wanted those boxes. She came here looking for those books for Patrick's room and the library. And she scared me, asking me about what your birth mom was like. She wanted pictures, to learn more about your past."

Marie wrapped the rosary around her hands. "I was so nervous. I didn't want her to have those boxes. I didn't even remember what was in them. So I wanted to make sure there was nothing in there that could harm you. That could make you remember that awful day. I needed to at least go through them before I gave them to her. But I never got a chance. She just took them."

"Do you have any idea what was in there?"

"I really don't. I packed them up so fast back then because I didn't want you to see anything. I thought I would go through them in time. But I could never bring myself to do it." She turned to face Mitch. "After your mom died and then your dad died in prison, I packed up their house before the bank took it. I thought one day I would give everything to you, but I was afraid..."

Mitch reached for Marie. "Afraid of what? Mom, please tell me. It could be important."

Marie searched his eyes. "You don't remember anything that happened back then, do you?"

"No, I don't."

"I was afraid that there was something in those boxes that would trigger something in you, and we would lose you forever. Just before Tiffany died, she showed up again at my doorstep. You have to understand something. Tiffany was very proper. She always called first.

So obviously, I was surprised when she just popped in. I knew something was up.

"She started asking me all kinds of questions about Natalie's death. She didn't realize your mom was a nurse. I lost it. I was so afraid that she would talk to you"—Marie looked at Mitch with fresh tears in her eyes—"and you would have another episode." Marie blew her nose. "I'm so sorry, Mitch. I just couldn't lose you."

Jacqueline needed Marie to stay on track. "So what did you tell her?"

"I told her a half-truth. That Natalie was killed by Mitch's father. That I thought it was an accident, but that since he was drinking, it was ruled vehicular manslaughter. I told her to leave it alone and to not, under any circumstances, talk to Mitch about it."

"Did she tell you why she was asking?"

"No. She just kept questioning me if I was positive Mitch's father killed her. And I just said that I didn't want to talk about it, and that she should drop it."

Mitch interjected. "But wait, Mom. Those boxes were at my house? Who else knew about those boxes?"

"No one, I swear. Only Tiffany, me, and—"

Mitch answered for her. "Patrick."

Marie could not stop crying, and Jacqueline regretted brainstorming in front of her. Jacqueline feared that she could have a heart attack on the spot.

Mitch acted first. "Mom, come here. This is not your fault. This is not your fault."

"I'm so sorry," Marie mumbled into Mitch's chest.

Jacqueline could feel that they were getting close to something important. "Marie, no one is blaming you, but this may be the vital information we need. Can you help Mitch?"

Marie looked up from Mitch's bear hug. She seemed to be

regaining strength from his embrace. "Yes. I can. I will do anything I can to help my son."

"Marie, I need you to focus. Back to Natalie's murder. What do you remember about it?"

Marie hesitated. "It's been such a long time. I never talked to anyone about it. Back in those days, we were common folk. The police didn't really investigate the murder." She looked at Mitch.

"Mom, it's okay. Please don't worry about me. My feelings are the least of my problems. Please tell us everything. It could help." Mitch held Marie's hand.

She looked at Jacqueline. "Mitch's parents didn't always fight. His father really loved his mom. I truly believe that. But then he got hurt again on the job. See, he had a lot of back pain from his football days, and no one had any money for fancy doctors. So Natalie said he drank to help with the pain. And then he lost his job. So money was tight, and they fought about it. A few times it got loud, but nothing serious. He never hit your mother, I swear. But that nosy woman, Viola Maury, called the cops a few times. People knew they were on hard times, but he wasn't abusive."

Marie took a deep breath. "Then Natalie was shot, and Mitch's father was passed out drunk on the couch. He always swore he didn't kill her, but they really didn't look for anyone else. He felt guilty for being drunk and not protecting you both. He hung himself in jail. People thought it was out of guilt for killing your mom."

Mitch's eyes searched hers. "Is that what you believed?"

"Your father asked me to bring you to him in prison. You saw him once, and the experience terrified you. For weeks, you had nightmares about the bars slamming and the guards. It was awful." Marie shook her head. Her fingers trembled as she reached for a Kleenex and wiped her eyes. She sighed heavily, her hands clutching the tissue tightly as if trying to squeeze the memories away.

Her voice quivered slightly. "That day, he gave me full custody and told me never to let you come again. He forbade me from even speaking about him to you. He wanted you to have a fresh start. He swore he didn't kill Natalie, but I think his guilt for being passed out drunk and not protecting you both overwhelmed him. The next day, he hung himself in his cell. I think he wanted to avoid the publicity of a trial.

"And Mitch, you kept mumbling something about how it wasn't your daddy, and that it wasn't your daddy's voice. But oh God, I'm so sorry." Marie hid her tearstained face. "I didn't listen. I just assumed you were trying to protect your father. With all the prior domestic calls, it was an open-and-shut case. No one saw anyone come in or out of the house that night. Including me."

"Do you believe Mitch's father killed his wife?"

Marie didn't hesitate this time. "I've had decades to think about it. No, I don't. Your father drank because he was in pain. Yes, he yelled at your mom. But I saw him with you before his accident. He loved both of you more than anything. He was a good man. It didn't make any sense. And the weird thing was I never heard anything about your dad even owning a gun.

"And that's what your dad said to me in jail the one time I took you. After he signed over custody, he said to me, 'If I did it, where did I get that gun?'"

Chapter 44

HE WATCHED AS THE DEFENSE ATTORNEY LEFT HER office. She really should improve her security. But one man's fault, or woman's, in this case, became another's advantage.

She was becoming a real problem. Her tenacity caused too much headache. When Mitchell chose her, it caused a landslide of emotions. First, disbelief. How easy could this get? She was a has-been. And her well-known tragedies became their assets. No one ever thought she'd be competent enough to handle this case.

But now, she was moving in on all fronts and putting the pieces together. This was not good. Not good at all.

They needed to get rid of her and quick.

Chapter 45

THE AIR WAS COOL AS JACQUELINE WALKED BRISKLY to the Philadelphia Public Library the next day, attempting to clear her head. Despite all the technology, Jacqueline found walking and doing research the old-fashioned way insightful. She played with her copy of the picture of Natalie Kluge in her coat pocket. Regardless of all the facts and information to the contrary, she knew it was the key. Tiffany put that picture in the bear for a reason. Now all she needed to do was figure out why.

As she walked down the street, she felt someone watching her. She turned around, scanning the faces. Nothing. No one she recognized. She backtracked a few steps, waiting for her father-in-law, or one of his cronies, to jump out at her. Nothing. Instead, she bumped into several people dressed in business attire trying to beat the lunch rush. "I'm sorry," Jacqueline said to no one in particular. They were all too consumed with their own lives to notice.

She stopped as the crossing light turned yellow, giving herself extra time to scan the area. Blank faces stared back at her. The city buzzed with people focused on themselves and drivers determined to get to point B as quickly as possible. The cars darted past the waiting pedestrians. Jacqueline was grateful for the sunny weather, despite the chilly air.

People moved in front of her, eager to be the first to cross. She stepped aside as a young mother tried to get herself and her baby playing in her stroller ready. She was too preoccupied with her thoughts about the case to save her place in the growing crowd. Someone was framing Mitch, but she had no evidence to prove it.

Only her instincts. She hoped her trip to the library would be fruitful. She had to find the connection between Natalie's death and Tiffany's murder.

Her phone buzzed and she looked down at a text from Lisa. The wife of the board member who'd changed his vote about the Harrison Investments election, Mrs. Wallingford, would talk to her. Before Jacqueline could view the address, the light finally turned green, allowing the crowd that had formed on the sidewalk to walk herd-like across the street. The child in the stroller dropped her toy in the crosswalk, and Jacqueline bent down to get it. The mother quickly thanked her and started running as the crossing hand started to flash. A man pushed Jacqueline, causing her to drop her phone.

"Damn it." Jacqueline reached down, trying to get it. She noticed the warning time on the crossing light ticking down, ten-nine-eight. A jogger, with his music blaring in his AirPods, kicked her phone further out as he too tried to beat the flashing hand. Six-five-four. She had to get her phone. She failed to notice that the light had changed to red, allowing the cars to start.

Jacqueline finally had her fingers wrapped around her phone when she heard it. The blaring of the horn. She looked up. A Porsche SUV was barreling down the street. Another set of pedestrians painted each corner. She had nowhere to turn as the bystanders screamed.

Chapter 46

"ARE YOU TRYING TO GET YOURSELF KILLED?" DAN yelled, his voice still trembling from the adrenaline coursing through him. He had grabbed Jacqueline just in time, yanking her back as the car sped by, its horn blaring. He guided her to a nearby bench, his grip firm on her arm. "Sit down, for God's sake!"

Jacqueline's whole body was shaking. "Oh my God, I can't believe that just happened."

Dan refused to sit. "I can. I told you, Jacqueline, this case is too dangerous for you."

"Stop. That had nothing to do with the Mitchell case. That was just sheer stupidity. I'm not sure I thanked you. I owe you one," Jacqueline said, brushing off the dirt. "How was I so lucky that you were there?"

She looked into Dan's bashful face. "Well, I called your office, and Lisa told me you were on your way to the library."

"If it's about the Mitchell case, friend or not, I can't let you jeopardize it."

Dan turned to face Jacqueline. "Someday, you're going to thank me for this."

"I doubt it. What now?"

Dan decided not to mince words. He handed her a copy of an old newspaper article.

"God, I hate your version of show-and-tell. What's this?" Jacqueline looked at it carefully. "Where did you get this?"

Dan ignored her question. "Jacqueline, what does it matter? Look at the picture. It's the same murder, the same type of gun."

Jacqueline shook her head. "So what? What does it prove? If I remember the report correctly, Mitch's father allegedly used a Glock 22. It's one of the most common handguns around. Mitch was eight when his mother died. I know you think he's the devil, but even you can't blame his mom's death on him."

Dan handed Jacqueline Mitch's juvenile record. "Read more, Counselor. I know you see the similarities. Mitchell was there. Just like his little boy. He was home when his father shot his mother to death. The neighbors called it a jealous rage. Sound familiar?"

Jacqueline scanned the papers. "It says the little boy was taken away in an ambulance." Jacqueline put the paper down. "Dan, I still don't get it. One has nothing to do with the other. Guess you are having a hard time finding this alleged mistress, huh?"

Dan stared at Jacqueline. "Jacqueline, come on. I know you see it. Mitch has his father's genes. He snapped, just like his father. You're the smart one. Can't you hear the prosecution?"

Dan paced the sidewalk, pretending to address the jury. "He suppressed the memory for years. He even says he doesn't remember how his mom died. He worked hard to overcome his background, to prove that he could fit in. He marries the beautiful socialite to help him with his image. But he slips up, just like his old man. Can't stay faithful to one woman. So when she confronts him about the affair, he snaps. Remembering how his father did it, he kills his wife in exactly the same way."

Jacqueline slow clapped. "You don't really believe that, do you?"

Dan leaned in so that his voice couldn't be overheard. His face inches from hers. "Yes, I do. This man is dangerous. Jacqueline, you need to stay away."

She stood up, seemingly forgetting her near-death experience. "No way. Are you working on anything other than railroading my client? Have you investigated that hospital case Tiffany was involved in? Did you know that she met with Dr. Fitzgerald the week before she died? And that he's disappeared?"

Dan stood. "That's not my job."

"Yes. It is. Dan, I know you. You want justice. I'm telling you that there is more to this case. I know they say that his father killed the mother. But did you actually review the so-called investigation of her murder? The police did nothing. They didn't even look for any other suspects."

Dan shook his head. "The father was convicted in a court of law, and there is no connection between the Westerfers and his mother, Natalie Kluge, except Mitchell."

Jacqueline scanned his face. "Do you know anything about Mitch's birth parents? What they did?"

Dan didn't answer.

Jacqueline forced eye contact. "Well, we do. And then there's that good Dr. Fitzgerald who is presently missing or in hiding. Did you talk to him yet?"

Dan smoothed down his hair, turning away. "I'm not sure what he has to do with her murder. He's a doctor, for God's sake."

"So that's a no?" Jacqueline asked, getting into his face.

"You're grasping at straws. Come on, Jacqueline. Do you have any idea how crazy this all is?"

"What are you hiding? I know you, Dan. Something is bugging you. Do you know that Patrick was holding a picture of Mitch's biological mother and that Tiffany was asking about the woman's death only days before she died? What if someone is setting Mitch up? I know you don't like him, but I also know you pride yourself on independent investigation. Mitch swears he wasn't having an affair. So who sent that anonymous text to Tiffany? And why anonymous? And why is Natalie Kluge's murder surfacing now? Dan, there has to be some connection. Something smells."

Dan threw his hands up, exasperated. "Jacqueline, I'm sorry, and I know this is hard to hear, but you're wrong. The only relevance of the mother's murder is that your client has the same temper as his father. It's in his blood. And if you don't believe me, let's ask his son. Here's a copy of the prosecution's motion to depose Patrick Mitchell, the eyewitness."

Chapter 47

DR. STAVROPOULOS WAS KNOWN ALL AROUND THE world as the leader in child trauma cases. He'd finally arrived, and Mitch couldn't wait to meet him. Mitch rushed over to the hospital only to be told to wait. And wait. According to the nurses, Dr. Stavropoulos insisted on speaking with no one except Patrick. Per the doctor's orders, he was given access to all Patrick's medical records, and then he wanted to examine Patrick.

Mitch just sat and waited, watching the second hand slowly tick around the clock. Work issues piled up, and his phone incessantly beeped, notifying him of emails and texts. He finally shut it down. He couldn't focus on anything other than Patrick. Since Mitch's time in foster care, he swore he would never depend on anyone for anything. And except for the last few months, he almost never did. His life revolved around control. And money became his vehicle. Always planning, always making things happen the way and when he wanted.

Yet as he sat in a cold hospital room some thirty-odd years later, after working himself to death, he'd returned to where he started. Random strangers controlled his life, but more importantly, Patrick's. His son's life was dependent on some so-called expert from California. If there is a God, Mitch needed his help yesterday. He had to do something fast before he exploded.

Eric walked in. "How are you holding up? Where's the doctor?"

"He needs to be alone with Patrick first. It's driving me crazy. I'm not sure how much more of this I can take. Talk to me about something. I couldn't read anything you sent me."

Eric sat down. "I know you don't want to hear this, but with the arrest, I think we need to appoint an interim CEO." Eric paused. "Don't kill the messenger, but I think we should appoint Harrison."

Eric picked the wrong time to talk about Mitch's resignation. "No way. Have you lost your mind? It'll be a cold day in hell."

"This isn't the time to be stubborn. I'll follow his every move, I promise. I'll make sure he does a good job."

"What are you talking about? You of all people know what a cheat he is. What's going on with you?"

"I'm just trying to protect you. You don't want the Westerfers as your enemies. Maybe if you recommend Harrison, they'll help you."

"Have you lost your mind? Don't want them as enemies? They're leading the charge on my arrest. You honestly think that there is anything I can do to make them change their minds? Harrison and Victoria are finally getting what they've wanted all these years, and then they are just going to say, 'Oh, I was wrong, I didn't see you kill Tiffany.'"

Eric stood up. "I'm at a loss. Mitch, you know you can't run the company with a trial looming."

Mitch had an idea that might work for everyone. "Make Katherine the temporary CEO."

"What?"

"You heard me. You know she's the right person for the job, and she's a Westerfer. That should appease Victoria."

"But..."

The nurse came out, indicating that the doctor would see Mitch now.

"Eric, I'm still the CEO. Just get it done." Mitch walked into the other room, failing to see the sweat forming on Eric's forehead.

Chapter 48

WHEN BILLY PAID GEORGEANNA, SHE FAILED TO EX-plain that "the files" equated to one big, unorganized mess. Boxes and papers spewed all over the cold basement with no labels or any visible sorting system. In contrast, no piece of paper, file, or box entered Jacqueline's office unless it was categorized, labeled, and color-coded. When Billy asked about Georgeanna's organizational system, she looked at him like he was speaking a different language. "Honey, he's lucky I took them. I didn't say I organized them."

Billy asked Georgeanna for a glass of water and got to work. It took several hours of literally looking through each piece of paper, but he recognized it immediately. Among all the bogus accident claims, divorce papers, and basic wills, he found it. Despite Scaggs's lack of an adequate filing system, he took surprisingly detailed notes. Billy began his review:

Interview Sheet

Date: *May 20th, 2019*

Name: *Maggie Brown*

Address: *300 Main Street, Apartment B, Attalla, Alabama*

Injury: *None (but woman hysterical)*

Problem: *Doctors are questioning whether she is her daughter's real mom.*

Payment: *Has cash!!! Paid $100 for consultation.*

Advice: *Calm down. Tell me the story.*

Billy wondered if she paid one hundred dollars before or after that advice. He turned to the next page. Scaggs apparently gave her at least an hour.

Lived in Alabama almost all her life except for the year she lived with some cousins in Philadelphia. After high school, wanted adventure—wanted to go to a big city. Parents said no to N.Y. Compromised—sent her to her cousins in Philadelphia.

Loved Philly. Got a job in a store at the Marketplace; in heaven. Then she started going out at night to the clubs, and she met him. Matt Lavelle. Love at first sight. Good-looking—tall, blond, and the bluest eyes she'd ever seen. She was in love, and she thought he loved her. "He told me he loved me." (Is she stupid?)

She finds out she's pregnant (shocker) before wedding. He bails—telling her too much responsibility. Not ready to be a dad.

She wanted to go home, but she couldn't. Ashamed. Had the baby by herself. Girl in "a big hospital in the city." Penn something. (Need to confirm. Says she still has the hospital bracelet and will bring it in.) Needed help; comes home to parents in Alabama.

Daughter's name: Amanda Brown. Loves her. Close to daughter. Grown daughter now very sick at City Hospital. Maybe cancer, Amanda needs transfusion. Drs. ran all these tests, and Mom offered to give blood. Then the tests came back showing that Amanda is blood type AB and Maggie is type O—no way Amanda is Maggie's biological child. (Has a copy of results.)

Billy reviewed the file. Stashed between all the scrap pieces of paper, he saw the blood test typing from City Hospital proving that Maggie could not possibly be Amanda's biological mother. Billy didn't like where this was going. He turned back to Scaggs's notes.

Mom scared. Doesn't know what to do. Doctors questioning her about how she got her daughter. Maggie going to bring in the papers.

Billy turned to the next sheet. It was dated the next day.

Paid: $125.

Brought in documents. Has the discharge summary and medical bands. Maggie definitely gave birth at Penn Central Hospital in Philadelphia, Pa in 1992. Confirms that she had a little girl. Pregnancy complications which required the doctor to put her under general anesthesia. Needed to have a cesarean.

Told Maggie I would call the doctors at City.

Maggie doesn't want to do anything now. Doesn't want Amanda to know anything about this.

Did the hospital accidently mix up the baby back in 1992? Possible since security nothing like it is today. Potential for big malpractice suit. $$$

Then there were several entries.

1/25
Tried to talk Maggie into investigating claim of baby mix-up. Won't talk to me. Amanda ill.

1/30
Went to hospital. Maggie still doesn't want to talk. Amanda very sick. Doesn't look good.

3/2
Saw Maggie at the hospital. Convinced that it was a baby mix-up. Big MONEY!! Need to follow up with Maggie.

3/12
Amanda died. Went to funeral.

4/22
Talked to Maggie. Told her that her real daughter may be out there somewhere. Thinking about the case!!!!

6/30
Maggie finally agreed to investigate claim. Signed retainer.

7/5
Talked to attorney in Philadelphia. Sent him retainer for $3000. Filing writ.

7/14
Filed writ.

7/20
Wrote to hospital. Going up there to investigate.

8/22
Met with board. Board scared. Told them I would go public with the news of the mix-up if they didn't meet my demands.

9/12
Got a call today. Wants to negotiate. Demanded 20 mil!!!

9/30

Hospital offer 10 mil, but Maggie can have no contact with her real daughter. Should I find out the name of the woman?

10/3

Talked to Maggie. Wants to at least know something about her daughter. Doesn't want to take her from the only mother she knows. We'll take the 10 mil. Also, the other family must be informed of the truth and offered a settlement as well.

10/6

Deal—Hospital paying 10 mil, but we can't ever know the identity of Maggie's real daughter per the other family's wishes. Convinced Maggie to give her up.

Billy reviewed the rest of the file, including the retainer, the hospital records, and the discharge summary. There was no specific mention of Tiffany, but one name leaped off the page. Maggie's doctor was one Marc Fitzgerald.

Chapter 49

JACQUELINE COULDN'T WAIT TO COLLAPSE INTO BED. She could feel her fuzzy pajamas and the La Crema chardonnay she'd put in the refrigerator calling her name. As she waited for the elevator, her phone rang.

"Hi, Lisa. I'm sorry I didn't come back into the office. I'm just exhausted." Jacqueline decided to omit her near-death experience as she already had too many people worrying about her.

"No worries. I just want to confirm that you have the meeting with Mrs. Wallingford in the morning."

Once inside the elevator, Jacqueline pushed the floor button. Almost home. "Yes. That's a big coup. Hopefully she can tell us something about this damn election." Jacqueline checked her watch. "Lisa, get out of there. It's late. We can figure it out tomorrow."

Jacqueline heard Lisa packing up. "Only if you promise to do the same. You need your rest."

For once, Jacqueline agreed. "I may lose you. I'm in the elevator."

"Okay, well, really quick. I did a lot of research on Dr. Fitzgerald. It seems like Harrison Investments gave money for his research and…"

The connection broke. Jacqueline rubbed her head. Almost there.

As she stepped off the elevator, she dialed Lisa back and then walked robotically toward her condo. Waiting for Lisa to pick up, Jacqueline unlocked her door.

This time she saw the man in the dark, a big imposing figure rushing at her.

Chapter 50

"DAD, YOU SCARED ME!" JACQUELINE SCREAMED. "What are you doing here?" She rushed to hug her father.

"I'm so sorry. I got here a few hours ago and decided to take a nap in that chair. I guess I never turned on a light. Your keys woke me up." Her father released her. "Jacqueline, you're shaking. Are you okay? Sit down."

Jacqueline gratefully accepted the chair. "Dad, you should've told me you were coming. I would've picked you up at the airport."

Her father sat across from her, not even attempting to hide his concern. "You aren't driving, are you?"

Jacqueline dismissed him. "Dad, I would've had my driver meet you. And just for the record, you know I can legally drive because I get an aura. I just choose not to. So please stop. I don't need a babysitter."

Jacqueline watched as her father's pale eyes filled with tears. "Jax, I can't say anything right to you anymore. Either I'm too tough or too protective."

Jacqueline put her hand on his leg to prevent him from walking away. "Dad, please, I'm the one who should apologize. I'm a mess. It's just that I hate people treating me as if I'm ready to break if the wind changes direction," Jacqueline said, her own waterfall about to spill over.

"No, I'm sorry for scaring you. And for the record, I do know you can drive. Oh, you're shaking. Is everything okay?"

Jacqueline nodded. Her father headed to the kitchen to get her a glass of water. "Just sit there, and I'll make us something to eat. I'm still allowed to wait on you, right?"

Jacqueline blushed. "Dad, you're the best. And yes, a home-cooked meal sounds amazing, but my cupboards are as bare as they get."

He opened the refrigerator. "I suspected that was the case. Hence why I stopped at the store before I came here. Now talk to me while I whip up your favorite."

Jacqueline smiled. "How's Caroline doing?"

Her dad got out the necessary ingredients and filled Jacqueline in on his trip. "So once I knew one daughter was doing great, I came home to check on my other one. The house looks beautiful, by the way."

The smells of garlic and butter filled the room. "Yes. Thank you. Your designer friend Denise did a wonderful job."

Her father came over to the table with two piping hot plates of shrimp scampi. "Eat before it gets cold." As they enjoyed their dinner, her dad confessed. "I noticed that Jack's room hasn't changed, though."

Jacqueline twirled her pasta. "Dad, please. Not now."

"Okay, okay. But you promised me that you were going to think about giving some of his stuff away. You know, there are a lot of little boys and girls who would love all that superhero stuff."

Jacqueline looked down at her plate.

Her father tried again. "Jax, it's not healthy to come home to that every night. Keep a few items, but the rest you should give away. I'm afraid to ask, but is his bedroom the same at the shore house?"

Jacqueline threw her fork down. "Dad, you know I haven't even been there since. Now, please. I'm in the middle of a big case."

Her father raised his hands, conceding. "Okay, we will table this discussion. But after it's over, we need to talk about it."

Jacqueline smiled. It felt good to have dinner company. Over wine, she filled her dad in on the latest developments and outlined her concerns. "I know his mother's death is somehow related to his wife's murder. I just can't figure out how. And the lead detective on the case is only convinced that my client did it."

Her father took a sip of his wine. "Who's the lead detective? Not that friend of yours, what's his name, Dan something?"

Jacqueline focused on her pasta. "Dan O'Neill. And Dad, don't go there. He's a stubborn pain in the ass."

"Really? I remember a time that a certain attorney thought his instincts were right on."

Jacqueline picked up her wine. "Well, they got a lot worse. He won't even look at the mother's murder."

"I don't know, honey. The woman has been dead for thirty years. And it doesn't seem like the two families ran in the same circles."

"Hence the dilemma. Anyway, thanks, Dad. Dinner was delicious. Just what the doctor ordered. And it's nice to confide in someone."

Her dad patted her hand. "It's exciting to see you at work. You're an amazing attorney."

"Thanks, Dad, that means a lot. I'm just worried about Mitchell's son. You heard he's in the hospital?"

Her dad put his fork down. "I did. And that's why I'm worried. This case may be too much for you. Have you had any episodes?"

Jacqueline started to clear the plates. "Dad, please. I don't want to talk about it. I'm fine. And before you ask, yes, I took my medicine."

Chapter 51

"THANK YOU, DETECTIVE, FOR MEETING ME ON SUCH short notice," Lisa said, shaking the elderly man's hand. At Jacqueline's suggestion, Lisa had pulled the reports on Natalie Kluge's murder. The detective on the case had retired but was willing to talk to her. A well-loved recliner faced the television playing the Penn State game. Two empty Miller Lite cans stood crushed on the end table next to a newspaper laying out the stats on the game. Next to them was an old police scanner.

"Are you kidding me? To be called detective again is like music to my ears," Art Jones said, gesturing for Lisa to sit. Following her eyes, he shut off the scanner. "Sorry. Old habits die hard. Please sit down. Tell me about your case."

Seeing her belly, Art asked, "I assume you don't want a cold one, but I'm afraid I don't have much else. Want a glass of water?"

Lisa accepted the chair. "No, I'm good, thank you."

"Oh, right, well, I have to admit that I'm excited to hear about something other than the damn news and grandkids," Art said. "How can I help?"

Lisa immediately got to the point. "I'm working on a case, and an old murder that you handled came up."

"Must be a real oldie, then," Art deduced, reaching for the file she held out. "Which one was it?"

"The murder of a young woman in the northeast. Her name was Natalie Kluge. Her husband was convicted of her death. You were the investigating detective at the time."

Art leaned back in his rocker, reading over the file. He grabbed his reading glasses and took a sip of his beer. He took his time.

"I remember this. Sure. Sad case. Beautiful woman. And the child was found at the scene. What can I do for you?"

Lisa treaded slowly. Having investigated a lot of detectives over the years, Jacqueline taught her that none of them wanted to be second-guessed. "Please forgive me, but did anything stick out about the husband? Or the child? The case in general?"

Art took another sip of his beer before he answered. "Are you asking me how confident am I that the husband did it?"

"Yes."

Art sat up in his chair and looked right at Lisa. "As confident as we could be, given the limited resources we had back then. Let me explain something. Today you kids have all those fancy tests and technology. You can pinpoint exactly where people are and have all those fancy videos. We just had good old folks and what they saw. This young couple had no one. I think the kid was finally adopted by the neighbor, right?"

Lisa was impressed by his memory. "Yes. He was."

Art sat back. "See, I remember that. No one asked about this case. The consensus was that this young couple was on hard times. He was a drunk, and he killed her. We had no evidence of anything else. We had no other suspects."

Jacqueline's demand for tenacity motivated Lisa. "Do you remember anything about the child? Where he was? If he said or claimed anything?"

Art hesitated. "Lady, you have to understand. Things were so different then."

Lisa tried to appeal to his conscience without insulting him. "Mr. Jones, we are not judging you. We know how hard it was then and now to be a police officer. But anything you can tell us may prevent an injustice today. Please help us."

Art leaned forward. "Okay, what I remember—and, to be honest, I never forgot it—was pulling that little boy out of the closet. He was scared, holding his hands over his ears, shaking. He was incoherent. But I do remember him saying, 'Not daddy, not daddy.' Then the ambulance took him away. It was a really sad scene."

Lisa took notes. "Another question. Do you remember if the wife worked?"

Art looked over the case notes, pointing. "Yes. See right here. She was a nurse. Worked at Penn."

"Did you investigate anyone from the hospital? Any suspects back then?"

Art again referred to the notes. "Says here we interviewed people she worked with. Came up with nothing. Everybody loved her. No complaints about her. Nothing."

Lisa nodded. "Did you think the husband did it?"

Art sighed heavily, toying with his beer can before he answered. "See, back then we had a lot of cases and no fancy shortcuts. Just good old-fashioned detective work. And we got credit for how many we closed."

Lisa leaned in. "Detective Jones, I'm just trying to solve a present murder. No judgment here. But if I'm hearing you right, it sounds like something is bothering you."

Art took off his glasses and rubbed the bridge of his nose, as if the weight of old memories were pressing down on him. "Like I said, all the evidence pointed to the husband. There wasn't anyone else we could pin it on. But there's something that never sat right with me." He leaned back in his chair, eyes distant, as if he were trying to recall the scene. "When we answered the neighbor's call about the gunshot, we found him passed out drunk. Couldn't even wake him up to tell him she was dead."

Art's voice grew softer. "She was shot in the head, no alcohol in her system, no defensive wounds. He was out cold. The gun was just sitting there on the coffee table next to him, and he had gunshot residue on his hand. Pretty clear-cut. But when we finally managed to wake him, well…" Art paused, looking at Lisa. "Let's just say the guy could win an Oscar for that performance. He didn't behave like a man who killed his wife. He was disoriented, barely able to stand. And we responded pretty quickly after the call. The notes should say. Think it was about ten minutes. But when he woke, he started screaming for her and his son."

Art sighed. "But there was literally no one else. And the question that always haunted me was if he was so drunk, and she wasn't, why didn't she defend herself?"

Chapter 52

DAN SAT AT HIS DESK, MAKING BASKETBALLS WITH crumbled paper. Waiting for Grady to get off the phone, he tossed another one toward the wastebasket and missed it completely.

"Mom, it's an ongoing investigation. You know I can't tell you anything more than what you read. Now, I have to go. Love you." Grady hung up the phone. "God, my mother is going to kill me. She is obsessed with the Mitchell murder."

Grady watched as Dan missed the wastebasket again. "What's got you in knots?"

Dan sat up in his chair. "What? Just because I missed one?"

Grady pointed to the mountain of wadded paper around his desk. "No, because of all the trees you're killing. What's your problem? What Jacqueline said to you yesterday getting to you?"

Dan got up and put the paper balls in the trash can. "I just don't like it. I feel like I'm missing something. And I don't like that we received that anonymous package last night with Mitchell's juvenile record and the info on his mother's murder. It just feels like someone has their own agenda."

Dan rubbed his temples. He didn't need more issues. Before he could figure out his next move, his phone rang.

"I'm looking for a Detective O'Neill?" the caller said.

"Speaking," Dan said into the phone, instantly regretting answering it as the man stuttered to get to the point.

"I really don't know if this is important. And I really didn't want to get involved, but my wife insisted," the man said.

The caller paused. Dan debated about hanging up. *Get on with it, buddy. I've had a shitty day.*

"You're the lead detective in the Mitchell murder, right?"

Dan sighed. He was tired of all the useless leads. He was about to hang up when the call got interesting.

"My name is Howard Hastings. I'm a neighbor of the Mitchells. We just got back from Florida, and I think my wife may have some helpful information about the case."

Chapter 53

"MRS. WALLINGFORD, THANK YOU SO MUCH FOR agreeing to meet with me," Jacqueline said, as she entered yet another impressive mansion the next day.

Despite being roughly the same age as Victoria Harrison Westerfer, their similarities ended there. Mrs. Wallingford seemed to have no interest in societal norms and traditional notions of elegance. In stark contrast to Victoria's meticulously styled hair, Mrs. Wallingford wore hers long and full, resembling an older version of Farrah Fawcett. Bleached blond, way too sexy and brash for the Junior League. Jacqueline would bet Mrs. Wallingford didn't own a set of pearls or an outfit to match.

Jacqueline smiled to herself as she followed Mrs. Wallingford into a light purple living room. She felt like she'd just entered a Lilly Pulitzer store on Palm Beach.

As if reading Jacqueline's mind, Mrs. Wallingford said, "I know it's a little much, but I love purple. Did you know it's the color of royalty?"

"It's lovely."

Mrs. Wallingford let out a nervous laugh. "Well, aren't you kind, sweetie. You and I know it's what people around here would call tacky, but my hubby let me be me. And I loved him for it. It's a shame no one else was as understanding. We were fine just the two of us."

Despite the woman's Southern charm, Jacqueline could tell she was nervous. Jacqueline had to get her talking. And fast. "Thank you for agreeing to meet with me."

"Well, I must admit, you have some pretty insistent associates. I didn't think that Lisa would ever stop calling me," Mrs. Wallingford admitted, half laughing.

Jacqueline noticed the woman kept glancing up at the portrait of a very attractive older man above the mantel. She took a guess. "Is that Mr. Wallingford?"

A huge smile crossed the woman's face. "Yes, it is. Mr. Theodore Wallingford. But I called him Teddy. My Teddy. Every day since he died, I'm so glad I insisted he sit for that portrait. I often find myself in here, talking to him. We were married thirty-five years."

Jacqueline watched as the woman admired the portrait. Love was all over her face. "Very handsome man."

"Yes, he was. And a good man, too. I'm not sure they make them like that anymore," Mrs. Wallingford said.

Jacqueline noticed the woman staring at her bare ring finger.

"What can I help you with?" Mrs. Wallingford sat down, facing the portrait.

"It's my understanding from speaking with Lisa that you have some information regarding the election at Harrison Investments four years ago," Jacqueline supplied, hoping to get the woman to talk. She noticed how Mrs. Wallingford kept staring at the portrait of her late husband. *Please tell her to talk to me*, Jacqueline pleaded to him. Maybe talking to inanimate objects was beginning to work.

Mrs. Wallingford played with her wedding band. "I'm sorry. I don't know why I am so nervous. I'm just not sure I should be speaking with you."

"Please, Mrs. Wallingford, it could be important."

She stared at Jacqueline. "Oh well. Here goes. I'm saying this because Mr. Wallingford always liked Mitch. Thought he was one of the good ones. Teddy always thought Mitch was the right person to run Harrison Investments. But Preston was so torn. He loved his son, but he was too good a businessman not to recognize Harrison's shortcomings. Harrison had no right to run any business, let alone that one. Teddy was always such a loyal friend to both Preston and Victoria."

As Mrs. Wallingford stood and moved to the fireplace, Jacqueline noticed the glisten of tears in her eyes. "Ms. Stone, I'm not sure I can do this. Betray Teddy." She glanced up at his portrait, her voice trembling with emotion. "I made my husband a promise, and we never broke our promises."

Jacqueline felt a pang of admiration for the Wallingfords' love, so pure and unwavering. She decided it was time for honesty. "Mrs. Wallingford, I'm not sure what the election has to do with Mrs. Mitchell's murder, if anything. But any information would be helpful. If you know anything about how Mitch got the CEO position, we would greatly appreciate it. We promise that we will only use it if it helps with the criminal action."

Mrs. Wallingford talked to the portrait. "Teddy, I think Mitch has a right to know. Sorry, Teddy, but you and Preston are both gone now, and the truth must come out. And it wouldn't hurt to knock that Victoria Westerfer down a few pegs."

Mrs. Wallingford turned to face Jacqueline. "One of the only advantages of old age is that you no longer care about such silly things as the social calendar or registry. Ms. Stone, I will tell you how Mitch got to be CEO."

Chapter 54

TYLER DIDN'T THINK IT WAS A GOOD IDEA. VICTORIA didn't care. She wanted to meet this infamous defense attorney, Jacqueline Stone, and find out what she thought she knew. No one came into her family's world and thought they could get the better of *the* Victoria Harrison Westerfer. Given her beauty, people often severely underestimated her ability. Like any master chess player, she blinded her opponents with her cunning ways, and before they knew it, they were her victims, following her agenda. Her network informed her of Ms. Stone's meeting with that gold digger, Barbara Wallingford. No one, especially some common defense attorney, would destroy the one thing Victoria had left. Her family.

A staff member announced the arrival. Victoria checked her watch. Punctual. Not late, but not too early. Victoria made her wait in the foyer for twenty minutes, testing her, baiting her to become unraveled. Instead, when the housekeeper led her into the library, Jacqueline walked into the room holding her head up high.

Victoria sized Jacqueline up immediately. She was appropriately dressed in a St. John suit. Victoria recognized it as last year's design. Jacqueline wore it well, though. At least she knew enough not to appear in business casual. Victoria glanced at the shoes, accessories, and Louis Vuitton tote bag. If she had better taste in clients, Victoria would probably invite her for tea.

Victoria did not offer her a seat.

"Thank you, Mrs. Westerfer, for agreeing to meet with me."

"Well, my purpose was not entirely unselfish." Victoria paused, despite knowing she had Jacqueline's full attention. "It's a shame."

"Excuse me?"

"From everything I could learn about you, you appear to have talent, but you obviously choose to waste it. You are making a grave mistake representing that monster, and I am hoping that I can convince you otherwise."

No response.

"Ms. Stone, I know of your reputation and how challenging your work can be. My family is well connected. I could make life a lot easier for you."

Jacqueline's tone rose. "Mrs. Westerfer, I'm not interested in an easy life. I want to do what is right. And I asked to see you because I need to know something."

Victoria dismissed Jacqueline's rejection of her offer with the wave of her hand, as if Jacqueline had no idea what she had just given up.

"Mrs. Westerfer, I just spoke with Mrs. Barbara Wallingford. It seems that your secret didn't die with her husband. Theodore told her about your plan."

Although Victoria was concerned, she refused to show it. "I have no idea what you're talking about."

"Mrs. Westerfer, I am not one of your servants or committee ladies. Mrs. Wallingford told me that it was you who instructed Theodore to change his vote to Mitch, and that's how Mitch won the election for CEO."

Victoria looked at Jacqueline. "If your accusation wasn't so serious, it would be laughable. Your so-called witness is nothing but a pathetic liar who hates me for all that I have.

"Let me tell you something about your witness before you rely on what she said." Victoria leaned forward, her voice dripping with disdain. "The whole world knew that Theodore married beneath him, and she was and never would be accepted into our world. The only reason she got invited to different events was because of my husband. My husband begged me to invite her, for his best friend's sake. So I invited her. I couldn't help it if everyone ignored her, like the lowlife she was."

Victoria noticed that Jacqueline stood erect, seemingly uncon-vinced. She obviously needed to be educated. "My Preston tried to explain to Theodore that his bimbo wife would never be accepted, but Theodore insisted. So I went along with the charade. Barbara's not a fool. Now that woman is trying to get back at me for all the times she was snubbed.

"Take this as a warning, Ms. Stone. If you try to use that filthy lie at your trial, I'll not only destroy her, but you as well. If you think you have problems now, your hell is only beginning. I did not, and would not, ever betray my own child. I always protect my own."

Victoria rose, indicating the meeting was over.

To her surprise, Jacqueline tried to interrogate her. "Mrs. West-erfer, I know you were the one who forced Wallingford to switch his vote. It's the only thing that makes sense for how Mitch could have gotten enough votes to win. The only question that remains is why? Why would you do this to your precious son? If you don't want to tell me, that's your decision. But I promise you that I will find out. Please rest assured that I will uncover whatever it is that you are hiding."

Jacqueline stood in front of the doorway. "And by the way, right now, we are hunting down Dr. Fitzgerald. Did you know Tiffany met with him the week she was murdered? We will find him."

This attorney confirmed Victoria's fears. Years of good breeding allowed her to hide her emotion. "If you want to rely on that woman, that's your choice. I just thought you were smarter than that. Shame on you. If that is all you have, good luck. You're going to need it."

Victoria walked to the library doors. She wasn't finished. She was going to bury Mitchell and his pretty attorney. "Oh, Tyler, since Ms. Stone is here, why don't you give her the papers personally?"

She walked away without so much as a goodbye.

JACQUELINE DIDN'T KNOW WHAT TO EXPECT, AND Tyler's apologetic face told her it wasn't good.

"I'm so sorry about this." Tyler handed Jacqueline the papers. "I tried to convince Mrs. Westerfer otherwise, but as you can see, the woman has her own mind."

Jacqueline glanced at the papers for permanent and sole custody of Patrick. Her blood started to boil. "How could she do this?"

Tyler turned away. "This nightmare just keeps getting worse. I hate what is happening to Mitch."

Jacqueline sympathized with the difficult conflict for the gentleman but was furious that he wouldn't help Mitch.

Tyler cleared his throat. "Ms. Stone, I just want you to understand. Victoria is convinced that Mitch killed Tiffany, and she is only concerned about her grandson."

Jacqueline didn't have time for Victoria's feelings. "Mr. Hines, my job is to protect Mitch and Patrick. You can tell Victoria that she will never get full custody of the boy." Just as the words spilled from Jacqueline's mouth, it hit her. Victoria's plan. "She wants to destroy him, doesn't she? She knows that these papers will completely distract Mitch. He'll be so crazy protecting Patrick, he'll have no time to help with his own case. How can you say you love him and let her get away with this?"

"Ms. Stone, that's not it. Victoria is sincerely concerned about Patrick."

Jacqueline looked at Tyler. He looked even older than he had a few weeks ago. "Mr. Hines, you have to help us. If she files those papers, it will kill Mitch."

"I know. I know. Trust me, you have no idea how heavy my heart is. If only I could help." Tyler wrung his hands.

"What? What is it?"

"I've been debating about whether to tell you, but Victoria left me no choice." Tyler stood up and closed the heavy cherry doors to the library. "Ms. Stone, I need to tell you something."

Chapter 55

AFTER AGREEING TO MEET MITCH AT THE HOSPITAL, Jacqueline ran to her office. Lisa left a message that she had some news, and Jacqueline prayed it was good.

"Did you find Dr. Fitzgerald?" Jacqueline asked as she entered.

Lisa trailed behind her as they headed to the war room. "No, not yet. We are still working on it. But what I did discover is that our Dr. Fitzgerald is intimately connected with Harrison Investments."

Jacqueline scanned the documents Lisa found. "But does that help or hurt us? Did you forget Mr. Mitchell is the CEO of that company?"

Lisa pointed to the page. "I'm going to ignore that. Look at the dates. Fitzgerald has been working with Harrison Investments since well before Mr. Mitchell came on the scene. Fitzgerald was just beginning his research as a young doctor when he connected with Harrison Investments."

Jacqueline kept reading. "Interesting, but how does Tiffany fit into that?"

Lisa shrugged. "I can't find any connection other than her meeting with him the week of the murder. But we've also noticed some discrepancies in the company's financial records, which we are currently reviewing."

"I had an interesting chat with Tyler Hines. Apparently, Ms. Katherine Conceillo did leave the office that day. Shortly before Mr. Mitchell."

Lisa reviewed her notes. "How could that be? I interviewed her secretary."

"But you also said they were very close. Mr. Hines said another security camera was recently installed that only he and Mr. Mitchell know of that monitors the private back stairway. Since Mr. Mitchell went out the front doors of the office, apparently they didn't think to check those cameras."

"Consider it done." Lisa scribbled on her pad. "And guess who also worked at Penn Central Hospital?"

"Who?"

"Natalie Kluge."

"Really. Interesting. Have we heard from Billy about the Alabama case?"

"No, not yet."

"Well, find Billy and find that doctor. He holds the key."

Chapter 56

AS JACQUELINE WALKED INTO PATRICK'S HOSPITAL room, her heart leaped.

Not only was he awake, but his once-vacant eyes now danced with mischief as he played his father in an Xbox game. But her joy quickly transformed into fear. As Patrick's condition improved, they couldn't hold off the other side from interviewing him much longer. Mitchell's last chance rested in Patrick's little hands.

"Gotcha, Dad."

Neither one looked up as Jacqueline entered the room.

"No fair," Mitch cried out. He saw Jacqueline. "Hey, there you are." Jacqueline noticed the question in his eyes. "Patrick, do you remember Ms. Stone?"

Patrick looked at his visitor, his blank expression saying it all. Jacqueline understood. To a nine-year-old, what happened to him when he was a little boy seemed like a million years ago. Jack would have been the same way.

Patrick greeted his father's guest. "Hi, Ms. Stone, it's nice to meet you." He held out his hand. Jacqueline remembered all the times John had gone over how you greet an adult with Jack. *Make sure you look them in the eye. And no wimpy hands. Strong, like this. If you have a hat on, always remove it first.*

Jacqueline accepted. "Thank you. It's nice to see you again. I'm sure you don't remember, but I met you years ago in Stone Harbor on the beach."

Patrick nodded politely, looking at his dad for help.

"Patrick, years ago, this remarkable lady saved your life. One morning, you woke up early and decided to go down to the ocean without me. The only problem was you didn't know how to swim." Mitch nuzzled Patrick in the arm.

"Where were you? Weren't you supposed to be watching me?" Patrick countered.

"Oh, it's always the dad's fault, I see. Anyway, we both owe this lady a lot."

"Well, thanks. I mean, thank you."

"No problem. Glad I could help." Jacqueline changed the subject. "So what's going on here? A little Xbox?"

"Yeah, I'm kicking Dad's butt."

Jacqueline smiled. She shot Mitch a "we need to talk" look.

"Patrick, why don't you see if you can beat that computer while I talk to Ms. Stone."

Jacqueline followed Mitch into an adjoining patient room, which Mitch had converted into an executive suite. Donating a wing to the hospital clearly had its advantages.

"Does he remember anything yet?" Jacqueline asked.

"No. He hasn't said a word about it. The doctor is calling it selective amnesia. When Patrick woke up, he acted as if nothing had happened. Apparently, it's very common for children who were traumatized to completely block out the whole episode. Dr. Stavropoulos has been working with Patrick to evaluate whether he is stable enough to discuss that day."

Jacqueline nodded, understanding "that day" was code for Tiffany's murder.

"Dr. Stavropoulos warned it could be years before Patrick remembers anything."

"Do they have any idea about what happened with Katherine?"

"No, other than something must have triggered him that caused the panic attack. I'm just glad he's feeling so much better."

Through the open door, Mitch watched his son playing his video game. Seemingly satisfied, he turned to Jacqueline. "Any news for me?"

Confident Patrick was out of earshot, Jacqueline filled Mitch in about her meeting with Mrs. Wallingford.

Mitch shook his head. "There must be some mistake. No way. Why? Why would Victoria tell Theodore to switch his vote? That year, since Preston had died, Theodore oversaw the vote. Under the bylaws, the vote is strictly confidential. But I personally spoke with Theodore, and he was voting in line with Preston's final wishes. I never knew which board members voted for me."

Jacqueline was just as confused. "Mrs. Wallingford didn't know why. She only knew that Victoria came to the house to talk to Theodore the night before the election. According to Mrs. Wallingford, Victoria told Theodore that you had to win the election. Obviously, she could not, and would not, vote for you herself. She needed Theodore to change his vote. Theodore asked her about his promise to Preston, and Victoria assured him that Preston wanted you to run the business. Apparently, it didn't take much convincing because Theodore always believed you were the right successor."

"I hear what you're saying, but it still doesn't make any sense. Victoria would never do that. She hates me. More importantly, she loves Harrison too much. He is her golden child. *The son*. These people, the Harrisons and Westerfers, they aren't regular people. It's not just about money. It's the social status. It was all I heard about. In the Harrison family, the bloodline, the son, was paramount. It was in *Philadelphia Magazine* when Victoria Westerfer gave birth to Harrison. No way would she tell Theodore to vote against her son."

Jacqueline thought of something else. "Maybe Tyler convinced her that it was the right thing to do?"

"No way. Tyler does everything Victoria wants, not the other way around. No, Victoria was adamant that Harrison was to be the CEO. She wanted that since the moment she gave birth.

"I remember when Tiffany was pregnant, Victoria kept saying that she hoped Patrick was a boy. She even suggested that if it was a girl, as if that was something horrible, the next time we should do that spinning thing. Apparently, Victoria had complicated pregnancies, the last one resulting in a hysterectomy, and she feared Tiffany would have similar problems."

Jacqueline was dumbfounded. She knew of the sperm spinning process that allegedly increases the chances of having a baby of the desired sex, but she didn't think a grandparent would care. "Why did she care whether Tiffany had a boy?"

Mitch shrugged. "I never understood that woman. She comes from a different world, one I will never understand. Tyler said Preston would divorce Victoria if he didn't have a son to run the business."

"Tyler knew Victoria back then?"

"Yes. Tyler's father was their lawyer before Tyler was. Apparently, Victoria's doctor had told the family after Katherine and Tiffany were born that her third pregnancy had to be her last."

"Told the family?"

Mitch confirmed. "Yes. The family. It was a family affair. Trust me. I'm surprised I was permitted to marry Tiffany. It wasn't easy. To this day, they think they have royal lineage in them. According to Tyler, the entire family was anxiously holding their breath, desperately hoping for a boy."

From everything Jacqueline had heard about Preston, that didn't seem like him. "Even Preston?"

"We never talked about it. But I think his family had their own hang-ups. He was old-fashioned, drove Katherine crazy, thought women shouldn't be in business. Back then, there really was a difference between blue bloods and the nouveau riche. The latter couldn't access the necessary circles and clubs or even the schools that were needed for certain social status and business connections. Preston was astute enough to recognize that he needed the Harrison family connections. And, he desperately wanted Harrison to take over the business. But he was also very disappointed in his son. They were

238 · MARY V. SLINKARD

nothing alike. Harrison only cared about spending money and hav-ing a good time. And, unlike Victoria, I think Preston recognized his son's shortcomings."

"Do you think that Tiffany could have somehow forced Victoria to get Theodore to change his vote?"

Jacqueline watched as Mitch's mind began to rewind. "At the time of the election, Katherine, Eric, and I were running around meeting with everyone we could to convince them to vote for me. We were exhausted and nervous and convinced that we had lost. I distinctly remember I was upset with Tiffany because even though she wasn't as involved in the business, she could be very persuasive with her dad and the board members. But she had no time for us. She was consumed with some hospital matter. And when I finally won, Tiffany said 'great' as if I'd ordered lobster for dinner. Convince Victoria to get Theodore to vote for me? I don't think even Tiffany could convince her mother of that, nor did my wife care enough to even try.

"I just can't see it. What could Tiffany do, or know, to make Victoria change her mind?"

Jacqueline had no idea, but she sure was going to find out.

Chapter 57

MARC FITZGERALD PACED THE CABIN, TIRED OF LIS-tening to his wife.

"Honey, you better come home soon. Everyone wants to talk to you. The cops keep calling. And that defense counsel won't stop coming to the house. They think you're the key to that Tiffany woman's murder. You need to come home and help."

Marc tried to stay calm as he poured himself a bourbon. "You didn't give anyone my cell phone, right? Promise me, Nora."

He could hear the concern in her voice. "Honey, this is ridiculous. You always like to help. What if you know something?"

"Nora, answer me. You didn't give them my number, right?"

"Don't yell at me. Yes, I listened. I told you I didn't say anything."

Relief flooded over Marc. "Okay, good. I'll be home soon. I gotta go."

Marc talked to himself as he paced. *If I cooperate, then maybe I won't go to jail.* He just wanted solitude. Peace and his fish.

A knock at the door. He opened it.

"Hello, Doc." The visitor handed Marc an opened bottle of his favorite scotch. "Let's enjoy this before you do anything stupid. I hope you don't mind. I had a couple of swigs in the car up here. Long drive."

Marc allowed his visitor in. "You need to do something. I have both the cops and the lawyer calling me." He had that sickening feeling like he'd had all those years ago when his tunnel vision for money to finish his research took over. He thought he was doing the right thing in the name of progress. What an idiot he'd been.

Marc slammed the door, the sound reverberating through the room. "I'm done. You have to do something. Go to the cops with me. Tell them it was an accident."

His visitor raised a hand, leaning casually against the wall. "Let's calm down."

"Calm down?" Marc paced frantically, running his hands through his hair. "Do you even understand? Tiffany had that letter. She thinks I did it. If I wasn't in the hospital that day, I swear she would've gone straight to the cops. Then, I call you and now, she's dead."

His visitor strolled over and sank into Marc's favorite chair, crossing one leg over the other. "Please stop. You just said it yourself. You have an airtight alibi. Now, I drove all the way up here. Why don't you offer me a drink?"

Marc hesitated, still holding the bottle.

"Marc, please. Let's have a drink and discuss things. What's the problem?"

Marc had to agree. Driving back to Philadelphia and facing charges didn't appeal to him. He threw out his bourbon and opened the hundred-year-old scotch. He remembered the first time he bought himself a bottle. The luxury of sipping something so expensive. He and his friends smoking cigars. Celebrating his success. *They don't serve this in jail*, Marc thought. He poured them two drinks. And gulped some down.

He handed one to his guest. "We need to figure this out. I should never have gone along with your plan."

"Oh, how we rewrite history. Now it's my plan? Who wanted the research? Needed money to fund all those developments? Say whatever you want to convince yourself that the ends justified the means. But it was a win-win situation."

Fitzgerald didn't want to debate the past. "What's going on? You tell me to sit out here and fish. But I have the cops and that attorney banging at my door in the city. I need answers. I'm running out of time and patience."

"For once, you're correct," his visitor said while Fitzgerald gasped for breath, holding his heart.

Chapter 58

"THE GOOD NEWS IS YOUR SON IS OUT OF THE CATA-tonic state, but he's still suffering from PTSD," Dr. Stavropoulos explained. "Most people think that PTSD only affects combat veterans or survivors of sexual assault, but it can happen to anyone who's been through a life-threatening event."

Jacqueline noticed that he left out murder, and apparently Mitch did too.

"Do you believe that he saw my wife's murder?"

"I can't say for sure. But given his actions, the nightmares and panic attacks, and his difficulty sleeping, I would say that he did."

"I feel like Patrick is trying to tell me something. Does that mean anything?"

"There've been several studies recently done on children with PTSD. We've seen a preoccupation with words or symbols, but the tests haven't been conclusive on whether or not they're related to the trauma."

"Will he ever be able to talk about it?"

Shock flashed across the doctor's face. Jacqueline realized how Mitch's question sounded.

"Doctor, I did not kill my wife," Mitch said. "I'm not hiding anything. I want my child to get better, and I'll do whatever it takes to make that happen."

The doctor held up his hand. "Listen, Mr. Mitchell, as a doctor, my primary concern is for Patrick's well-being, not your innocence or guilt. I'm here to ensure he is mentally and physically okay. I've examined your son, and I can assure you he is physically fine."

"I'm sorry. It's just that I can't stand to think that people wonder if I killed my wife."

The doctor shrugged. "To answer your question about whether he will ever talk about that day, it depends. There's no definitive treatment for PTSD, but I've had a lot of success with exposure therapy. I'd like to try it with Patrick."

"What would it entail?"

"I've tried to establish rapport and create a very safe and controlled environment for Patrick. What we would do next is help the boy relive the frightening experience to help him work through the trauma of it. Patrick will be exposed gradually and taught relaxation methods so that he can learn to stay calm while recalling his experiences. Through this process, we'll be trying to teach him that he doesn't have to be afraid of his memories." Dr. Stavropoulos paused. "I want to be clear. There is no set time frame. There is no overnight cure. Some people are never able to articulate or even remember the event."

Mitch's knuckles turned white as he grabbed the edge of the table. "My sole concern is Patrick. Can you assure me that someday— and I don't care how long it takes—Patrick will be okay? Are there any side effects of this treatment?"

Dr. Stavropoulos met Mitch's intense gaze calmly. "What are you asking? Could he regress?"

"Yes. I want to understand what my options are." Mitch's voice wavered. He leaned forward, gripping the edge of the table as if to ground himself. "Doctor, do you have any children?"

"Yes. A boy and girl," the doctor replied, his tone measured and steady.

Mitch's eyes bore into the doctor's. "What I need to know is if this were your child, would you opt for this treatment?"

For the first time, Jacqueline finally saw some compassion in the doctor's eyes. Gone was all the medical terminology. Instead, Jacqueline saw two fathers dealing with a tragedy. She felt as if she and Mitch were holding their collective breath as they waited for the doctor's response.

"Yes, I would. We need to help Patrick deal with what he saw so he can begin to heal," the doctor said, his voice softer now.

Mitch's shoulders relaxed slightly, though tension still radiated from him. "So we should try the exposure therapy?"

"Mr. Mitchell, your firm handles investments, right?"

"Yes."

"Then I'm sure you know the answer. Just like every one of your clients wants reassurances that the investment will increase in value and make them money, so do my patients want a sure thing. I can't guarantee anything, but I'm good at what I do, and I think I can help Patrick." The doctor looked at Jacqueline. "And I don't want any pressure from you. I know Patrick could help your case, but I must treat him according to his needs, his timeline, not yours."

Jacqueline nodded. "Dr. Stavropoulos, I assure you, you will have no problems with me. But as Mr. Mitchell's lawyer, I must ask. How accurate is this exposure therapy?"

"What do you mean?"

"Is it an actual memory of what happened, or could the brain block out the true events if they are too painful or difficult to remember?"

"Do you mean could Patrick remember someone else, like let's say the bogeyman killed his mom, when in reality it was Santa Claus, because it would be too painful?"

Jacqueline wanted to smack the doctor. "Yes."

"No. I've never seen that. Instead, what I've seen is the patient being unable to retrieve the entire memory because it was too painful. For example, he could remember going upstairs, watching a show. He might be able to tell you all the specifics, like what was on, the channel, what episode. But just when you actually get to the trauma, in this case the murder, his mind refuses to go there. It's simply too painful." The doctor paused as if to let the explanation sink in. "The mind is an incredible machine."

"We understand. Just help Patrick, please," Jacqueline said. *And if it's not too much trouble, help our case*, she thought.

Chapter 59

THERE WAS NO REASON TO WAIT. WITH MITCHELL'S blessing, they were about to start the exposure therapy. The only problem was the doctor wanted to be alone with Patrick, and Mitchell insisted on being in the room. "I need to be there if he needs me," Mitchell said.

"I don't think I'm making myself clear. It won't work if you're in the room," the doctor repeated for the fifth time.

"But what if he needs me?"

"I'll call you. Again, it won't work unless it's just him and me. And Mr. Mitchell, your son should be everyone's primary concern. I need to create an environment where Patrick feels completely free to say whatever he saw."

"You mean if he thinks I killed Tiffany, he'd be afraid to say it in front of me?"

"Yes."

"But I didn't kill my wife."

"Then you won't object to waiting in the other room," the doctor said calmly.

Jacqueline broke in. "Doctor, just so we are clear. This session and all your notes are confidential under the doctor–patient privilege. Mr. Mitchell still has control over medical issues. Your opinions cannot be discussed or given to anyone, including the police, until we say so. Does everyone understand?"

With all in agreement, the doctor left to prepare for the session. The hospital staff put small cameras in the room so that Mitch and Jacqueline could watch it from next door. On the screen, they stared at the makeshift playroom. As instructed, Mitch had brought some of Patrick's things from home.

Mitchell broke the silence. "Really? Patrick is supposed to believe that this room is safe? That it's a playroom? Give me a break. He's nine. He recognizes a hospital room."

Jacqueline interjected. "Please, let the expert do his thing. Now, go, and do as the doctor instructed."

Mitch met Patrick in his hospital room and wheeled him to the playroom. Away from the hospital room that had been his home for weeks, Patrick's face grew pale. "Patrick, you remember Dr. Stavropoulos, right?"

Patrick nodded.

Mitch handed Patrick his favorite stuffed animal. "Here's Bear. He's going to be with you when you talk to Dr. Stavropoulos."

"Dad, what's going on? I don't want to be here. I want to play my games."

Mitchell took his hand. "Patrick, it's okay. You and the doctor have been working together, right?"

As if on cue, Dr. Stavropoulos appeared, smiling brightly. He bent down closer to Patrick's height. "Hey, Patrick. It's great to see you again. Tell Dad that you're allowed to call me Dr. S.," he said in a conspiratorial tone.

Patrick smiled.

Dr. Stavropoulos pointed to some figurines in the room. "I know they're not as exciting as Xbox, but do you mind if you and I stay in here for a few minutes and talk? I promise your dad is just on the other side of the door. Is that okay?"

Patrick nodded his head.

Mitchell reluctantly got up to leave. He kissed Patrick on the top of the head, like he had when Patrick was a little boy. Patrick didn't move or respond. He just sat there.

Mitchell joined Jacqueline in the adjoining room. "He'll be okay," Jacqueline reassured.

"I hope so."

Mitchell watched with amazement as Dr. Stavropoulos started the interview and got Patrick to smile. He was no longer the stuffy doctor with the fancy degrees. His mannerisms changed. He was playful and childlike. Mitch noticed that the doctor had even changed out of his fancy suit into khakis and a polo shirt. *No wonder he's as successful as they say*, Mitch thought as the doctor created a fun, safe environment for Patrick.

After what seemed like forever, the doctor began the serious part of the process. "Now, Patrick. I want to talk to you about what happened at your house."

"I don't want to talk about it. I want to play a game."

"We can play a game later, I promise. Patrick, look at me." The doctor waited until Patrick looked up. "I want you to know that you will have a lot of time to play games and have fun with your friends like you used to. Would you like that?"

Patrick nodded. Mitchell noticed that his son almost smiled.

"Good. Now, I need you to talk to me about what happened so that I can help you. Would you like that?" Patrick turned away from the doctor.

The doctor moved around so that he was in front of the boy. He held Patrick's hands. "I promise you that I can help you. It won't be as scary if you talk about it."

Mitchell watched as Patrick, with intense focus, began building the LEGO set, deliberately avoiding the doctor's gaze. "No, I can't. It's so scary."

"Okay, let's not talk about what happened to your mom. Let's talk about what happened before. You weren't feeling well that day, right?"

Patrick seemed to calm down. "Right. Mom said I didn't have to go to school because I felt sick."

"Did your mommy make you chicken soup?"

"She said she would, but then she forgot. She told me to get in bed and try to sleep. Then she came upstairs and kissed me. She was sad. She was crying. I told her not to cry. I told her I felt better. Mommy laughed at that. She told me I was so funny. She called me her beautiful boy. I told her to stop. I'm not beautiful. Only girls are beautiful."

"Your mom sounds like a great mom."

"She is. She even said I could play my video games in my room. I never got to play on school days. She said Dad would be home soon, and I could play with him. But she said I had to stay in my room until she came to get me."

"What happened next?"

"I fell asleep." Patrick opened his eyes. "I fell asleep, and my mom came up in my room and shut the TV off. But I heard her. She gave me Bear and stuck him under my arm." Patrick leaned over to whisper in the doctor's ear. "My mom loves Bear almost as much as I do. She said he was like a second son."

The doctor took Bear from Patrick's lap. "Is this Bear?"

Patrick beamed proudly. "Yep, that's him. I love him. Don't tell my friends because I'm too old for him. But when I'm sick, I like him. He's like a pillow."

"I can see why." The doctor gave Bear back to Patrick. "What happened next?"

"I can't talk about it."

"Why not?"

"Because I didn't listen."

"Patrick, you didn't do anything wrong. You need to know that."

"Yes, I did. I was bad."

Dr. Stavropoulos looked at Patrick. "Why do you think you were bad?"

"Because Mom told me to stay in my room. She told me not to leave. I didn't listen. Mom hates when I don't listen." Patrick was crying now. Mitch moved closer to the door dividing him from his son.

"Patrick, it's okay. You left your room, right?"

Patrick nodded. "I heard a crash. And I wanted to make sure Mom was okay. But I didn't want her mad or to make her cry. So I sat there."

"Patrick, tell me what happened. No one is going to be mad at you."

The child looked around the room. Then he pulled on the doctor's sleeve so that he would bring his ear closer to Patrick's mouth. Mitchell could barely hear him whisper. "Mom said Dad was coming. I heard a voice. I yelled out, 'Dad? Is that you?'"

Patrick hid his face in the doctor's shirt. The doctor held him. "Patrick, you are okay. It's safe in here. No one is going to hurt you."

Patrick just shook his head, his face buried in the doctor's chest. "But they were shouting."

"Who was shouting?"

"Them."

"Did you see them?"

Patrick just nodded.

The doctor pressed on. "Where were you?"

Patrick hid his face in the doctor's lap, covering his ears with his arms. "I was on the steps. I knew Mom would be mad. She hates when I don't listen, and she told me not to leave the room. But they were yelling." Patrick started to cry. He leaned into the doctor for comfort, shielding his mind from the ugliness.

"Patrick, I'm here. No one can hurt you, I promise. Please tell me what happened next."

Patrick shook his head. His voice changed, growing deeper, as if mimicking an adult. "No, no, I can't. No, I can't."

Patrick grabbed the doctor's shirt as if he wanted to crawl inside it for protection. "No, Daddy! Don't hurt Mommy!!" Patrick screamed just before he collapsed.

Chapter 60

JACQUELINE HUNG UP THE PHONE FOR THE THIRD time. She had been calling Mitchell since he left the hospital, but she couldn't find him anywhere. Not knowing where else to turn, she decided to go back to her office and see if she could make sense of it all. But she couldn't concentrate. Patrick's words kept haunting her. She knew if the police were somehow able to interview Patrick, it would be over. But she refused to believe Mitch did it.

Lisa met her at the door. "How did it go? Was the exposure therapy helpful?"

"Not exactly." Jacqueline filled her in on the devastating news as they sat in the war room, staring at her Think Board. "Lisa, what are we missing? I know there is some reason why Tiffany put that picture of Natalie Kluge in his bear."

They sat in silence. The security footage from the garage confirmed that Katherine did leave the office early, so that gave her opportunity. Could Katherine have killed her own sister? Was she the alleged mistress? Jacqueline was sure that she was hiding something, but what? And what was the Natalie connection? Jacqueline thought about the other voice Mitchell had heard as a little boy. Could there have been someone else in the Kluge house that night? Was Mitch's dad set up? Was it Dr. Fitzgerald?

The phone rang, breaking into Jacqueline's thoughts. Billy. "What did you find out?"

"You were right, Jacqueline. Dr. Fitzgerald did have a malpractice case. I emailed you the details."

Jacqueline listened to Billy for a minute, then ended the call. "Lisa, I don't care what you have to do. Find every property that Dr. Fitzgerald owns. We need him. Now."

Chapter 61

MITCHELL SCURRIED OUT OF THE HOSPITAL BEFORE anyone had time to close their mouths after Patrick's shocking confession. Mitch had to get away. He couldn't face any of them. Especially Jacqueline.

He'd set his escape plan in motion weeks ago. On the way over, he instructed his corporate lawyers to have everything ready. He'd received confirmation of their completeness. Now he just had one thing left to do. When he devised his plan, he never expected to use it. But his past required it. For the umpteenth time in his life, he was glad he was a planner.

His heart broke as he signed the documents. He loved Patrick more than anything, and the thought of never seeing those gorgeous blue eyes again almost broke him. But he made a promise that, unlike him as a child, Patrick would always have the best. And he intended to keep that promise. Patrick, his pride and joy, was no longer a Mitchell.

You don't have to worry anymore, little guy. I won't ever hurt you again, Mitchell said to himself as he entered the offices of Harrison Investments for the last time.

Chapter 62

KATHERINE SAT AT HER DESK, STUNNED BY MITCH'S request. She had prayed and dreamed about this moment. God, she had even done the unthinkable to achieve this moment. To win. But instead of being elated, his demand crushed her.

She shut her eyes to think. There had to be another way. She was a Harrison, and for the first time in her miserable life, she was determined to act like one. Harrisons always got their way, and it was about time she got hers. But how? How could she make things right? Could it possibly have been only a few weeks ago when life seemed so good?

She looked at her wedding picture. Eric's beautiful face smiling back at her, with Mitchell and Tiffany at their side. Eric's eyes appeared to adore her. But Tiffany stood directly next to her. Were those loving glances really meant for Tiffany? Was Eric declaring his love for her, yet longing for Tiffany? And then there was Mitch. In his perceptive way, had he known about Tiffany's insecurities? Her need to be front and center? Is that how the bond among them disintegrated so quickly? Did they ever really have a true bond?

She shut her eyes, and the image of Eric holding Tiffany barged in, destroying all the happy memories. His strong, muscular arms wrapped around her so tight, just the way Eric had held Katherine once. Tiffany's signature long blond mane draped over his shoulders. *Damn Tiffany. Why did she have to ruin everything? She had it all— the most handsome, wealthiest man in town, a beautiful child, a beautiful home. Why couldn't she have just left my husband alone?*

Katherine made up her mind. She, too, took in the office for the last time.

Chapter 63

FINDING THE ADDRESS FOR THE POCONOS PROPERTY that Dr. Fitzgerald owned was the easy part. It was getting there that took time. As Lisa drove up to the fishing cabin, she was surprised by the scene.

Gone was the serenity. In its place, crime scene tape surrounded the lake. Lisa scanned the area, her eyes landing on the youngest, and thus most inexperienced, officer. She decided to use her pregnancy to her advantage. "Excuse me..." She approached him, her voice soft and trembling. "I'm looking for a friend of mine, Dr. Marc Fitzgerald? Isn't this his home?"

The officer glanced around nervously, clearly searching for someone more seasoned to take over. Lisa knew she only had a few seconds. Placing her hands on her stomach, she let her shoulders slump and her eyes droop in a convincing display of fatigue and desperation. "Please, sir," she implored, her voice tinged with worry and exhaustion. ""I drove all the way from the city. What's happened?"

The officer hesitated, clearly torn between protocol and compassion. "I'm sorry to inform you, miss, but Dr. Fitzgerald died of carbon monoxide poisoning. Faulty heater. It's been really cold up here, and he probably hasn't been here that often. Didn't have it serviced." His sergeant called him over sharply, breaking his moment of indiscretion. "Sorry. I shouldn't have said all that. I have to go."

Lisa thanked the officer and headed back to her car. *A faulty heater? I don't think so*, she thought as she grabbed her phone.

Chapter 64

AFTER LISA FILLED HER IN ON DR. FITZGERALD'S death, Jacqueline decided to find out what had really happened to him.

"Where is he?" Jacqueline demanded as she barged into police headquarters, finding only Grady at her desk.

"I'm sorry, I don't know where Detective O'Neill is, but…" Grady trailed off as Dan appeared by the elevator holding a file.

"Hello to you, too, Counselor," Dan said. "I get that you're stressed, but you have no right to demand anything. Can we be civil please? Like, 'Hello, Detective. Do you have a minute?'"

"You know I don't have time for this," Jacqueline said. "Is that Dr. Fitzgerald's autopsy report?"

"Why do you ask?"

"Because you and I both know that it is just too convenient that Dr. Fitzgerald, who my firm has been looking for, suddenly dies from carbon monoxide poisoning. Now are you going to hand it over?"

"Well, technically it's not related to your case." Dan waved the report, toying with Jacqueline. "But I may share it if you give me something in exchange."

"Like what?"

"I want a date to interview the kid."

"No way. Not yet," Jacqueline said, standing firm. "But I'll divulge a bombshell if you agree to let me see that report now."

Dan took a sip of his coffee. "It better be good."

"My team just found out that Dr. Fitzgerald and Ryan Mitchell's birth mother, Natalie Kluge, worked together at Penn Central Hospital."

Dan kept his promise, handing Jacqueline the report. "I'm not sure how that helps since the doctor is now dead, and it wasn't carbon monoxide poisoning, as they first assumed. The medical examiner ruled it a homicide. Apparently, his wife went up to find him after he wasn't answering her calls. They found him quick enough, so they were able to run some blood tests. Toxicology report found traces of succinylcholine chloride—the drug normally used to paralyze patients during surgery—in his blood. But too much of it can be lethal."

Jacqueline's face lit up. "Wait. So that drug also could make it look like carbon monoxide poisoning, and if blood tests aren't done immediately, there would be no evidence?"

Dan nodded. "Exactly. Succinylcholine chloride is metabolized quickly, so if they hadn't drawn Dr. Fitzgerald's blood in time, we might never have known."

Jacqueline had another thought. "And that's more evidence that my client didn't kill his wife. You know Mr. Mitchell couldn't have killed Fitzgerald because he was here. He has an ankle bracelet on him."

Dan held up his hands. "Hold it a minute. It means nothing of the sort. Mitchell could have an accomplice, or it could be completely unrelated to Mrs. Mitchell's murder."

But Jacqueline was already running for the elevator. She had an idea. But she needed to find Mitch.

Chapter 65

DAN AND GRADY WATCHED JACQUELINE LEAVE.

"Why didn't you tell her what else we found?" Grady asked.

Dan shrugged. "Because she didn't ask." He grabbed his jacket from the back of his chair. "Grady, let's go. I want to follow her. She's planning something, and I want to drop a bombshell of my own."

Chapter 66

JACQUELINE RETURNED TO HER OFFICE, PUSHING aside her exhaustion. She had to revisit something she read earlier. They were on the brink of a breakthrough, but that meant the killer should be getting nervous too. The revelation that Dr. Fitzgerald's death wasn't an accident had given them an edge, but it was only a matter of time before the killer realized they were closing in. Fitzgerald had to be connected to Tiffany's death. Tiffany had seen him right before she died. Moreover, Fitzgerald had signed Preston Westerfer's death certificate, right around the election, and Harrison Investments had funded Fitzgerald's research. Jacqueline needed to uncover the link between Westerfer and Fitzgerald. But she also needed to find Mitch. *Damn you, Mitchell. Where are you?*

Jacqueline rubbed her temples, feeling a headache coming on. She grabbed the Tylenol from her top drawer. She should go home and sleep like the rest of the team. Or at least take her medicine. She felt her pendant. She had her backup if necessary. But her need for a clear head outweighed her need for medicine. Plus her inability to find Mitch swirled around in her head, making sleep all but impossible. She felt the sand in the hourglass vanishing.

Her office door flew open.

"Lisa, is that you?" Jacqueline turned.

"No, it's me." Mitch's impressive build filled the doorway.

"Mitch, where have you been? I've been calling you."

"I know. I'm sorry."

"It doesn't matter. I'm turning myself in."

"Are you kidding? You're going to give up just like that?"

Mitch pulled out her client chair and sat. His face did not change.

Neither did his resolve. Instead, it penetrated the air, making Jacqueline feel like a child wanting to throw a tantrum yet knowing it would have no effect on the parent. He removed some papers from his chest pocket and laid them on her desk. "It's over. I've asked Katherine to adopt Patrick. I've just gotten a call that Patrick is doing much better and they want to release him. Marie is picking him up now. I couldn't see him. I can't cause him any more pain. I'm turning myself in."

He mirrored the shell of the person Jacqueline had become when she lost John and Jack. Now she understood. In that moment when Patrick said those words, he killed his father. "Mitch, you can't do this. You have to fight. I have an idea."

"No, Jacqueline, we can't. Patrick is afraid of me now. And for whatever reason, he thinks I killed his mother. I won't have the prosecution interrogate him or use him and scar him for life. He needs to go home and forget about everything, including me. What if something worse happens to him? I'd rather be in jail than let that happen."

Jacqueline moved to the other client chair, forcing Mitch to face her. "What I heard Patrick say was 'No, Daddy,' and then 'Don't hurt Mommy.' It was two different thoughts."

Pain showed in Mitch's eyes. "Don't make this any harder than it already is. Did you not see the fear in my son's eyes? Do you think I want to give up on my child? My life?"

Now it was Jacqueline's turn to be angry. "No, I don't. The Ryan Mitchell I know doesn't give up on anything, especially his son."

"Jacqueline, I'm done. I'm not in the mood for lawyer tricks. You may be able to manipulate words, but I'm not about to play games with my son's life, his mental stability."

"I'm not asking you to play games. I'm asking you to trust me. You're too close to this. A few days ago, you learned about your own mother's death. You've convinced yourself that you somehow have bad genes, and that all of a sudden after thirty years of working hard and accomplishing all your dreams, you cracked and became like the father that you barely knew. I don't buy it. I won't buy it. Your mother's murder is the key to all of this."

"What are you talking about?"

Jacqueline couldn't look at him. "I don't know yet. But I have an idea. I don't have time to explain, but I need your help."

"Well as much as I would like to bet on your instincts, our time is up. And don't tell me it's not. That asshole detective is going to interview Patrick any minute, and I won't let it happen. I won't do it to him."

"Maybe I can..."

"Stop. Like you said, I'm the client. You have to do what I say. It's over."

"Listen to me for five minutes. Your life is worth that, right?" She looked at Mitchell with determination in her eyes. Jacqueline had one last argument. "Okay, think about this. Let's say the doctor is right, and the memory of traumatic events can cause a person to snap. Maybe seeing Tiffany murdered brought back those horrible memories for you, and that would explain your blackout."

Mitchell tilted his head. "Now you're scaring me. Are you trying to get me the death penalty?"

Jacqueline continued. "No, listen. That explains why you can't remember those precious few minutes, and why you didn't call 911. If you follow the prosecution's assumed theory, you killed Tiffany because of some alleged adultery she discovered. But your memory of the affair, if there was one, would not be blocked. According to the police, they have an anonymous text as proof you were unfaithful. So, did you have an affair? Fight with Tiffany about it?"

"Jacqueline, you know I didn't. I never had an affair. But we have no evidence to refute the affair either. I was in those hotels at the times it says I was. But I was alone. I swear. Working. I'm sorry, Jacqueline, I know you are trying, but we have nothing. And I won't sacrifice Patrick. He's the only thing I did right. Now will you come with me to turn myself in, or do I have to do this by myself?"

Jacqueline decided to come clean about her plan. It wasn't iron-clad, but Mitch wasn't giving her a choice. "Since you're hell-bent on turning yourself in, we're going to try something first."

Chapter 67

"I'M NOT SOLD ON THE IDEA, BUT GOING TO JAIL ISN'T appealing either, so I guess I have nothing to lose," Mitch said. He placed all the required calls. He told the Westerfers he needed them to come to his house for Patrick's sake. "That's the one and only reason anyone of them would even consider this."

Jacqueline was convinced that the deaths of Dr. Fitzgerald and Natalie Kluge held the key to unraveling the case, though the exact connection still eluded her. With a sense of urgency pressing down on her, she resolved to orchestrate an intense confrontation, hoping that the pressure would force someone to confess and reveal what they knew.

"All set?" Jacqueline asked Mitch as they waited in his private office. She looked down at her ringing phone and ignored Dan's call for the third time.

Mitch nodded. "This is a big gamble. I hope you know what you're doing."

Jacqueline nodded back, radiating unwavering confidence despite the nagging doubt in the back of her mind. She was certain Dr. Fitzgerald was involved, but the specifics remained frustratingly out of reach. Ignoring her reservations, she forged ahead, since Mitch had forced her hand.

They proceeded to the great room.

The setting had clearly unnerved everyone. Tiffany's blood still stained the carpet. Victoria Westerfer sat facing the window. Gone were any type of niceties and appearances. Victoria despised Mitch, and she didn't care who knew. Tyler Hines stood behind her, in protective mode. Jacqueline noticed Katherine and Eric were on the opposite side, holding hands, sitting on the edge of their chairs. Upon further inspection, Jacqueline realized Eric was pressing his hand down on Katherine's knee, preventing her from rising. Not surprisingly, only Harrison charged at them.

"What the hell is going on?" Harrison Westerfer demanded, jumping up from his seat. Still dressed in his stuffy sports coat with the leather elbow patches from an afternoon of trapshooting, he launched into a tirade like a spoiled child. Gone was the smug face of the country-club kid. "And why isn't Mitchell behind bars? I came here solely because of Patrick, but when we are done here, I'm going to march up to the commissioner's office and demand your head on a platter. You have about five seconds to explain. You interrupted a very competitive shooting match."

"Mr. Westerfer, if you'll give me a minute. Please sit down," Jacqueline said.

Harrison wagged his finger at Mitch, who looked like he wanted to break it off. "Here's what you don't understand. See, you work for *us*. It's *our* company, always has been, not the other way around. How dare you summon us like servants." Harrison placed his face inches from Mitch, flushed red.

Mitch stood still, facing off.

"Mitch, don't," Jacqueline reminded him. "If Mr. Westerfer will please sit down, I'll explain."

Harrison stood in place, his nostrils flaring.

Tyler Hines grabbed him by the arm, leading him to a seat. "Please, Harrison, this is very disturbing for your mother. Let's hear what the attorney has to say."

Harrison was not finished. "Do you have any idea of the embarrassment I just faced among my colleagues at the club?" He looked at his mother. "Did you call the DA like I told you? How is he allowing this to happen?"

Before Victoria could answer, Jacqueline attempted to get

control of the situation. "Everyone, please. Let me speak. I'll tell you some important discoveries out of courtesy to the family, and mainly to Patrick, but I won't have a shouting match." Jacqueline knew the clock was ticking.

No one responded. Harrison grunted as he moved toward the window.

Jacqueline began. "Mr. Mitchell's neighbor has come forth with some information." Jacqueline turned to face Katherine. "Mrs. Conceillo, would you like to tell the group your involvement, or should I?"

As all eyes turned to Katherine, she appeared to wilt instantly, and the floodgates opened.

Mitch forced her to look at him. "Katherine, tell us what?"

Eric stepped in front of Mitch, his expression tense. "Ms. Stone, what the hell is going on? You can't do this. My wife has nothing to say." He turned to Mitch, his voice firm but apologetic. "I'm sorry, but we are not saying anything until we have retained counsel. Katherine is not going to be your scapegoat."

"This is outrageous. My sister didn't kill Tiffany," Harrison shouted.

"That is correct," Jacqueline said. "Your sister Katherine didn't kill Mrs. Mitchell. But Katherine was at the scene moments before. We have an eyewitness, a neighbor, Mrs. Hastings, who saw Mrs. Conceillo leaving the house just minutes before Mr. Mitchell arrived."

Jacqueline looked directly at Katherine. "And we know that Katherine sent the anonymous text to Tiffany. Katherine had access to Mitch's calendar and his schedule. And if I'm not mistaken, Mrs. Conceillo believed Mrs. Mitchell was having an affair with you," Jacqueline said, pointing directly at Eric.

The room tensed as Jacqueline approached Eric.

"Which I assume, Mr. Conceillo, you can clear up for all of us," Jacqueline said, pausing for emphasis.

Eric's eyes widened and his face flushed. He opened his mouth as if to defend himself and then stopped. Instead of speaking, he took a step closer to his wife. His silence was telling. *He's hiding something, but not an affair with Tiffany.*

Jacqueline continued. "Because Katherine thought Tiffany was having an affair with Eric, she sent the anonymous note as an act of revenge, falsely claiming that Mr. Mitchell was cheating on Tiffany. It was a calculated move intended to make Tiffany experience the pain of betrayal. I suspect that years of being compared to Tiffany and feeling inadequate finally came to the surface."

Jacqueline's words hung in the air, charged with tension. "But once Katherine set everything in motion, regret consumed her. She rushed over to stop her sister from confronting Mitch."

Jacqueline pressed on. "But after telling Tiffany the truth, Mrs. Conceillo didn't like the way her sister responded. That's when Katherine threw the vase. The vase has her fingerprints on it, by the way.

"Tiffany didn't care about the alleged affair. She had something much more important on her mind that day."

Jacqueline let the weight of her revelation hang in the air, hoping to provoke a reaction. She paced around, looking at the suspects, before stopping at Victoria, who abruptly stood.

"Tiffany knew a secret. A secret that involved the now-deceased Dr. Marc Fitzgerald and your family," Jacqueline said, her voice steady but charged with implication. She paused, her eyes scanning the room, baiting someone to crack under the pressure and reveal how Fitzgerald was connected to Tiffany's death.

It wasn't working.

Jacqueline pressed on. "See, Mrs. Westerfer, when we discovered Dr. Fitzgerald didn't die of natural causes, we also found that someone went to serious lengths to make us think he did." Jacqueline held up some papers. "As you will see from the medical examiner's report, his death was made to look like an accident. And that got us thinking about another person who conveniently died. Your husband, Mr. Preston Westerfer. And Dr. Fitzgerald signed off on this death certificate, correct?"

No response. Victoria remained stoic, but Jacqueline saw the flicker of fear in her eyes. She wasn't breaking, not yet.

"The late Dr. Fitzgerald was keeping your secret, wasn't he?"

Jacqueline watched as Victoria recoiled with each word, moving closer to the window as if it could free her from confinement. Although she shook her head, her whispered denial lacked credence.

While everyone stared at Victoria, Jacqueline sent a quick text on her phone. She continued speaking. "You realized the secret is going to come out. You can't hide it forever. Your husband didn't die of natural causes, did he? Instead, Tiffany figured out that someone murdered her father because your husband wanted Mr. Mitchell, not your son…"

Before Jacqueline could continue, the doorbell rang, and Dan and Grady came bursting in. Grady was holding up a black bag.

"Sorry to interrupt this little family gathering, but there have been some developments," Dan said.

Harrison looked relieved. "Thank God you're here. Please tell me you've come to arrest this man." He pointed at Mitchell.

Dan ignored Harrison. "Actually, as a result of some new evidence, we're dropping all charges against Mr. Mitchell."

A gasp echoed through the room. Jacqueline tried to hide her own surprise.

Harrison spoke first. "This is outrageous. What are you talking about? And what the hell is in that black bag?"

Grady lifted the satchel. "This old thing?"

"It may look like a jewelry bag," Dan said, "but it holds something much more priceless and relevant. Mr. Westerfer, would you care to explain?"

Victoria's façade melted and only a grieving mother remained. "Please stop. I saw that monster kill my daughter with my own eyes. Where is the commissioner? I demand to see him," she cried, black lines of mascara streaming down her face.

Jacqueline almost felt sorry for the normally elegant woman. Almost.

Harrison suddenly charged at Dan. "Are you a complete idiot? It's him," he screamed, pointing at Mitchell. "He's responsible for destroying our family. For stealing my company." Fury all over his face, Harrison turned to Dan. "How much is he paying you?"

Victoria jumped in between the men. "Please stop."

Tyler stepped toward Victoria, obviously outraged. "This is preposterous. Why are you putting Mrs. Westerfer through this?"

The invitees were unraveling just as planned. Dan turned to Mitchell. "And you, of all people, are not going to believe what we found."

Dan pointed to Grady as she held up the black bag. Victoria almost fainted as Grady revealed its contents.

Chapter 68

BILLY DECIDED TO GIVE UP AND GET SOME REST. HE'D tried several times to reach Jacqueline, but she wasn't answering her cell phone. He couldn't remember a time when she didn't. Lisa had filled him in on their boss's plan, but he was anxious to speak to Jacqueline herself, because boy, did he have this one wrong. He rarely bet, but his gut had told him the Maggie Brown litigation was somehow relevant. It was just too coincidental that Mitch's mom was her nurse and that it involved Penn Central and Dr. Marc Fitzgerald. Yet if Jacqueline was able to prove Mr. Mitchell's innocence and get them to drop all the charges against him, he didn't need to know that his mom most likely was involved in an accidental baby switch. Wouldn't exactly help their client relations.

But that wasn't his department. Totally Jacqueline's call. Besides, it was over thirty years ago, and back then hospitals had far fewer security standards and protocols around deliveries of babies. It was only after numerous lawsuits that hospitals had instituted security bracelets for the infants and their parents. Although it was a shame it happened. That baby mix-up discovery could go in a drawer, or a fire, for all Billy cared.

Billy left the file in the middle of Jacqueline's desk as he closed the office for the night. As he locked the door, he didn't hear the phone ringing.

Chapter 69

HARRISON FELT THE SWEAT DRIPPING ON HIS FORE-head. They couldn't possibly know he'd killed his father. No way. He'd been meticulous about wiping his prints off his father's nitro-glycerin pill bottle, carefully tidying everything up in the room after their last big fight.

But doubt gnawed at him. Maybe they had something on him after all. Why did they keep bringing up his father's death? Years of drug use had left his brain in an almost constant state of paranoia. Damn, he shouldn't have smoked so much this afternoon at the club. Harrison watched as the detective toyed with them, holding what he claimed was the gun that shot Tiffany. Were they going to try to pin that on him? Harrison's mind spun out of control looking for ways to get out of the room. He was suffocating.

That bitch of an attorney broke through his panic. "Is that the murder weapon used to kill Mrs. Mitchell?"

Stay calm, he told himself. "What are you idiots doing? Mitchell killed my sister. What is this show? What are you holding? I don't have time for this. Take him back into custody."

The female officer looked at him. "Yes and no. It is the murder weapon, but it doesn't have Mr. Mitchell's prints on it."

"Of course, it doesn't," Victoria said. "Mitchell's not a complete fool. But he did it. Please tell me that is what these theatrics are about. Please get me a water, my dear."

Harrison stood frozen in disbelief as Tyler crossed the room to the small mini fridge. *Damn it, Tyler, do something! What the hell are you doing?*

The officer was unrelenting. "Mrs. Westerfer, it's over. We know Dr. Fitzgerald didn't die of natural causes. The late Dr. Fitzgerald was keeping a family secret, wasn't he?"

Harrison watched in horror as his mother just stood there, speechless. She actually looked afraid of these imbeciles. Not Victoria Harrison Westerfer. Not his strong mother. *Damn it, Mother, remember who we are.*

Harrison felt paralyzed. His world was crashing down around him. Did Dr. Fitzgerald uncover the true cause of his father's death? Panic surged as he struggled to recall. Who was Dr. Fitzgerald again? He wasn't going down without a fight.

No, I won't let Mitchell win.

The inquisition of his mother was too much for him. "You animal, you did this to us," Harrison screamed, pointing a gun at Mitch.

He barely registered Tyler rushing toward him.

It was too late.

The gun went off.

The gunshot echoed in his ears.

Chapter 70

ONCE AGAIN, VICTORIA WAS IN MITCH'S HOUSE WITH her dead child. This time, however, she was surrounded by family as Tyler, Katherine, and Eric tended to her care. Grady's precise shot had killed Harrison Westerfer instantly. Uniformed police had responded from all areas, and the room was overcrowded, but completely secured.

Emergency personnel tended to Mitch's injury, where Harrison's bullet pierced his left shoulder. A few more inches, and he wouldn't have been so lucky. He most likely needed surgery, but he was going to live. But he refused to leave until he got answers.

Mitch unleashed his anger on Dan. "What the hell kind of show are you running here? You wanted to push him to the brink. Well, congratulations. Are you satisfied now?" He pointed to Victoria sobbing on the floor.

Dan ran his hand through his hair, looking weary. "Wasn't exactly the plan." He took a deep breath. "According to Tiffany's datebook, we know she recently visited Dr. Fitzgerald. We believe that somehow Tiffany discovered that Harrison killed his father Preston Westerfer to stop him from appointing you as CEO at the last minute, Mr. Mitchell. We surmise that Harrison assumed that once Preston was out of the way, the company would automatically go to him. Yet, when that didn't happen, he began plotting his revenge against you.

"Since Dr. Fitzgerald signed the death certificate, Tiffany went to see him. When Harrison found out Tiffany was talking to the doctor, he feared she was going to expose him and killed her. We received an anonymous tip from someone at the club that Harrison, in a drunken stupor, had been bragging about killing his sister. We are still searching for this witness but they correctly led us to Harrison's locker at the club, where we found the murder weapon with his fingerprints all over it. What remains unresolved is whether he acted alone when he killed Dr. Fitzgerald."

Mitchell ran a hand through his hair, troubled. Tyler stepped closer, his expression concerned. "Mitch, do you want me to go with you to the hospital?" He asked quietly.

Mitchell shook his head, managing a small, appreciative smile. "Thank you, Tyler. I'll be fine. But will you check in with Marie? She's watching Patrick, and I don't want them to be worried."

DAN AND JACQUELINE STEPPED OUT OF EARSHOT OF the family.

"Do you really believe Harrison killed his sister? It still doesn't make sense. Don't you think this is all too convenient?"

"Jacqueline, stop. For once, be happy. It was a clear case of self-preservation."

Jacqueline shook her head, still not convinced. "I just can't believe Mitch's mother's death had nothing to do with it."

"Jacqueline, it's over. The evidence is clear. We know there was foul play with Fitzgerald and we found the gun in Harrison's locker. Fitzgerald must have confessed to Tiffany about keeping Harrison's secret and she was going to go to the police. He had to stop them both. Now, please. Accept the win and go get some rest."

Jacqueline interrupted. "Dan, I just don't agree. I think there's more to this case."

Grady tapped Dan on the shoulder. "Captain's on the line. And he's not happy."

Dan looked at Jacqueline. "Jax, I'm sorry. I have work to do. Go home."

Chapter 71

"COME ON, BOSS, WE SHOULD GO OUT AND CELE-brate," Lisa said.

"Absolutely not. You stay at home and take care of that newest member of ours. You need your rest. You did an amazing job. I'm very proud of you and Billy."

"Only if you promise that you're going home as well?"

"Of course," Jacqueline lied as she opened the office door.

"What's going on? I can hear it in your voice."

Jacqueline headed straight for the war room. "I don't know, Lisa. Something about Harrison as the killer doesn't sit right with me. Katherine's behavior and Patrick's reaction when he saw his aunt finally made sense—he must have seen her at the scene the day of the murder." Jacqueline hesitated, unsure how much to reveal to Lisa.

"But...?" Lisa waited.

"I can't shake this feeling. I was convinced that photo of Mitch's mom was Tiffany's dying message. Like she was trying to tell us something. And now, there's the death of Dr. Fitzgerald." Jacqueline realized Lisa was still on the line.

"I'm sorry, Lisa. Go get some rest. Enjoy the night off."

Jacqueline fell into her chair, even more perplexed. "Come on, Think Board, what am I missing?" she muttered, glaring at the empty room as if the walls could answer her. None of it made sense. She didn't buy the story about Harrison being the killer—there had to be more. But what? And, how did Tiffany discover that Harrison killed their father? What did she know?

Jacqueline replayed the interrogation with Marie, scouring every word, every pause. Mitch's past, Tiffany's obsession with it—there was something there. But what? And then there was the Scaggs case, Dr. Fitzgerald's involvement. "What the hell am I missing?" It was right there, just beyond her grasp, taunting her.

Jacqueline didn't like any loose ends, and the present solution had plenty of them. Her determination to figure it out fueled her. She cracked open one of the files Billy had left on her desk. A sticky note on top of the file read *Call me*. She glanced at her watch. Not at this hour. Exhausted from the emotional roller coaster, she started a pot of coffee. Her watch alarm sounded, reminding her to take her medicine. No way. She couldn't afford to slow down. The answer existed somewhere in that room at Mitch's house.

Armed with coffee, Jacqueline noticed she had a message on the office line. She hit play. "Huh, this is Georgeanna from Alabama. I just wanted to tell Billy that I remembered what Scaggs was singing. I don't know if this is helpful. But anyway, y'all know that song, 'Thank heavens for little girls, they grow up in the most unusual way'? Well, Scaggs kept singing 'Thank heavens for little boys...' Not sure if it means anything. Anyway, hope that helps. Bye now."

As Jacqueline grappled with what in the world that might mean, her phone rang.

Chapter 72

MITCH WASN'T SURPRISED WHEN SHE ANSWERED ON the first ring.

"How are you feeling?" she asked him.

"I'm surprised you answered. I was hoping you were home sleeping," Mitch said, ignoring her question.

"Not exactly. Are you okay?"

"Yes. I'm waiting for the doctors. I'm hoping if I annoy them enough, they'll let me leave soon."

"Great. Is there anything you need?"

Mitch hesitated. "Well, I just wanted to thank you for everything and, uh, to apologize."

"Please don't," Jacqueline said, almost too quickly. "Anything else?"

Mitch decided to tell Jacqueline his plan. "I'm going to call Katherine."

"I don't think it's a good idea. She shouldn't talk to you. She may be facing charges for interfering with a criminal investigation. You could compromise her case."

Mitch hadn't thought about that. "Jacqueline, I just need to see her and understand why she did what she did."

"That's your decision. And hers."

"Thanks. By the way, where are you? Please don't tell me you're in the office?"

"No, I'm at home. I'm just finishing up a few things. Listen, why don't I come see you in a little bit?"

She's lying. Mitch could hear it in her voice. "Okay, sure. Take your time."

A nervous laugh on the other end. "Okay, thanks. Gotta run."

"Sure. I'll see you later," Mitch said to a dead phone. He looked at his visitor. "That was strange. Jacqueline just lied to me. She's not letting it go. She doesn't buy that Harrison killed Tiffany."

Chapter 73

JACQUELINE JOLTED AWAKE, SHOCKED THAT SHE had actually fallen asleep. How could she let that happen? The Mitchell case—its facts, loose threads, and unanswered questions—lay scattered in front of her, taunting her exhaustion. Yet, she wasn't ready to confide in Mitch. She had to figure this out. After all, she didn't know if it had anything to do with Tiffany's murder. But, the answer had to be there, buried somewhere in the chaos.

Jacqueline grabbed the Penn Central file from the discovery pile. She knew the date of the baby mix-up seemed familiar. She looked at her Think Board with all the different suspects. All their essential information. Hoping the connection stared back at her. Mitch's mom died one week after Amanda Brown was born. She leafed through the file Billy had brought from Alabama. The records confirmed what Jacqueline feared—Mitch's mom was the obstetrics nurse on duty that night. Her name was right next to Dr. Fitzgerald's as the attending physician on the hospital records for the deliveries of Amanda Brown *and* Harrison Westerfer.

Could Mitch's mom have been responsible for the mix-up? What had Tiffany learned? The baby mix-up was never made public since the record was sealed when they settled, so what damage could it have done to the hospital? Even if Natalie was responsible for the switch, it would have to be a mistake. Clearly, Mitch's mom wouldn't...

What if the mix-up wasn't an accident at all? What if someone arranged for the Westerfers to get a boy? Mitch said Victoria was anxious to learn the sex of the baby when Tiffany was pregnant with Patrick.

Jacqueline laid all the pieces out on the table, putting them in chronological order.

The baby switch occurs. Victoria gets Maggie Brown's son. Accident or on purpose? Natalie Kluge is Maggie Brown's nurse. Dr. Fitzgerald delivers both babies. Victoria gets the son she always wanted.

Mitch's father allegedly killed his mother a week later.

Dr. Fitzgerald becomes the chief of obstetrics and makes his millions with the licensing of his new developments. He receives the research money from the shell company of Harrison Investments.

Marie said Mitch kept mumbling something about how it wasn't his daddy, not his daddy's voice. Did Natalie hide him somewhere too? A closet? *As a mother, what would I do?*

Mitchell's dad is arrested but swears he didn't kill Natalie.

Over three decades later, the Brown litigation is filed, claiming a baby mix-up, at almost the same time as the election at Harrison Investments. Preston Westerfer dies. Tiffany and Victoria learn of Harrison's true identity and Tiffany uses it to get Mitch the CEO position. But Victoria can't vote for Mitch. Harrison would know. So she gets Theodore to change his vote.

But, then what? Tiffany has what she wants. What did Tiffany do next to give someone reason to kill her?

Jacqueline looked back over her notes. Her interviews. Tiffany was investigating something else about the hospital. She was trying to find out about Mitch's past. She got the boxes out of Marie's house. Tiffany stumbled on that picture of Natalie as a nurse at Penn. Did that lead her to start looking into Natalie's death?

Then Tiffany is found dead.

Dr. Fitzgerald is also murdered.

Who's left?

Jacqueline stared at the pictures of the murder scenes. Both women let their killer in. They knew him. And both women were shot in the back of the head, running away from their attacker. She looked over the information again.

Tiffany got the boxes from Marie. They had to hold the key.

What was she missing? Jacqueline grabbed the catalog Lisa had made of the contents. Pictures, baby clothes, baby books, Dr. Seuss. Didn't Mitch say something about how his mother loved to read?

Jacqueline threw open the boxes and flipped through all the books. Nothing.

But did Tiffany find something? Where would she hide it?

Jacqueline looked back at the catalog. What was in the room where Tiffany died? The photo albums. She flipped through each of them, finding nothing. And then finally...

A paper slipped out from between the pages.

It was a note from Natalie to her husband.

If something happens to me, please investigate Dr. Fitzgerald. I did something awful, and I am so sorry. We need the money so desperately, and you are so hurt and angry all the time. I thought it would be harmless. Dr. Fitzgerald kept saying it was harmless if the babies were switched. Both were getting healthy babies. I convinced myself it was okay. And the Westerfer family was thrilled to hear they were having a boy. No one wanted to see or know anything else. Just that it was a boy.

Both women were so happy. Oh babe, I'm so sorry. What did I do? Dr. Fitzgerald is coming over. I think he's bringing the money, but we can't keep it. I can't live with myself. I met that young girl, Maggie Brown. She was all alone and excited to have a baby. She didn't want to know the sex. She wanted to be surprised. And she was due at the same time as Mrs. Westerfer. So, we convinced her she needed a cesarean even though she didn't.

Dr. Fitzgerald said the Westerfer family would take care of Maggie, pay all her hospital bills. But it wasn't right. I need to make it right. I need to tell Mrs. Brown what I did. But Dr. Fitzgerald said to wait.

If anything happens to me, it's because of the baby switch.

Please take care of Ryan. I love you both so much. I truly thought it would solve all our problems and no one would get hurt.

Yet, Fitzgerald is dead. He had to be working with someone.

Just then, Jacqueline looked at where Tiffany put the note. In the photo album. And, right there...

Almost as if on cue, her phone buzzed. Thinking Mitch was calling back, she grabbed it. An anonymous text with a picture of a boy with blond ringlets resting soundly. In a Green Arrow bed.

Come alone if you ever want to see him alive again. Call the cops and he dies. I'm watching you.

There was no address. She didn't need it. She knew that place by heart.

Chapter 74

HE STARED AT PATRICK, WHO WAS SLEEPING SOUNDLY in the superhero bed, at the images of the Green Arrow shooting arrows at imaginary villains under Patrick's curls. The sedative had worked well. Patrick should be out for a while.

He looked at his watch. Any minute now. He thought about sending another text, but he'd calculated the trip from Center City to Stone Harbor in late winter. She had a few minutes. It will finally be over. He wondered for the umpteenth time how it had come to this. So many times he thought he'd reached the pinnacle of his life. Gained everything his heart desired. Only for it to be threatened again.

He looked around the little boy's bedroom. A life-sized version of Batman on the wall stared back at him, the caption underneath stating, *You only have your thoughts and dreams ahead of you. You are someone. You mean something*. Designed to motivate its occupant every morning. Next to Batman, shelves lined the walls with every imaginable action figure. Pictures of a father and son playing super-heroes filled frames next to the bed. Regrettably, they didn't help the former resident of the room. And they sure as hell weren't going to help his mother now.

What a waste. She must have been a good mom. He admired the bookcase lined with classics. He returned to the reading chair in the corner. It was almost over. And then he would just begin again. He still had his money. His freedom. No crazy lawyer was going to destroy him now.

She'd dug deeper than anyone else. Seeing her argue with the detective had shaken him. Then the call with Mitch, the wiretap—it confirmed his fear. She was getting too close.

Just like Natalie. Just like Tiffany.

Tyler's jaw clenched. He'd been naive before, thinking they wouldn't push. But they did. And he took care of it. This time, though, it was different. His freedom was at stake. He turned toward the window, listening to the waves crash below. The plan had to work. She had left him no choice, just like the others. She wouldn't let it go.

She would now, though. For Patrick.

Chapter 75

"DAMN IT, DAN, PICK UP," JACQUELINE DEMANDED.
"Redial," she yelled at Siri as she turned her eight-year-old BMW
SUV off the Garden State Parkway. The smell of the bay and salt air
evoked feelings of nostalgia that hit her like the first song of the holi-
day season. She returned to her once-happy place. Long walks next to
the ocean, evenings on beach chairs until the sun went down and the
air turned chilly, lazy nights of ice cream cones and card games with
family. Now, hell waited for her.

Each minute passed like a ticking bomb. *Dan, where are you? Now
you leave me alone?* Jacqueline screamed as she floored the gas. An
emotional storm raged inside her. She refused to lose Patrick. She
grabbed the gun she had in the office before she left, but she needed
backup. How could she have let this happen? The nightmares, the
images, and Patrick's struggle to tell them something all came back to
her, flooding her mind with uncontrollable anger.

The killer was in her home. The dream house she'd built with
John, where they were supposed to grow old and babysit their grandkids together. Where all her future memories died, along with John
and Jack. Until tonight, the house had sat empty, deserted. A physical reminder of her struggle—unable to let go of it and unable to live
with it. He knew that. He had the upper hand.

But she couldn't understand his endgame. What did he want
with them, and how did he think he was getting away with this?
Horns from oncoming cars brought her back to reality, and she
swerved back into her own lane. The wind seemed to get under the
Beemer, teasing it to turn over, as she pushed the SUV to its limit.
She couldn't, wouldn't let it happen again. The picture he sent played

over and over again in her mind. She gripped the steering wheel so hard the blood drained from her knuckles. No, it would be different this time. It had to be.

But feigning bravery couldn't suppress the memories. The loss. The pain. The panic swelled with every moment she was behind the wheel. She wiped her eyes with trembling hands, trying to focus on the white dotted lines of the road. Finally, Jacqueline pulled the tired BMW into the long dirt pathway leading to the gray-shingled bungalow. Through her tears, she saw the dim light of her phone's wallpaper. The picture of her boys. Her superheroes. She could do this.

She left Dan a message and went into the house alone.

Chapter 76

AS SHE EXITED THE BIMMER, THE LATE-WINTER WIND whooshed around her, forcing her to pull her cardigan closed. Ocean waves crashed below her in the distance, threatening doom. She didn't even look for help. Stone Harbor turned into a ghost town in March. She tried her phone. No cell service. She was alone. Except for him. Yesterday she would never have believed he could harm Patrick. Today all bets were off. *Please, Dan, look at your phone.*

Jacqueline slipped on the gravel path. She turned the knob of the front door, finding it unlocked. She raced up to Jack's bedroom. She had to get to Patrick. As she opened the bedroom door, her nightmare sat there, waiting for her. Just like she feared.

"You realize that this is all your fault, right?" he said.

She wiped off the sweat pouring down her face, trying to focus. It wasn't her baby, but Patrick in that bed. She couldn't blow her second chance. *Go to Patrick*, she demanded of herself. *Check to see if he's breathing.* But her feet refused to move. "Please tell me you didn't..."

He looked straight at her. "Why the hell couldn't you just leave it alone?" His face was swollen, tears creating a sheen on his face as he stepped into the light from the nearby window. "I'm sorry. But I can't go to jail."

Chapter 77

"GET OUT OF MY SON'S ROOM," JACQUELINE DE-manded.

She stood in the doorway, her heart pounding as she clutched the gun she had taken from her safe. Her hands trembled, and she cursed herself for never letting Billy teach her how to use it. She took a deep breath, trying to summon the courage she desperately needed to confront the bastard standing before her. "It's over, Tyler. I know what you did."

"Me? You did this," Tyler said, pointing his gun at Patrick's head.

"Please. Put your gun down. I know you don't want to do this."

Tyler laughed bitterly. "Of course I don't. What I wanted was to be with my family. With Victoria. With Mitchell. But no, you couldn't drop it, could you?"

His voice rose, each word dripping with anger. "I set the whole thing up, you fool. I gave you your big win, Mitchell his freedom, and I got my life. I wrapped Harrison up in a bow. Why the hell couldn't you just have accepted it and gotten back to your life?"

His eyes blazed with fury as he glared at Jacqueline. "You had everything you needed. Why couldn't you just let it go?"

Jacqueline moved into the room. "Think about Victoria. This will kill her. You don't want that. You've always loved her, haven't you?"

"Congratulations, Counselor. I'm impressed. You've lived up to your old reputation. And yes, you're correct. I love Victoria, always have. Everything I ever did was to keep her happy."

"I saw you two in Tiffany's photo album. Tiffany put Natalie's confession in there. She was trying to warn Mitch. You two looked very much in love. That was in college, right?"

"Correct again. We were. But damn Victoria's father. *The* Bryon Harrison. He thought he was better than everyone else. Gambling the family's fortune away. Victoria paid the price. She was forced to marry Preston. And keep all the money in the family. I was just their lawyer's son."

Jacqueline moved closer to Tyler. She had to get him away from Patrick. "The police are on their way. For Patrick's sake, drop the gun."

"You're a terrible liar. I know you wouldn't risk the kid's life. We're all alone here, right? How are you holding up, my dear? It must be so hard. The boys look so much alike. Must have been horrific when your son died."

Jacqueline tried to stay focused. "You did all this for Victoria. So that she would have the son she needed. Tyler, I know you're a good person. I know you never meant for any of this to happen. Natalie wasn't supposed to die."

"Why can't you women just listen?" Tears swelled in Tyler's eyes. "All I wanted was to make Victoria happy. It was all supposed to be so easy. Everyone wins. But no. Natalie couldn't live with herself. She threatened to go to the hospital board. I didn't want to kill her. I tried to reason with her."

"I believe you. That's why you took care of Mitchell all those years. You felt guilty about Natalie, so you wanted to make sure her son was okay. You did that on your own. To make it right."

"Exactly. I didn't mean to leave him orphaned. I helped him. I gave him everything. The scholarship. The counseling. I made sure he had a better life than he ever would have. His damn mother was just supposed to take the money. You know that, right?"

Jacqueline moved toward Tyler and Patrick. "I do. I also know you tried to get Tiffany to drop it. You didn't want to hurt her either."

"Thank you. Someone finally gets it. I did. When Tiffany first found the connection between the settlement and Natalie, I told her

286 · MARY V. SLINKARD

to forget about it. Mitch didn't want anyone to talk about his past. I even had Marie tell her to drop it. But she insisted on digging into the murder."

Jacqueline nodded. "This whole thing was one big mistake. Now, I know you don't want to harm Patrick."

Tyler's hand trembled as he gripped the gun. "I really don't. How could I hurt this boy?" His voice faltered, breaking. "I've loved him like my own grandson." He reached out to touch Patrick's head.

Seeing the anguish in his eyes, Jacqueline almost moved to take the gun. But in a sudden flash of anger, Tyler slammed his hand against the nightstand. "But he knows," Tyler said, shaking his head. His eyes imploring Jacqueline.

"We can work something out. Let's end it now. Too many people have gotten hurt. Patrick has his whole life ahead of him."

Tyler shook his head. "I was hoping the same thing. I prayed to God that Patrick didn't see me. But I checked. I visited him at the hospital. Luckily, Katherine unknowingly took the blame for that when Patrick panicked. I slipped out, and she never saw me. But it confirmed my fears. He knew it was me. He's been trying to tell his dad all along. Poor kid's been traumatized. Just like Mitch. I never wanted any of this."

Jacqueline had to stall until Dan got there. "Explain something to me. The 'other family' in the Brown litigation was the Westerfers. After the board heard of the lawsuit, Tiffany figured out that Harrison wasn't a real Westerfer and she used that to get Mitch the CEO position."

Tyler's face twisted with anger as he spoke. "That's correct. Tiffany used Harrison's identity against Victoria to make sure he never became CEO. Harrison, that idiot, thought the company was his, but he blew it all on smoking and drinking. Damn fool," he said, waving the gun around. "And Preston, that conniving puppet master, pitting the two boys against each other. Thought it was funny. Hoping

Harrison would learn from Mitch. But his love of money and the company won out."

Jacqueline's mind raced as she tried to keep Tyler talking. She needed to buy more time until help arrived. "But did Harrison kill his father?"

A sarcastic grin spread across Tyler's face as he waved the gun at Jacqueline. "You're apparently the smart one. What do you think? Makes sense, doesn't it? Victoria always feared Harrison overheard her and Preston arguing. Bloodline or no bloodline, Preston knew that brat Harrison wasn't capable. He was adamant that Mitch be CEO. Then suddenly, Preston's dead? Harrison conveniently finds him after a heart attack? Don't need to be a rocket scientist to figure that out. But, Victoria never wanted to know."

Tyler started laughing uncontrollably. "By the way, good use of *secret*. Victoria was afraid of her secret coming out that Harrison wasn't her son and Harrison..."

Jacqueline forced herself to stay calm, asking more questions to keep him distracted. She needed to get him away from Patrick. "Victoria's father Bryon and you planned this all along, right? Dr. Fitzgerald went along with the scheme, falsifying the medical records and assuring Victoria she was having a boy, giving her no reason to doubt that Harrison was her son—until Maggie Brown came forward with the truth. And Victoria still doesn't know you and Fitzgerald planned the entire ordeal and you killed Natalie, does she?"

Tyler tilted his head slightly, a slow, mocking smile spreading across his face. "Very good, Counselor. Mitch sure knows how to pick women."

Jacqueline moved closer to Tyler, hoping to grab the gun. "Please, let us go."

"You know I can't. I tried. I really did try to give you an out. I set Harrison up to take the fall. He only caused Victoria pain. But no. No, that wasn't enough for you," Tyler shouted, his face contorted with rage. He stood up abruptly, knocking the chair over in the process. His eyes locked onto Jacqueline's and he pointed the gun at her, his hand trembling with the intensity of his emotions. Each step he took toward her radiated his frustration and anger.

Jacqueline instinctively took a step back, her heart pounding in her chest. It was working. She was getting him away from Patrick. "I can help you. I can explain how Natalie's death was an accident. We'll work something out."

Tyler let out a menacing laugh. "It's really a shame. Your instincts are good. But it's too late. Just not good enough."

"Please. Let's end this. You can't harm Patrick."

"I have no intention of harming Patrick. You are. This is your fault, and now you have to fix it. Just like the others."

"You're never going to get away with this. They will figure it out."

"Really? Think about it. Everyone knows how difficult the loss of your family has been. You really should get better security. I bugged your office the first time I came to see you. Don't underestimate the old man." Tyler waved his finger at her. "Tsk-tsk, my dear. I laid the groundwork in your office. The bloody Green Arrow? Saw the pictures on your desk. Nice touch, don't you think?"

"You sick bastard."

"Now, now. Name calling is beneath you. How do you think I became so successful? Through careful planning and being extremely opportunistic. When Mitch hired you—or should I say, sent me to hire you—I was concerned. First, I didn't think you were good enough. But then when you actually made some headway, I knew I needed a plan B.

"I always have a backup plan. I think the headline will read 'Brilliant defense attorney frees handsome client whose only son looks remarkably like her dead child. After the case, she kidnaps the child, never to be heard of again.'"

"You'll never get away with this," Jacqueline repeated.

"Oh yes, I will. And thank you for bringing the gun. It works perfectly. Everyone knows how stressed you've been. How much you came to care for Mitch and Patrick. Haven't your colleagues all remarked that it may have been unhealthy for you to take on this case?"

Tyler paused for a response. "No matter. You don't need to answer. But you should never play poker, my dear. Don't worry. A lot of women would never be able to do what you did without breaking down. I think it will play out something like this..."

He paced around the room, seeming to think out loud. "You came to Mitch's house to relieve me. Makes sense. You were Mitch's attorney. What did I know? I thought you seemed preoccupied, but I just assumed it was from the case. Yet this time was different. Now that the case is over, you were afraid that you would never see Patrick again. You couldn't handle that.

"So, instead of taking Patrick to the hospital to see his dad like you said you would, you brought Patrick here," Tyler said, his voice growing more erratic. He ran a trembling hand through his disheveled hair. "You have enough money that you think you can just go anywhere with Patrick and start a new life. I was thinking car accident. But this works out much better. Murder–suicide. This will work."

Tyler's movements became more frantic. He waved the gun around wildly, his breathing shallow and rapid.

"Just tell me one thing," Jacqueline said, trying to keep her voice steady. "How did Tiffany figure it out?"

Tyler laughed, a horrible sound that echoed through the room. "I know what you're doing, young lady. You're stalling. You know about Natalie's confession. How many times do you think I will underestimate you damn women?" He took a step closer, anger dripping from each word. Gone was the distinguished father figure, replaced with a dark, vengeful presence. Tyler's face twisted into a cruel sneer as he recounted the events, his hands shaking with rage.

"You are just like Tiffany. Can't give it up. Tiffany couldn't either. She brought the confession to me," he continued. "Asked if Dr. Fitzgerald killed Natalie." He let out another ugly laugh. "Do you believe Tiffany found that confession in those boxes she took from Marie?"

Jacqueline kept her hand steady. She could do this. "Tyler, I don't want to shoot you, but I will. Please, let's end this now."

Jacqueline pointed the gun at his chest. She remembered what John taught her about archery, hoping it would work. *Aim small, miss small.*

Tyler moved closer, laughing. "You won't shoot."

She had to protect Patrick. She pulled the trigger. Click.

Jacqueline's eyes widened in shock when Tyler didn't fall back. Instead, he whacked her in the face with the butt of his gun. The force of the blow shoved her against the wall. She dropped like a rag doll to the floor.

"Obviously you're new at this. You might want to try it without the safety next time."

Chapter 78

JACQUELINE CAME TO WITH A POUNDING HEADACHE. Her left eye was almost closed shut from where he struck her with the gun. Blood dripped from the side of her face as she lay facedown on the floor. She could feel from the vibrations of the floor that Tyler was pacing. She was out of options. He had her gun. Her phone. And despite his old age, his physical frame would overpower her.

Her involuntary moans caught his attention. "Finally, you wake up. It's about time. Clock is ticking."

Think, goddammit. "You won't get away with this." It hurt to speak.

Tyler laughed. "Oh yes, I will. I'm finally going to tie up all those loose ends. Now, I need you to get up. Finish this."

"Why?" she mumbled.

"Because it needs to look like a murder–suicide. I can't have you lying on the floor. Now get up."

Jacqueline willed her left eye to open, trying to search for anything that could serve as a weapon. The bed blocked most of her view, and she needed to buy time. Tyler grabbed her arm, attempting to pull her up, but she used all her weight to remain on the floor.

"Well, you're heavier than you look," Tyler said.

Jacqueline needed to keep him talking, distracted. In her present state, she could barely move, let alone get the gun away from him. Her body felt like lead, every movement a struggle.

"Why Fitzgerald?" she muttered weakly, her voice barely above a whisper.

"This better not be another stall tactic." He bent down to examine her face. "Don't think about going anywhere," Tyler said as he planted a firm foot on her back, constraining her to the floor. "I guess I can at least answer your questions. See, Fitzgerald wanted money for his research. I wanted to get rich. We concocted the baby swap to secure Preston's fortune with Victoria's family."

Jacqueline twisted her body underneath his weight. The pressure of his foot only allowed her to stretch her arm.

"Patience, my dear," Tyler chided. "Fitzgerald was weak. He was always suspicious that I had something to do with Natalie's death, but after a few years, he let it go. Then Tiffany had to stir the pot, ask all kinds of questions about Natalie. Confronted him about some letter Natalie wrote. I couldn't let her tell Victoria. I needed a scapegoat. And I wasn't about to let Mitch take the fall. I worked too hard on that kid. Harrison was the perfect patsy. But now there's you. You couldn't let it go."

Then Jacqueline saw it. Her answer. Her final chance to right this wrong. She moved her hand under the bed and her fingers grazed it, but it was just out of reach. "Mitch will never believe you."

"That's where you're wrong, my dear."

Jacqueline stretched closer to it. "Oh, no."

"A wasted talent, truly. You could have been an excellent attorney." Tyler stopped as she strained her back against his leg. "What's wrong, my dear? Are you having another seizure?"

Tyler turned her body over. Jacqueline started convulsing. "Oh, no. There really isn't time for this. I need to get going," Tyler said, checking his watch.

Jacqueline intermittently shook and froze her extremities, then closed her eyes, feigning unconsciousness.

"You're pathetic. I thought you'd have put up a better fight. I've got to get moving. Just one final step to complete our staging. I need you up on your feet. We don't want any inconsistencies with forensics, now do we? Let's avoid giving our detective friend anything to worry about with bullet trajectories, and gunpowder residue, and the like."

Tyler leaned down to pull Jacqueline to her feet. It was the break she needed. She stretched her hand until it finally reached the shiny metal arrow under Jack's bed. It was her final gamble to save Patrick.

Tyler froze at her sudden movement. Jacqueline quickly rolled back over to face him and drove the arrow straight into his chest. He fell toward her, pushing the arrow even deeper. Blood spouted from his chest, and his face immediately lost all expression.

Chapter 79

THE AMBULANCES AND COP CARS CAME IN THREES. Jacqueline's summer home was bathed in a sea of red and blue, drawing the few winter residents out of their homes. Jacqueline imagined this was the most excitement their sleepy town had seen since Labor Day.

Detective O'Neill and Mitchell arrived on the scene, weaving between all the vehicles in the driveway. They approached the front steps, their faces tense. As they reached the door, Jacqueline burst out, cradling a groggy but alive Patrick in her arms. "Now you two show up," she said.

"Dad, Dad," Patrick cried, his small voice weak as he slowly regained consciousness.

Mitch turned to Jacqueline, his voice raw with emotion. "I knew I was right to trust you. I just didn't know how much that trust would be tested. Thank you for never giving up on me or Patrick. You saved us both this time. You're truly an amazing woman."

"Jax, how? How did you do it?" Dan asked.

Jacqueline gave Patrick a conspiratorial smile. "It was easy. My son Jack helped us."

She thought it best to clarify. "I remembered that he kept his bow and arrow set under his bed. My superhero boys and I captured the bad guy. I fooled Tyler into thinking I was having a seizure, and that gave me just enough time to surprise him. Despite what you think, I still got it."

Dan smiled. "I never should have doubted you."

Jacqueline hugged him. "No. I gave you reason to worry. But not anymore. With the help of my superheroes, I'm finally okay."

Epilogue: Six Months Later

"I DON'T LIKE IT," DETECTIVE DAN O'NEILL SAID, HIS voice crackling with concern over the cell phone. Even though Jacqueline wasn't with him, she could vividly picture him pacing the floor.

Jacqueline had been making significant strides with her therapist, working through her issues and finding a healthier balance. Her therapist had even given her the green light to stay involved with Mitch and Patrick. While Patrick and Jack shared blond hair and had been close in age, the similarities ended there. Jacqueline had realized she had been projecting her own desires onto Patrick, but now she was embracing the differences between them.

Coming to terms with the tragic deaths in her own family was a slow process. Despite the official report of the accident, she still harbored doubts. Her heart ached with unresolved questions, but she was determined to move forward, step by step.

"Well, I'm sorry, but you really don't have any choice. And I didn't ask for your opinion," Jacqueline said. She knew this last line was a punch to the gut, but she was exhausted. They had been over this numerous times, and she was losing patience. Since publicity over the Mitchell case, requests for representation had been pouring in. The money was exciting, but the influx of work was a bit overwhelming for her small firm. So on top of maximizing the business, she and Lisa were interviewing people to help. The last thing she needed was Dan's overprotectiveness.

"I'm serious. This is dangerous."

Jacqueline laughed. Dan was and always would be a good friend, but he would never trust Ryan Mitchell, no matter how innocent he was of any crime.

"I'm sure it's many things, but dangerous is not one of them."
Jacqueline pulled up to her destination. It still looked as grand as she
remembered. "Gotta go," she said as Ryan Mitchell opened her door.

"Let me guess. Mr. Muscles is not happy."

Jacqueline put up her hand, silencing any discussion about Dan.
The animosity between them was tiring. "We're not talking about
him today. This is about Patrick."

Mitch leaned in, but Jacqueline turned her head, offering him
her cheek instead. She and Mitch had become close over the last few
months, leaning on each other for emotional support. Mitch had also
enlisted Jacqueline's help to finally seek justice for his biological parents. With Tyler's confession and their newfound knowledge about
the baby switch, along with a few political favors, Jacqueline suc-
cessfully petitioned the court to exonerate Mitch's biological father.
Next, Mitch had moved heaven and earth to give his biological parents the burial they deserved. The service was intimate, attended only
by Marie, Jacqueline, Mitch, Patrick, and Eric and Katherine, who
had spent the past few months working on their own relationship.

Jacqueline's mind returned to the present as Patrick came out to
the car, waving to her. She didn't want to admit it, but one of the
highlights of her days was seeing him. She didn't think she would
ever tire of seeing his beautiful face.

As Jacqueline walked toward the Westerfer mansion, she caught
Mitch staring at her with those loving eyes, just like he had so many
years ago when she saved Patrick. Yet it was too hard for Jacqueline.
As much as she cared for him, her heart was still with her own family.
She avoided Mitch's eyes as she spoke. "Mitch, I'm so proud of you.
You won't regret it. I truly think Victoria wants to make amends."

After Victoria found out the truth, she reached out to Jacqueline
when Mitch refused to take her calls. Despite the fact that Victoria
had finally come to her senses, Mitch knew that her vendetta against
him could have cost Patrick his life. As they walked into Victoria's

home, Jacqueline couldn't help but worry about getting involved in someone else's family affairs. But she truly believed Victoria's heart was in the right place. Moreover, having lost her own family, Jacqueline intimately knew how important family is and always would be. Patrick could never have enough people who loved him in his life.

As they walked up to the grand mahogany door, intricately carved with detailed scrollwork and adorned with brass accents that had weathered to a deep patina, Jacqueline felt a shiver of apprehension. She glanced at Mitch, whose gaze lingered on her, filled with an emotion she couldn't quite place. Dan's voice echoed in her mind, his worry palpable even from miles away. Two men, both important in her life, both pulling her in different directions. The uncertainty of what lay ahead left Jacqueline ambivalent. She couldn't quite figure out which path her heart would ultimately follow, but a sense of gratitude for the opportunity put a smile on her face.

Before they could ring the bell, the door flew open. Jacqueline watched as Patrick launched himself into Victoria's waiting arms with a delighted squeal. Victoria scooped him up, her face glowing with pure happiness as she spun him around. The room filled with their shared laughter, a sound so sweet it momentarily chased away Jacqueline's doubts and fears. In that moment, surrounded by love and family, she allowed herself to believe that everything maybe, just maybe, might turn out okay.

She felt a smile cross her lips, wholeheartedly enjoying the genuine love she was witnessing, her heart feeling light for the first time in a very long time. Just then the buzz startled her, interrupting the momentary joy. The vibration emanated from her jacket. As she reached to retrieve her phone, her heart sank. Her smile vanished as quickly as it had come, replaced with sheer disbelief as she read the message.

A text from Lisa.

Jacqueline, call me immediately. It's Urgent!!! There's new evidence about your family's car accident—you need to hear this!

Jacqueline's legs threatened to give way beneath her. The car accident. The tragedy that had shattered her world, haunting her every step... She couldn't believe what she was seeing. Could this message hold the answers she had been desperately seeking—or would it expose a truth she wasn't ready to face? Her pulse raced as she glanced at Ryan. Holding up her phone, she signaled to him with a faint shrug that work was calling. She turned to call Lisa. The laughter behind her faded completely as she pressed the phone to her ear. Lisa answered on the first ring.

"Jacqueline, are you sitting down? You're not going to believe this..."

About the Author

While law may have been her initial passion, **Mary V. Slinkard**'s heart has always belonged to the world of mysteries. After a successful two-decade career as a commercial litigator, Mary's love for fiction persisted, inspiring her to blend her legal expertise with literary finesse as a suspense author. With each novel, Mary presents readers with a fresh and gripping take on the classic mystery genre. Alongside her writing, Mary cherishes her role as a devoted wife and mother of four in the suburbs of Philadelphia. Join Mary in her literary adventures and explore the captivating world of mysteries through her masterful storytelling.

Seizure First Aid
How to help someone having a seizure

As an individual living with epilepsy, Mary is deeply committed to raising awareness and educating others on how to properly care for someone during a seizure. Her passion for this cause has inspired her to donate a portion of the proceeds from this book to the Epilepsy Foundation, an organization that has been instrumental in her journey. For additional resources, support, or to learn more, please visit Mary's website or connect with the **Epilepsy Foundation Eastern Pennsylvania** at www.efepa.org.

1 **STAY** with the person until they are awake and alert after the seizure.
✓ **Time** the seizure   ✓ Remain **calm**
✓ Check for **medical ID**

2 Keep the person **SAFE**.
✓ Move or guide away from **harm**

3 Turn the person onto their **SIDE** if they are not awake and aware.
✓ Keep **airway clear**
✓ **Loosen tight clothes** around neck
✓ Put **something small and soft** under the head

Call 911 if...
▶ Seizure lasts longer than 5 minutes
▶ Person does not return to their usual state
▶ Person is injured, pregnant, or sick
▶ Repeated seizures
▶ First time seizure
▶ Difficulty breathing
▶ Seizure occurs in water

Do NOT
✗ Do **NOT** restrain.
✗ Do **NOT** put any objects in their mouth.
✓ Rescue medicines can be given if prescribed by a health care professional

EPILEPSY FOUNDATION
EASTERN PENNSYLVANIA

efepa.org

919 Walnut St, Suite 700
Philadelphia, PA 19107

215-629-5003

This publication was created by the Epilepsy Foundation, a nationwide network organization, and is part of our END EPILEPSY® awareness campaign. This publication is made possible with funding from the Centers for Disease Control and Prevention (CDC) under cooperative grant agreement number 1NU58DP006256-04-00. Its contents are solely the responsibility of the Epilepsy Foundation and do not necessarily represent the views of the CDC. EFA440/PAB0220   Rev. 02/2020   ©2020 Epilepsy Foundation of America, Inc

www.ingramcontent.com/pod-product-compliance
Lightning Source LLC
Chambersburg PA
CBHW020840060726
PP18531500001B/2